"This book may cause the earth to shake in certain political circles—justifiably."

Dr. Martin Rudner, Director of the Canadian
Centre of Intelligence and Security Studies,
Norman Paterson School of International Affairs

"Every responsible citizen of Canada, the US, the UK and other Western countries should read this book."

Christopher Ondaatje,
Times Higher Education Supplement

"an arresting look at the reality of terrorism"

The Gazette (Montreal)

"*Cold Terror* is a chilling book. Drawing on 12 years of experience writing on terrorism, journalist Stewart Bell has compiled an impressive case that Canada has become 'an unofficial state sponsor of terrorism.'... a bold and impressive effort to confront a critical but neglected aspect of Canadian life."

The Ottawa Citizen

"This book should alarm Canadians. It is a story of negligence, complacency and corruption that should disabuse them of the illusion that their country is a force for global peace."

Winnipeg Free Press

"impressive reportage . . . [Bell] makes it too easy to become enraged with our slack system and contemptible political leadership."

The Western Standard

"stunning and chilling"

The Edmonton Journal

"... an unvarnished look at how Canada became a haven for terror groups ... raises valid questions about why the country failed to act, time and again, in identifying and expelling the bad guys."

The Vancouver Sun

"Back from deadly terror-fronts from Afghanistan to the West Bank, Canada's leading chronicler of terrorism makes this wrenching discovery: more and more roads to terrorism start and finish in Canada."

David B. Harris,
Director, INSIGNIS International,
Terrorist Intelligence Program

"*Cold Terror* recounts a disturbing array of short-sighted policy decisions, from CIDA funding Islamic charities that supported terrorism to senior political leaders attending meetings of terror-supporting domestic organizations..."

Canadian Jewish News

"... a bold and impressive effort to confront a critical but neglected aspect of Canadian life. If Canadians genuinely desire to be compassionate and constructive world citizens, this is an issue, and a book, they cannot afford to ignore."

Avery Plow, *Times-Colonist* (Victoria)

COLD
TERROR

Also by the author
The Martyr's Oath: The Apprenticeship of a Homegrown Terrorist

COLD
TERROR

HOW CANADA NURTURES AND EXPORTS TERRORISM AROUND THE WORLD

STEWART BELL

BICENTENNIAL
BICENTENNIAL
1807
WILEY
2007
BICENTENNIAL
BICENTENNIAL

John Wiley & Sons Canada, Ltd.

Library and Archives Canada Cataloguing in Publication Data

Bell, Stewart, 1965-
    Cold terror : how Canada nurtures and exports terrorism around the world /
    Stewart Bell.— 2nd ed.

Includes bibliographical references and index.
ISBN-13: 978-0-470-84056-6
ISBN-10: 0-470-84056-0

1. Terrorists—Canada. 2. Terrorism—Canada—Prevention.
3. National security—Canada. 4. Terrorism I. Title.
HV6433.C3B44 2006   363.320971   C2006-905214-X

Production Credits
Cover design: Ian Koo
Interior design: Adrian So R.G.D.
Printer: Tri-Graphic Printing Ltd.
Anniversary logo design: Richard Pacifico
Photographs courtesy of Stewart Bell unless otherwise noted.

Printed in Canada
1 2 3 4 5 TRI 10 09 08 07 06

TABLE OF CONTENTS

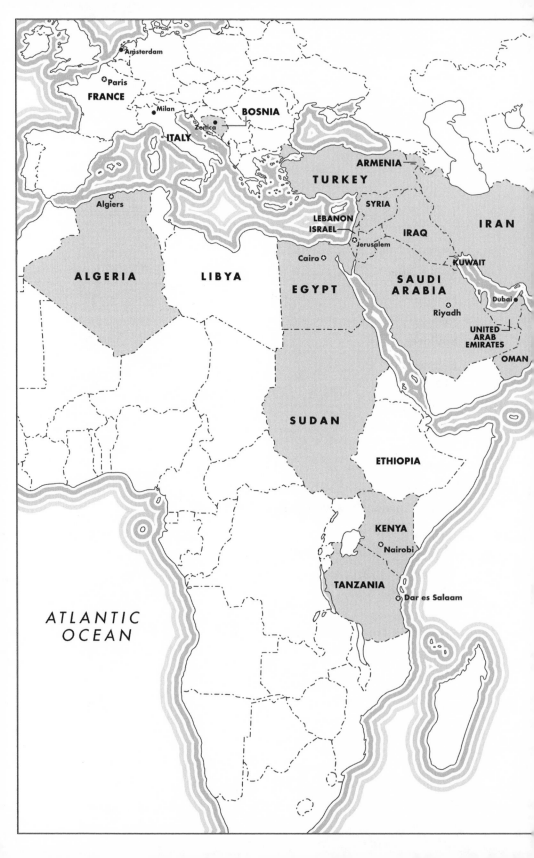

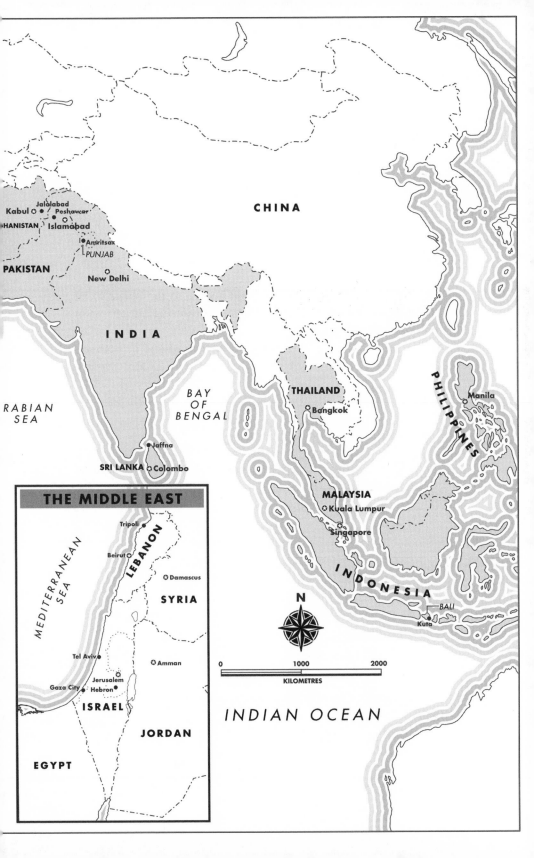

CHINA

Kabul ○ ● Jalalabad
● Peshawar
HANISTAN ● Islamabad
PAKISTAN
● Amritsar
PUNJAB
○ New Delhi

I N D I A

RABIAN
SEA

B A Y
O F
B E N G A L

THAILAND
○ Bangkok

PHILIPPINES

Manila ○

● Jaffna
SRI LANKA ○ Colombo

MALAYSIA
○ Kuala Lumpur

○ Singapore

I N D O N E S I A

THE MIDDLE EAST

Tripoli ●
LEBANON
Beirut ●
○ Damascus
SYRIA

M E D I T E R R A N E A N
S E A

Tel Aviv ●
○ Jerusalem
Gaza City ● ● Hebron
ISRAEL

○ Amman

JORDAN

EGYPT

BALI
Kuta ●

N

0   1000   2000
KILOMETRES

I N D I A N   O C E A N

"I am not aware at this time of a cell known to the police to be operating in Canada with the intention of carrying out terrorism in Canada or elsewhere."

Canadian Prime Minister Jean Chrétien,
in the House of Commons,
September 17, 2001.

"That's really just a bum rap."

Canadian Prime Minister Paul Martin, on CNN,
responding to concerns that Canada has been soft on terror.
December 5, 2004.

FOREWORD BY DR. ROHAN GUNARATNA

The Context

The most noteworthy aspect of Al Qaeda in the post–9/11 environment has been its broadened appeal among the Muslim community. Al Qaeda's ideology and operational methodology of suicide (martyrdom) has become popular, widespread and accepted by like-minded jihad groups from Australia to the United Kingdom, the United States and Canada. After inventing itself as a popular movement, the network has maintained its course despite sustained pressure by the United States and its allies. Its resilience, intransigence and failure to yield have surprised many, and its followers, both cradle and convert Muslims, have become even more committed in its jihad campaign (holy war). Al Qaeda has become more resolute in achieving its strategic goals.

In the face of adversity, the global jihad movement has demonstrated an extraordinary ability to generate a post–9/11 vision of perpetual war against the West. The periodic arrests in Canada, the United States, the United Kingdom, Continental Europe and Australia demonstrate the adaptive nature of the constantly evolving network. It no longer needs to send operatives from Afghanistan; there are young first- and second-generation politicized and radicalized Muslims living in the West willing to carry out its avowed mission. Even if Al Qaeda leadership is hunted down and the group destroyed, its mission of attacking the West articulated by bin Laden as a religious duty and popularized by Al Qaeda will continue.

Threat Context

As a migrant-receiving nation, Canada today faces a significant terrorist threat. First, the periodic influx of migrants—especially migrants from conflict zones—means that newcomers are vulnerable to terrorist indoctrination and recruitment. Second, the operation of the well-entrenched and established support networks on Canadian soil will seek to politicize and radicalize them. Third, Canada has emerged as an important gateway to the United States, the primary target of multiple jihad groups.

The vast majority of Canadian migrants and diaspora are peace-loving citizens who respect Canadian laws and norms. Nonetheless, there is a tiny minority driven by events in their homeland as well as by global events that seek to support and participate in violence both in their homelands and even in their host country—Canada. As the recent arrests in Canada demonstrates, the threat facing the country is recurrent and enduring. To aid in understanding the context and the evolving nature of the threat to Canada, there is no book as exhaustive as *Cold Terror*—a book authored by Stewart Bell in the shadow of 9/11, a strategic event that transformed the world.

Three significant developments mark the post–9/11 threat environment:

- The dismantling of a state-of-the-art terrorist and guerrilla training and operational infrastructure in Afghanistan.
- The dispersal of Al Qaeda and formation of a multi-headed global jihad movement that is resilient and difficult to combat.
- The emergence of Afghanistan and Iraq as two frontiers of jihad, with a profound effect on Canadian Muslims.

As Mr. Bell's book illustrates, Canada has featured prominently in each one of these stages. At least a dozen Canadians received training in Afghanistan. Many Canadians participated in Jihad campaigns from Chechnya to Kashmir and Iraq. A few hundred Canadians are angry about the suffering of Muslims in Iraq, and some of them want to seek justice and others revenge by attacking targets at home and overseas.

Identifying the Threat
Managing migrant and diaspora communities in an age of globalization is a challenge. It is especially a challenge for a country that is committed to preserving the ethnic and religious character of its migrants and diasporas. In fact, Canada prides itself in the way it treats its visitors and immigrants. However, Canada must take into consideration the realities of the post–9/11 environment. Mr. Bell's book contributes considerably toward both identifying and explaining the threat to a point that no other author has been able

to accomplish before. His book highlights two key problems that Canada must address.

First, there must be nation-wide recognition that the current Canadian political and administrative structure and system is susceptible and vulnerable to misuse and abuse by terrorist and extremist groups. As Canadians are trusting and want to be politically correct, terrorist and extremist groups have been able to mobilize support within their communities. These terrorist and extremist groups have been able to accomplish this feat by infiltrating Canadian host institutions such as the Canadian political parties, including mainstream political parties. Canada must develop tough legislation that will preclude politicians and officials from becoming subjected to constituency and electoral pressure.

Second, terrorist and extremist groups have successfully penetrated the migrant and diaspora community institutions. Operating through front, cover and sympathetic organizations, terrorist and extremist groups have built networks for propaganda, recruitment, procurement and other support activities. Canada must not fear to legislate against groups and individuals that seek to support or conduct terrorist attacks regardless of whether it is in Canada or overseas. By lobbying through human rights and other civil society organizations, terrorist groups have been able to block and delay Canada from passing appropriate legislation. In protecting Canada's national security, its law enforcement and security and intelligence agencies are as good as the powers given to them.

The Way Ahead
As illustrated by Stewart Bell, the threat facing Canada is evolving. The Canadian response must be proactive and dynamic. In developing its counter-terrorism structures and procedures, Canada must not be too far behind other western migrant- and diaspora-hosting countries. As the threat groups learn from each other, so should the Canadian security and intelligence and law enforcement authorities seek to keep up with the knowledge and technology developed by other countries to fight terrorism and extremism.

As Mr. Bell explains, no country, including Canada, is immune from the threat of terrorism or extremism. Canada, which has an image for working closely with Asian and Middle Eastern countries, must draw from global best practices in countering politically motivated violence. To better understand the changing environment, Canada should play a key role in building bridges between the West and countries that need assistance to fight terrorism. On the ground, Canada should encourage governments to move from cooperation to collaboration—building common databases, participating in the exchange of personnel and in joint training and operations, transferring resources and expertise, and sharing experience. In the face of emerging and current threats, the Canadian authorities must constantly assess the strengths and the weaknesses of Canada's security architecture and seek to close its gaps and loopholes. As there is no standard textbook for fighting the contemporary wave of terrorism, governments must maximize the successes and minimize the failures.

In fighting the contemporary wave of violence, Mr. Bell's research shows that intelligence-led law enforcement operations have proved to be the most effective. However, such operations need to be coordinated with parallel political and diplomatic activity. As media shapes public opinion, and public opinion is critical for fighting terrorism and extremism, media must be brought in as a partner. As public support is pivotal, it is so critical for the government, political parties and the intellectual elite to engage the communities, especially the communities vulnerable to terrorist and extremist penetration. In the early 21st century, the fight against terrorism and extremism has transformed into a multi-dimensional fight requiring multi-pronged, multi-agency, multinational and multi-jurisdictional efforts.

As Canada's most respected writer on terrorism and conflict, Mr. Bell promises much for the future. We are all indebted to him for his contribution to counter-terrorism research and more importantly, increasing the public awareness and understanding of the contemporary threat.

Dr. Rohan Gunaratna is Head of the International Centre for Political Violence and Terrorism Research at the Institute of Defence and Strategic Studies in Singapore, and author of Inside Al Qaeda: Global Network of Terror *(Columbia University Press).*

INTRODUCTION

HOW DO YOU TELL A MOTHER her son may be a terrorist? Asha Muhayadin is a mother of five who works on the packaging line at a Toronto bakery, and a Muslim refugee from Somali. I met her when I was researching the case of her son, Yasin, who was arrested in August 2005. He and his friend Ali Dirie had taken a rented Buick down to Ohio and loaded up on illegal firearms and ammo. As they were crossing the border back into Canada at Fort Erie, they were pulled over and searched. Customs agents found a loaded Hi-Point semi-automatic strapped to Yasin's groin. Ali had two semis hidden in his pants. They pleaded guilty and were sent away to serve federal time in Kingston.

Something about the case had not seemed right from the start. Toronto was flooded with illegal guns in the summer of 2005, but Yasin and Ali were not gangsters; they were devout young Muslims who had worshipped at the Salaheddin Islamic Centre, a mosque in the immigrant-rich city of Scarborough, Ontario that had repeatedly surfaced in counter-terrorism investigations. Why were they bringing guns into Canada? "That's the million dollar question," Ali's brother Jafar had told me when I met him at a Tim Hortons coffee shop one afternoon.

On June 3, 2006, at a news conference near Toronto's international airport, the Royal Canadian Mounted Police (RCMP) claimed to have solved the mystery. In an operation that had started the day before and continued through the night, police tactical teams had rounded up a group of mostly young Muslim men accused of training at a rural property north of the city and assembling truck bombs that were to be detonated by remote control at the Toronto regional headquarters of the Canadian Security Intelligence Service (CSIS) and the Toronto Stock Exchange.

A sample of the evidence seized during the raids was laid out on a table for the benefit of the TV cameras—a bag of ammonium nitrate, a cell phone–triggered detonator, a handgun, a computer hard drive, a door that had been used for target practice, and camouflage fatigues. A senior CSIS official said the group had been inspired by the ideology of Al Qaeda. A dozen adults and five juveniles were charged altogether. Their names were listed on a news release. Yasin and Ali were on the list. The charge sheet accused them of smuggling firearms for terrorist purposes.

As soon as the press conference was over, I got in my car and drove to Asha's place. What I was going to say to her, I was not sure. I started writing about terrorism and extremism in the late 1980s, shortly after Sikh militants in Vancouver, where I grew up, placed suitcase bombs on two Air India planes, knocking one out of the sky, killing 329 people. Since then I had been shot at by the Taliban; detained by Pakistani military intelligence for getting too close to an abandoned guerrilla training camp; and warned by Canadian police that the Tamil Tigers were looking for me. I had forced a politician to resign by exposing his connections to neo-Nazis; walked on a blood-soaked carpet after a Hamas suicide bombing; chased a terrorist fundraiser through a Toronto parking lot; and confronted one of Canada's most notorious terrorist ringleaders at the front door of his Montreal townhouse.

I was the first journalist to tour Canada's top secret signals intelligence headquarters, the Communications Security Establishment; I triggered a police investigation by reporting on a leaked intelligence report; and I mined the Access to Information Act and other sources to compile what may be the largest collection of documents on Canadian terrorists in private hands. I had met with accused terrorists, their victims, and the men and women charged with keeping their countries secure from terror, and given lectures on my reporting to community groups, the RCMP, CSIS and the Canadian military. But I had never had to tell a mother that her son had just been charged with terrorism.

Asha covered her head with a green scarf and let me in. As I took off my shoes, I saw that she was with her best friend and her son Abdul. The apartment was small and sparse. There was a tiny kitchen, a TV stand and a wooden cradle that held a copy of the *Koran*. On top of her factory job, Asha has her own home business, Asha Clothing. It's the only way she can scrape by. I started talking. I told her about the RCMP news conference, and I showed her the press release that named Yasin and Ali. At first, she got mad. She raged for half an hour about how all Muslims are called terrorists these days and how her son's life was over, not to mention her own. "He's not a terrorist," she said. "This is not fair." But then she turned to her friend and sobbed loudly into her shoulder. Abdul asked me if he could make a formal statement for the newspaper. He said that his brother was "a pure-hearted guy" and could never do something like that, and that terrorism goes against Islam. "Our religion forbids it, it is totally forbidden to kill civilians. If you kill an innocent person, they're supposed to kill you. That's shariah." An hour later, I left them, apologizing my way out the dented metal apartment door. I felt like I had thrown a hand grenade into the room.

The arrests of the Toronto 17, as they are known, were a sharp shock for Canada. Many Canadians have long lived under the impression that they are insulated from terrorism because of domestic altruism and foreign policies they judge less aggressive than those of their southern neighbor. Canadian troops are not fighting in Iraq; they are peacekeepers in blue berets who bring kindness to troubled lands, or so the theory goes. Why would anyone want to attack Canada? Just five days before the arrests, the Deputy Director Operations of CSIS, Jack Hooper, had testified before the Senate Committee on National Security and Defence. He explained that Canada had a problem with terrorists in general, and homegrown terrorists in particular. His testimony was met with incredulity by Members of Parliament, while the media speculated he was exaggerating to try to coax more money out of the government. The reaction reflected the way terrorism was generally seen in Canada, as someone else's problem, not Canada's concern.

In reality, whether its citizens realized it or not, Canada long ago became a source of international terrorism and an operational base for world terror—a country where the planet's deadliest religious, ethnic and political extremist movements had set up shop. According to the latest annual report of CSIS, released in 2006, "A relatively large number of terrorist groups are known to be operating in Canada, engaged in fundraising, procuring materials, spreading propaganda, recruiting followers and conducting other activities." The arrests of June 2006 were simply the latest variant of a problem that had been festering for two-plus decades.

Armenian terrorists were the first to realize Canada's potential as an offshore base in the early 1980s. In 1985, Air India Flight 182 was blown out of the sky by a bomb planted by Sikh extremists from British Columbia. Then came the Tamil Tigers of Sri Lanka, as the promise of a more peaceful post–Cold War world order was shattered by the rise of ethnic nationalism and religious extremism. Next came the Middle Eastern groups, the Palestinian factions and the Lebanese Hezbollah. U.S. intelligence authorities awoke to Canada's role in world terrorism in 1997, when Gazi Ibrahim Abu Mezer crossed into the United States from Canada to blow up the Atlantic Avenue subway in Brooklyn. When police and members of the FBI Joint Terrorism Task Force raided his New York apartment on July 31, 1997, the morning of the planned attack, Abu Mezer and a Palestinian colleague, Lafi Khalil, detonated their explosive suicide vests and were shot. Bombs were found in the apartment.

By 1998, every major terrorist group in the world was operating in Canada. Ward Elcock, who was CSIS Director at the time, testified that, "With perhaps the singular exception of the United States, there are more international terrorist groups active here than any other country in the world." The Canadian Senate subcommittee on security and intelligence wrote in its 1999 report that Canada had become a "venue of opportunity" for terrorists. "Most of the major international terrorist organizations have a presence in Canada."

On December 14, 1999, Ahmed Ressam of Montreal, who had trained at Osama bin Laden's camps in Afghanistan, built a massive bomb in Vancouver and tried to cross the border to blow up Los Angeles International Airport. The Ressam case is considered by intelligence analysts to be a pivotal moment for Canada. A "Secret" CSIS report describes it as "a watershed event in the evolution of the Sunni Islamic threat in Canada, changing the perception of Canada from terrorist safe haven to active operational environment." One of the recruiters who convinced several of the 9/11 hijackers to voyage to Afghanistan for training had been the imam of a Montreal mosque.

Standing before a room full of reporters in Washington, D.C. almost three years after September 11, 2001, U.S. Attorney General John Ashcroft and FBI Director Robert Mueller announced that intelligence sources had detected that Al Qaeda was again trying to strike inside America. Terrorists intended, Ashcroft said, to "hit the United States hard." Since 9/11, Osama bin Laden had certainly made no secret of his desire to do so, and the bombings two months earlier in Madrid had underscored that Al Qaeda was still capable of organizing mass casualty attacks within Western countries.

Mueller went on to say that the FBI was looking for seven Al Qaeda members in connection with plots to attack the U.S. There was the American Muslim convert Adam Gadahn; Aafia Saddiqui, a Pakistani woman; two others, Fazul Abdullah Mohammed and Ahmed Khalfan Ghailani, who had played roles in the 1998 bombings of the American embassies in Kenya and Tanzania; and Adnan Shukrijumah, who had been part of a plot to detonate a dirty bomb in the United States. But it was the remaining pair that was of particular interest.

Abderraouf Jdey had trained with the 9/11 hijackers and recorded a "martyrdom video," which was found at an Al Qaeda base in Afghanistan. The other, Amer El-Maati, was a licensed pilot who wanted to hijack a plane and crash it into a U.S. building, according to the FBI. Both were suspected members of Al Qaeda; both had professed their desire to kill for their cause; both were considered "a clear and present danger to America;" and both were on the loose.

Both were also Canadians.

To some this sounded like a verse of "Blame Canada," but the press conference highlighted a cold truth: Canada had a terrorism problem. In the weeks preceding the Washington press conference, for example, a Canadian was arrested in Ottawa on charges that he was part of a plot to build an ammonium nitrate bomb to be detonated in the United Kingdom; a young Canadian from Windsor, Ontario was arrested in Gaza after he was recruited and trained by Hamas to kill Jews in North America; and Abdurahman

Khadr of Toronto went on national television to confess that his was an "Al Qaeda family." A year earlier, another Canadian, Abdullah Warsame, had been arrested in Minneapolis. An immigrant from Somalia who moved to Toronto in 1989, Warsame had attended two terrorist boot camps in Afghanistan, where he had met bin Laden, whom he found "inspirational," an FBI affidavit says. Although he wanted to move permanently to Afghanistan, Al Qaeda apparently considered him more useful in Canada and had paid for him to return to Toronto in April 2001.

The FBI was becoming so concerned about Canada that it distributed a classified bulletin warning: "We believe Al Qaeda continues to have a terrorist infrastructure in Canada, one with documented links to the U.S. While many border security measures have been implemented since 9/11, the vast expanse of the 4,000-mile-long U.S. northern border, with eighty-six official points of entry and various unofficial crossings, may still provide opportunities for operatives to penetrate U.S. national security, particularly if Western passports are used."

Canada is not the only country with a terrorism problem. But it has unique troubles because of the nature of its society, its immigration system, its proximity to the United States and because, compared to its allies, it has historically done so little to fight terror. By failing to take appropriate action early on, Canadian political leaders opened the door for the world's major security threat, Al Qaeda. Since its inception, Al Qaeda has had an active presence in Canada. "Al Qaeda has operatives and intelligence gatherers in Canada," says an internal CSIS report written in the days after the September 11 attacks. The report names several Al Qaeda agents, including a Toronto convenience-store clerk and a teacher at a Toronto Muslim school.

At least two major Al Qaeda networks have operated in Canada, the Montreal-based Groupe Fateh Kamel and the Ahmed Khadr group, based in Toronto, in addition to several smaller ones such as the Kassem Daher Network. "Al Qaeda's global links, including to residents in Canada, and its use of sleeper agents— small groups of covert operators sent to infiltrate countries until called upon to attack—make its activities unpredictable and a threat to the security of Canada," the report says.

What are terrorists doing in Canada? The short answer is: everything. In the 1970s and 1980s, terrorist groups could rely on the Soviet Union, Libya and other sympathetic countries for funding, weapons and a base of operations. This state sponsorship of terror was a way for nations to engage their enemies by proxy without getting their own hands dirty. Since the end of the Cold War, however, state sponsorship has declined and terrorist groups have been forced to become more self-reliant. Cut off from the benevolence of their state backers, terrorists have had to establish their own international support networks to raise money, purchase material and spread the gospel of militancy. Functioning like global corporations, these terror support networks have offices throughout the world, run by terrorist-bureaucrats, those engaged in the mundane but nonetheless crucial activities that feed the international organization with money, passports, information and legitimacy. A French prosecutor who convicted members of the Montreal Algerian cell observed: "You can hijack a plane with a [box] cutter, but you need false documents to get on the plane."

Canada is the land of opportunity for terrorist groups seeking money to finance their bloody campaigns. Jobs are plentiful; welfare is generous. Everyone who sets foot in Canada is entitled to all the rights of a Canadian citizen. It is easy enough to set up a charity dedicated to a worthy humanitarian cause and launder the money instead to terrorist causes. In fact, until December 2001, it was perfectly legal to collect money in Canada for terrorist groups. Canada's Anti-terrorism Act now forbids the practice, but enforcing the law has proved difficult, in part because it is not retroactive, meaning it cannot be used to prosecute terrorists for crimes committed before its enactment. FINTRAC, the federal government agency that monitors suspicious banking transactions, said in its 2005 annual report to Parliament that $180-million had flowed to terrorist groups from Canada in the previous 12 months.

The other type of fundraising is the criminal kind. Police and corporate investigators looking into organized crime used to follow the money trail to mobsters or bikers. Now they are finding that those behind organized crime are terrorist groups such as the Tamil Tigers. Terrorist groups in Canada are involved in bank fraud, migrant smuggling, credit and debit card fraud, mortgage fraud, extortion, theft and money laundering. The RCMP calls it "criminal extremism"—crime for the sake of supporting terror.

Terrorists have long used Canada as a hiding place, both before and after attacks, as a recruiting ground and as a propaganda base. Terror is a weapon that seeks to psychologically hammer its opponents into submission, and it therefore requires lobbyists, front organizations and Internet sites to spread the terrorists' message. Canada hosts all three. Terror propagandists also organize pressure campaigns against those who threaten the cause. I have had my own experiences with this tool of terror. After writing an article about Islamic terrorists recruiting on a Canadian Internet site, I received more than three thousand e-mails in a single day, some of them containing overt threats. "Please don't write like this or I will fuck your mother, father, brothers and all you know," said one. Another said: "I kill you if I find you."

Canada's terrorism problem is responsible for untold carnage. It generates severe problems within Canada, especially in refugee communities, where extremists have seized control of community institutions. Refugees who come to Canada to start a new life should not have to live under the thumb of the same radicals that forced them to leave their homelands in the first place, but that is exactly what has happened. If Canada is going to admit refugees from war zones, it should be doing more to protect them after they get here so they can make the transition to becoming full Canadians rather than being forced to keep fighting the wars they thought they had left back home in Sri Lanka, Pakistan, India or the Middle East.

Canadian-based terror also creates risks for Canada's allies and Canadians traveling abroad. Canadian terrorists have spilled blood around the world. They are known to have taken part in the 1993 World Trade Center truck bombing in New York, as well as suicide bombings in Israel and bombings by the Provisional Irish Republican Army; political killings in India and the murder of tourists in Egypt; a 1996 truck bombing in the heart of Colombo, Sri Lanka, that killed close to one hundred civilians; the 1995 bombing of the Egyptian embassy in Islamabad, which killed seventeen; and the Bali bombing of October 2002, which killed more than two hundred innocent people. A Canadian was part of the group blamed for the 2003 bombing of Western housing complexes in Riyadh. In 1985, Canadians were behind one of the deadliest terror attacks in history, the Air India tragedy.

In an era of globalized travel and business, when people venture far from home for work, pleasure and public duty, governments must think about the safety of their citizens abroad. Another danger is that, when they travel, Canadians will be looked upon with suspicion by governments that have lost faith in Canada's ability to rein in terrorists. Maher Arar, the Syrian Canadian who spent a year in a Damascus jail after being deported by American authorities, may well have been a victim of this.

Canada's approach to counterterrorism has undermined not only its security but also its Canadian foreign policy and stature among nations. Although it aims to be a force of peace in the world, in some countries Canada is not seen that way at all. In Sri Lanka, Canada is the country that for years allowed the Tamil Tigers, the world's leading practitioners of suicide bombings, to operate freely and raise money that bankrolled terrorism and a brutal civil war. The same was true in India, which suffered through years of Sikh terrorist violence originating in Canada. Israel has had to deal with Canadian terrorists, and so have France, Italy, Turkey, Saudi Arabia, Singapore, the Philippines, Indonesia, Egypt and Pakistan, not to mention Canada's closest partner, the United States.

"To many Americans," says a report published by the Washington, DC–based Center for Immigration Studies, "the longest undefended border in the world now looks like a 4,000-mile-long portal for terrorists." Canada risks being isolated and perhaps even punished if it does not do its part against terrorism. And if Canada does not take care of the terrorists on its own soil, someone else will, and better that CSIS and the RCMP should tackle Canadian terrorists than Mossad or the CIA.

As the arrests in Toronto should remind Canadians, Canada is itself a terror target. Intelligence reports indicate that financial buildings, government offices, shopping malls, tourist attractions and mass transit across the country have been covertly videotaped, possibly by terrorists looking for targets. "Current intelligence suggests that economic and symbolic targets such as Parliament Hill, nuclear power plants and the Toronto transit system may have been subject to reconnaissance by extremists," says a Canadian government intelligence assessment dated April 2006. "There are individuals and groups in Canada who are involved in fundraising, money laundering, communications and planning acts of violence in Canada and abroad."

In April 2003, Pakistani authorities arrested two senior al-Qaeda operatives near Peshawar. In the "pocket litter" of one of the men, police found a list of Toronto landmarks, including Union Station and the Eaton Centre. One of the men was linked to a 9/11 planner, and the other had ties to Ramzi Yousef, who bombed the World Trade Center in New York in 1993. In the face of such threats, Canada has put itself at greater risk by tolerating terrorist support networks. Terrorists who feel comfortable enough to raise money and forge passports in Canada will not hesitate to stage attacks here as well; almost every terror group since the Armenians has done so, resulting in assassination attempts against several visiting dignitaries and Ottawa-based diplomats. It should come as no surprise that Al Qaeda has plotted attacks against Montreal Jews and the U.S. embassy in Ottawa. In the eyes of Al Qaeda, Canada is the enemy, as bin Laden has confirmed in one of his tape-recorded messages. "For Sunni Islamic extremists," says a classified CSIS report, "Canada is no longer regarded as simply a safe haven for criminal and logistical support activities. Canada is a viable terrorist target."

Canada values its law and order. Its symbol around the world is the Mountie in scarlet. So how did the country become a troublesome hub of world terror? To some extent Canada is naturally prone to terrorist infiltration. It is largely a country of immigrants. People settle in Canada from all over the world, and some bring with them the hatreds and causes of their homelands. Canada also has large ethnic communities, where terrorists can hide out, raise money and recruit. And Canada is right next door to the United States, the Great Satan in the eyes of many terrorists. "There are a variety of factors which explain why Canada is vulnerable," according to former CSIS Director Elcock. "Our borders and coastlines are long. Our society, like all developed countries, is comparatively wealthy—a source of technology, of equipment and funds. As with other democracies, our openness and respect for rights and freedoms limit the ability of the state to suppress terrorism in a ruthless, repressive fashion."

But there is more to it than that. Federal policies and the government's longstanding reluctance to confront the challenges of terrorism are also important factors. A U.S. Library of Congress study said terrorists were increasingly using Canada as an operational base because of its "generous welfare system, lax immigration laws, infrequent prosecutions, light sentencing, and long borders and coastlines ... These factors combine to make Canada a favored destination for terrorists and international organized crime groups."

Perhaps as important as Canadian policy is Canadian complacency. For many years, few Canadians seemed to realize the extent to which their country was been exploited by terrorists. In a poll conducted early in 2006, only 4 percent of Canadians ranked the war on terror as the most pressing foreign policy issue facing the government, and surveys have also showed wavering and sometimes soft support for the Canadian military mission in Afghanistan. Canadians generally do not recognize they are at war against terror. Instead of standing up to its foes, as Canadians did in the wars of the twentieth century, we have wrung our hands about counterterrorism measures; we worried that they might be infringing too heavily on our human rights and civil liberties; we worried that maybe they weren't even necessary. The Senate security subcommittee's 1999 report concluded that when it comes to terrorism, "considerable complacency ('it can't happen here') persists among the public-at-large."

This complacency was long fed by complacent politicians. In its handling of each of the major terrorist groups that operate in Canada—the Sikh extremists, Tamil Tigers, Hezbollah and Al Qaeda—the government has missed important opportunities to shut them down and has displayed an astounding level of indifference to nations afflicted by terrorism. The Canadian branch of the Babbar Khalsa, a Sikh terrorist group, was allowed to register as a charity, allowing mass killers to give tax receipts for blood money. The Liberal Cabinet refused on three occasions to add the Tamil Tigers to its list of designated terrorist groups, even though it is one of the top targets of Canadian counterterrorism investigators. It took a change of government in 2006 to finally get the Tigers blacklisted. Bill Graham, when he was the minister of foreign affairs, also resisted outlawing Hezbollah because he said it was a collective of "teachers, doctors and farmers." Ahmed Khadr, a close associate of bin Laden, was financed by the Canadian International Development Agency, and when he was arrested in Pakistan, Canada's prime minister intervened and he was released.

The lackluster response of Canadian politicians can be partly understood in the language of partisan politics. Some Members of Parliament hold stridently anti-American views, or at least recognize the political benefits of publicly denouncing the United States, and this sometimes finds expression on matters related to terrorism and counterterrorism. In addition, organized opposition to counterterrorism comes mainly from immigrant, refugee and ethnic lobby groups, which complain that their members are unfairly targeted by security measures. The Liberals have generally been reluctant to do anything that might anger the voters represented by these lobbyists. And so whenever counterterrorism was raised in Parliament in the months before 9/11, the Liberals responded by accusing the Opposition of racism and even anti-Canadianism.

In the logic of political strategy, to take a stand against terrorism was to risk losing the support of interest groups that buy influence by promising to deliver ethnic voting blocks. Securing the support of such lobby groups was apparently more important to these Parliamentarians than the security of Canadians. The president of the Montreal chapter of the World Tamil Movement, ruled by the federal court in 1997 to be a Tamil Tigers front organization, told me how he had helped a Liberal party candidate during the 2000 federal election campaign. "She came to our event, she was shocked, so I told her, 'Madam, my one word will give all the votes for you.' I told her and it was done; all the Sri Lankan votes went to the Liberals here in Montreal."

If many Canadians have no realistic understanding of the threat posed by modern terrorism it is partly because their government has historically displayed little interest in having a full and frank debate on the topic. The leading political parties hardly mentioned national security during the federal elections of June

2004, which saw the Liberals returned to power, and January 2006, which saw them replaced by a Conservative minority. The government strategy has been to deny that Canada has a problem, because to admit that terrorists are operating from Canada might prompt the United States to impose additional security measures at the border, which would slow trade and hurt the economy. So the government spin has been that Canada has an image problem, but not a terrorism problem.

The suggestion that there is a Canadian link to international terrorism was long met not with resolve but with outrage by Canadian politicians and more recently its ambassadors in Washington. While Canadian officials finally admitted that Canada could be an Al Qaeda target, they would not entertain the suggestion that Canada has failed to pull its weight in the war on terror. Just as Jean Chrétien told the House of Commons there were no terrorists in Canada, his successor Paul Martin told CNN that concerns about Canada's approach to security were just "a bum rap." This state of affairs proved frustrating for Canada's security agencies, which were consistently feeding terrorism intelligence up the food chain, only to have it ignored for partisan political reasons. In May 2000, prime minister-to-be Paul Martin and his cabinet colleague Maria Minna were warned ahead of time that they were scheduled to attend a dinner hosted by a leading Tamil Tigers front group in Toronto, but they went anyway. The Privy Council Office tried to deal with this problem in May 2000 when it wrote a memo to the prime minister concerning "contact of ministers with groups or individuals who may have undesirable connections." It mentioned that cabinet ministers are constantly being invited to functions, some of which "have undesirable links with terrorism." The Jerusalem Fund for Human Services, World Tamil Movement, Kurdish Information Network and Babbar Khalsa were singled out for mention as "front groups operating in Canada." But the report concluded that "there is no reason for undue alarm, or for ministers to restrict their agendas."

The trouble with this kind of approach was that it was concerned only with the politics of associating with terrorists; it failed to address the underlying problem that Canadian political leaders were being skillfully manipulated and co-opted by radicals until eventually they gave more credence to the exaggerations and propaganda of front groups than to their own intelligence professionals. An immigration official told me how he works all day at trying to get terrorists out of the country, and then watches as politicians court these same violent organizations for votes. When he gets home, his wife sometimes asks him why he even bothers. "I honestly don't know what to tell her," he said. Canadian counterterrorism officials have been forced to fight two wars—one against terrorists and the other against the Canadian politicians who pretend that terrorists either do not exist or are not a threat to Canada. "If anything should be a priority, it's the security of the nation," a veteran Canadian intelligence chief told me. "That that should be sold for cheap political gain outrages me."

The public was so often told there was no problem that citizens saw no need for solutions, particularly the kinds of compromises and intrusions necessary to fight terrorism effectively. Even after September 11, whenever a Canadian terrorist was arrested or deported, lobby groups turned what should have been an intelligence success into an opportunity to attack the intelligence services. When a suspected Al Qaeda sleeper agent was arrested in Montreal in May 2003, Islamic organizations portrayed it as an "inquisition against Muslims." Likewise, when the Federal Court of Canada ruled that Mahmoud Jaballah was a member of the Egyptian Al Jihad, as CSIS said he was, that was portrayed as an example of Canada's intolerance.

On December 10, 2002, a Pizza Pizza delivery man named Mohamed Harkat was arrested in Ottawa by an RCMP tactical team. A CSIS investigation had determined he was a member of the bin Laden network and that he had trained in Afghanistan. Harkat is an Algerian who came to Canada in 1995 and married a French Canadian named Sophie, all the while, according to CSIS, concealing his links to terrorism. He received large amounts of cash from points overseas, worked in Pakistan for a Saudi aid organization tied to bin Laden, and was a friend of Fahad Shehri, a Saudi deported for terrorism in 1997. "Prior to arriving in Canada, the Service believes that Harkat engaged in terrorism by supporting terrorist activity," CSIS wrote. "The service furthermore believes that Harkat has engaged in those activities as a member of a terrorist entity known as the bin Laden network, which includes Al Qaeda." The evidence was not to be taken lightly. Zubaydah himself had identified Harkat to authorities after being captured in Pakistan.

Days after the arrest, Sophie Harkat gave reporters a photograph of her husband of two years and said she stood by him "200 per cent." In the picture, Sophie and her mother are smiling as they embrace Mohamed. The symbolism is striking, though unintended: Canadians embracing a suspected terrorist. A support group was soon formed to lobby for Harkat's release. An Internet site was launched, featuring photos of Harkat and letters concerning his "fight for justice." Harkat was a victim of "racial profiling and scapegoating," it said. "Stop the insanity," Mrs. Harkat pleaded. She claimed that CSIS lies and breaks the law, and that she knew Harkat had done no wrong because, "In my husband's eyes, I can read innocence." In March 2003, Mrs. Harkat and forty others staged a demonstration in downtown Ottawa. She waved a placard reading "Save My Husband, My Friend, My Love, My Hero."

Activists in Montreal have also set up an Internet site seeking "Justice for Adil Charkaoui," a Moroccan whom CSIS calls an Al Qaeda sleeper agent. Although Charkaoui denies ever going to Afghanistan, both Ressam and Abu Zubaydah, who facilitated entry into bin Laden's training camps, have said they met him there. Ressam says they trained together at the same Al Qaeda camp. "We demand the release of Adil Charkaoui," reads the web site.

After Hassan Almrei, a forger in the Al Qaeda network, was arrested in Ontario, a Toronto woman befriended him and offered to post a $10,000 cash bond to secure his release. "We would be happy to welcome him into our home," said the woman. "We're all eager to have Hassan move in with us." The point here is not the guilt or innocence of these men. That is for the courts to determine (as of this writing they have sided in almost all respects with CSIS). What is troubling is the single-minded focus of Canadian activists, academics and politicians, on the rights of accused terrorists, without regard for the right of Canadians to defend themselves from the threat of terror. If this is how Canadians treat captured members of the bin Laden network, with hugs and protests, while the intelligence agents charged with protecting Canadians are called liars and cheats, no wonder terrorists view the country as a haven. "Canada," a Russian security official once told an RCMP officer in Moscow, "is the land of the trusting fools."

While terrorists can count on their own strident lobby, lobbying in favor of counterterrorism has been all but nonexistent. When a Tamil Tigers leader and an Iranian government hit man, who were both facing deportation, went to the Supreme Court of Canada to argue they should not be sent back to their homelands, eight lobby groups intervened in the case, all in favor of the terrorists. Nobody came forward to speak for ordinary Canadians who did not want their country to become a safe haven for terrorists. The only mainstream organizations that have consistently lobbied against terrorism were Jewish community groups, because Jews are so often the targets of terror, although several new groups have now formed, such as the Canadian Coalition Against Terror, which includes victims of Air India, 9/11, Palestinian suicide bombings and other attacks. One of the group's first aims is to get legislation through Parliament that would make it easier for victims of terrorism to sue the financial and state backers of terrorist organizations.

Over the past two decades, the government agencies charged with national security did their best given the lack of political support for their work but they were unable to stop the parade of terrorist organizations into Canada. Security background checks are routine, but it is no easy task to investigate someone whose home is halfway around the world, especially if there is war and upheaval in the country, and if migrants are not forthright about their past or even their true identity. The regions from which new Canadians come are not the kinds of places that keep accurate records, and so Canadian authorities are unable to properly screen for terrorists. "There are no databases," a former senior Canadian intelligence official told me. "And if there are, they are totally unreliable." And CSIS lacks the resources to screen as thoroughly as it would like to. Jack Hooper, the agency's Deputy Director of Operations, testified in May 2006 before the Senate Committee on National Security and Defence that 90 percent of immigrants from Pakistan and Afghanistan were not being carefully checked before being admitted to Canada. "That may be inadequate," he said.

Canadian intelligence authorities have been disrupting terrorist groups and tipping off police when there may be grounds for criminal charges. But even when everything works as it should and terrorists are caught in Canada's security screening system, the worst fate they suffer is usually deportation. And even then, many of those ordered out of the country never leave. Under the Canadian system, they are allowed to launch appeal after appeal after appeal. Government counterterrorism agencies can spend years building a case against a terrorist, at a cost of over $1-million per investigation. Canada's immigration system, however, is so cumbersome that few of those arrested ever get deported. The Canadian leader of the Tamil Tigers, Manickavasagam Suresh, was arrested in 1995 as a threat to national security, but in the summer of 2006 he was still here. Some terrorists have been arrested, released on bail by immigration judges, and then just disappeared. A former high-ranking Canadian security official told me, "We as a country collectively have lulled Canadians into a false sense of security by not taking seriously the cases that have come forward from the intelligence community in Canada."

The director of CSIS said as far back as 1998 that Canada was at risk of developing a reputation as a terrorist haven. "The wanton use of violence to achieve political ends is contrary to our core political and moral values," Elcock testified. "I do not believe that Canadians want their country to be known as a place from which terrorist acts elsewhere are funded or fomented. We cannot ever become known as some R&R facility for terrorists. In other words, and I will be as blunt as I can be, we cannot become, through inaction or otherwise, what might be called an unofficial state sponsor of terrorism." Following the 9/11 attacks, the government finally did the obvious—it tightened airport security, passed the Anti-terrorism Act and gave more money to security and intelligence agencies. But by then, through negligence, indifference and open support for violent organizations, Canada had already become an unofficial terrorism sponsor. Canada was in many ways a case study of what could happen when politicians let down their guard against security threats and willfully ignore warnings for partisan reasons, even as their allies and citizens are suffering the consequences.

Former Prime Minister Jean Chrétien used to boast that the United Nations Human Development Index ranked Canada the best country in the world in which to live. During the past two decades, it has also become the best country in the world for terrorists to make their home. An official at the Department of Foreign Affairs once told me that in the past, when there was a terrorist attack somewhere in the world, the department would routinely check the names to see if there were any Canadians among the victims. "Nowadays, we check both ends," he said. What he meant was that officials must now also run the names of the bombers to see if they were Canadians, because increasingly they are.

The government of Stephen Harper, which took office after winning a minority of seats in Parliament on January 23, 2006, was quick to send out the message that it intended to take a harder line against terrorists. It was the first government besides Israel to sever ties with the Hamas-controlled Palestinian Authority. It added the Tamil Tigers to Canada's list of outlawed terrorist groups and committed to rebuilding the armed forces and enhancing international security intelligence gathering efforts. The largest counter-terrorism sweep in Canadian history, the round-up of the Toronto 17 (later 18, following the arrest of yet another suspect), took place under the Conservative watch, and Prime Minister Harper said on the day after the arrests, "It is a dangerous world and we cannot escape it by turning a blind eye to it." Canadian attitudes about terrorism may have also hardened since the arrests, with 62 percent agreeing in a survey that without national security, civil liberties were no more than theoretical. Or maybe not. Following the Toronto arrests, Senator Colin Kenny recalled participating on a hotline radio show on terrorism. Of the fifteen callers, fourteen said they were not concerned about terrorism and the fifteenth said if anything were to happen, the Americans would take care of it. "As a general proposition," CSIS Director Jim Judd testified, "I am not sure that the average Canadian understands many of these issues."

In a paper published three weeks after the arrests in Toronto, the Center for Strategic and International Studies in Washington, D.C. optimistically declared that "any perception of Canadian complacency about terrorism within its borders is now behind us." The government certainly encouraged that perception by sending a team of senior officials to Washington to spread the word that all was well. But as Kenny, Chairman of the Senate Committee on National Security and Defence, wrote in the *National Post*, despite the government's rush to reassure, major problems remained unaddressed. The RCMP needed as many as five thousand more personnel, and CSIS remained short-staffed as well, he said. He said it would probably take Canada a decade to "get up to speed" on monitoring and countering threats at Canada's airports, sea ports, borders and inside neighborhoods where extremism incubates. He criticized the government's rush to reassure Canadians and their allies.

"The public doesn't need calming," he said. "The public needs the truth."

PROLOGUE

AHMED RESSAM LOOKS MUSCULAR and tough in his police photo, a sneering menace in a tight T-shirt, but in person he looks weak and scared. His eyes are dark and sunken deep into a gaunt face with a perpetual five o'clock shadow. His clothes, camel-colored sweater over a white undershirt, hang loose on his bones. Some say it's the malaria he picked up at Osama bin Laden's training camps, or maybe it's the stress of having been captured in the act by his sworn enemy.

Every morning it's the same routine. He arrives at the Federal Building in downtown Los Angeles in a vehicle protected by heavily armed guards wearing sunglasses. The sheriffs take him up the elevator to the courtroom, unlock his handcuffs and step back against the wall as he sinks into a chair to the left of the judge, crosses his legs in a way that makes him look effeminate, and puts on the headset that allows him to hear the translation of the day's legal proceedings.

Throughout the trial, I find myself staring at Ressam, as if I expect him to betray some semblance of the Islamic holy warrior we all know him to be, perhaps an outburst against infidel America or something more subtle like a sinister grin. This is, after all, a man so devoted to the Islamic jihad that he built a massive bomb using the method he learned in Afghanistan, stashed it in the trunk of his car and tried to drive to Los Angeles International Airport during the peak travel season.

I watch Ressam so much that I fear I am neglecting the witnesses summoned to detail his movements. Here he is, face to face with the nation he has been taught to despise: America, the Great Satan, enemy of Islam, supporter of the Little Satan, Israel. But still he never slips. He never looks more dangerous than a librarian, and that may be the scariest part of all.

The prosecutors explain how Ressam left his home in Algeria, how he was indoctrinated into the world of radical Islam by other expatriates, how he wanted so badly to fight for the cause of jihad that he flew to Pakistan, disguised himself as a woman and trekked through the mountains to a desolate camp in eastern Afghanistan to learn the tradecraft of terror—the weapons, the explosives, target selection, the art of concealment.

After months of training, Ressam returned to his base, a country that was harboring every major international terrorist organization on the planet, a country where terrorists were building bombs, raising money for weapons, plotting, recruiting and then going out into the world to spread terror.

That country is Canada.

How did Canada get this way?

I

SPILLOVER

"DEATH TO her!" the crowd shouted.

"Indira Bitch," a lone voice called.

"Death to them!"

"Hindu dogs."

"Long live ..."

"Khalistan!"

"Long live ..."

"Babbar Khalsa!"

Madison Square Garden is a shrine of hockey, the arena where Phil Esposito, Brad Park and Wayne Gretzky wore New York Rangers jerseys, but on this day in July 1984, it was transformed into a temple of hatred. A Canadian named Ajaib Singh Bagri took to the stage at the founding conference of the World Sikh Organization and delivered a sermon that seethed with rage. It was a potent combination of scripture and propaganda that used religious imagery to make its point: a Sikh nation separate from India was the will of God. "When the blood of martyrs is spilled, the destiny of communities is changed," Bagri began.

Bagri was a forklift operator at the Tolko Industries plywood plant in Kamloops, British Columbia. He was also a devout Sikh preacher who had immigrated to Canada from India in 1971 at the age of twenty-two. He helped build a temple in Kamloops, and could be found there regularly, serving food, performing hymns called *kirtan*, or doing maintenance. "I did carpentry, plumbing and daily cleaning," he said. He preached around the province and was general secretary of the Sikh Cultural Society. He also served with the Babbar Khalsa Society, which he called "a British Columbia society that promoted Sikhism." The Babbar Khalsa Society was a registered charity in Canada, but it was much more than just another nonprofit religious group. It was the Canadian branch of the Babbar Khalsa, one of India's largest terrorist organizations, whose members pledge to "take revenge on all those who insult the Guru Granth Sahib [high priest]; all those who are against the Panth [Sikh religion]; all those police officers who oppress Sikh youth and police informers who act against Sikhs." The founder of the Babbar Khalsa's Canadian wing, Talwinder Singh Parmar, had been wanted by officials in India since 1982 for six counts of murder stemming from his suspected role in police killings.

"Long live ..." the congregation continued.

"Sant Jarnail Singh Bindranwale!"

"Long live ..."

"Sant Jarnail Singh Bindranwale!"

Bindranwale was an obscure Sikh priest who came to prominence in Indian politics as an ally of prime minister Indira Gandhi. When Hindu nationalism gained ground in India in the early 1980s, Sikhs began to fear for their place in the country, setting off riots and hunger strikes in the Punjab, the state where they were the overwhelming majority. Bindranwale became an increasingly fundamentalist and militant advocate of a separate Sikh state. His followers set up guerrilla training camps and began killing Indian police officers. Bindranwale set himself up at the Golden Temple in Amritsar, turning the holiest of Sikh shrines into a fortress.

On June 6, 1984, Gandhi struck back with Operation Blue Star, sending troops to the temple. Hundreds were killed in the gun battle that ensued, including Bindranwale himself. The symbolism of the operation was quickly harnessed by extremist leaders, who held it up as proof that the Indian government wanted to wipe out the Sikhs. There were mass demonstrations around the world, including in Vancouver, where fifteen thousand demonstrated outside the Indian consulate, and at Madison Square Garden, where Bagri rallied North American Sikhs in a speech captured on videotape.

"Any speaker from here who will say 'Hindus are brothers' will be deemed a traitor of the community," Bagri told his audience.

"Death to ..." the audience shouted.

"Traitors of the nation!" yelled the slogan raiser, who leads the congregation in chants.

"Will create Khalistan ..."

"Will sacrifice ourselves."

"Will create Khalistan ..."

"For the retribution of sacrifices."

Bagri spoke about the Babbar Khalsa (BK) organization, which promotes the objectives advanced earlier by the Babbar Akali movement of the 1920s. The aim of BK is to avenge the deaths of Sikhs killed in defense of the faith and establish a Sikh fundamentalist state called Khalistan, Land of the Pure. The BK has worked in cooperation with other Sikh militant groups such as the International Sikh Youth Federation (ISYF). The Canadian branch was involved in raising money, and since it was a registered charity, it could issue tax receipts to its donors. "Sikh militants in North America are a source of financial support for terrorist activities," states a Canadian Security Intelligence Service (CSIS) report. "In Canada, Service investigation has revealed that funds are raised through the collection of moneys from Sikh communities in Canada and transferred to the leadership based in Pakistan and India. In Canada, the Babbar Khalsa Society of Kamloops, B.C., used its charitable status in order to raise funds for the cause."

Bagri urged Sikh families to offer up one youth to the organization, which he called the army of the timeless and immortal. "Yes, there must be our handshake with the Hindus; we will shake hands. Where? On the battlefield."

"Blessed be he who utters ..." the slogan raiser yelled.

"God is truth," the congregation replied. "Long live ..."

"Babbar Khalsa."

Amid this outpouring, Bagri was somehow able to find a spot to inject some humor, joking that it was not his fault his speech was taking so long since the congregation was eating up half his time with its chants. His focus eventually turned to the age-old beef of terrorists, that they are not really terrorists. "A Sikh who saves the honor of his sister, he is branded as a terrorist, separatist extremist. A Hindu who rapes our sister's modesty in the presence of a crowd of five or six thousand people is given the title of a patriot."

Throughout his speech, which was delivered in Punjabi, Bagri seemed to be trying to convince his audience that Sikhs would have to fight for Khalistan. (Bagri's speech has been entered as evidence at his trial; the defense has disputed the Crown's translation and its significance.) In the past, Sikhs would ask for their demands to be fulfilled but those days were gone, he said. "Today the Khalsa have to clash iron with iron ... No one hands a nation over to anyone, whoever gets it gets it by their own strength. We have to find that strength. Where will it come from? From the feet of the Lord."

Those unable to fight, he said, should work double shifts and collect money. "All should be ready. If we don't get up even now, those forlorn in India, in Punjab cannot get up. On us are their hopes ... the community has lots of money, the community has lots of blood."

"Long live ..."

"Babbar Khalsa."

"Long live ..."

"Babbar Khalsa."

"Long live ..."

"Khalistan."

"Avenge the shed blood."

"I make of you a request," Bagri continued. "Retribution is to be taken from these Hindus. Some say the word of retribution should not be used. I say, we know only this."

"Blessed be he who utters ..." the crowd responded.

"God is the truth."

It was in this heated climate that CSIS was born on July 16, 1984. Until then, national security had been the domain of the Royal

Canadian Mounted Police (RCMP), Department of National Defence and Department of External Affairs. After the Second World War, the focus was Cold War counterespionage and countersubversion—keeping a watch on the Soviet spies working out of Ottawa and weeding out the communist plants that had infiltrated the federal government. Canada's first major terrorism threat came from the Sons of Freedom Doukhobors. Beginning in the 1920s, this small Russian religious sect, which settled in Canada's West, carried out a terrorist campaign that was to span almost four decades and include more than a thousand arson and bomb attacks. Portraying themselves as a repressed minority whose religious beliefs were not extended tolerance by the mainstream, Doukhobor fundamentalists turned to terrorism to coerce change in government policies. Locals described it as a small civil war and complained to Ottawa of living in a state of terror. Police had little success in stopping the attacks, but a concerted police effort finally paid off, resulting in dozens of arrests that broke the extremist movement in the early 1960s.

The first wave of international terrorism came to Canada just as the Doukhobors were fading from the scene, when Cuban exiles opposed to the dictatorship of Fidel Castro staged a series of attacks against Cuban interests, mostly in Montreal. Ethnic nationalist tensions in Yugoslavia played out in Canada in the 1960s and 1970s, as Serbs and Croats traded potshots. The Arab-Israeli dispute also turned violent in Canada in the 1970s. But the terrorist threat was largely dismissed by Canadians because it was concentrated in only a few pockets of the country and the targets tended to be diplomats and others outside the mainstream.

The 1976 Montreal Olympic Games forced Canadian authorities to pay closer attention to foreign terrorist organizations. The previous Olympics, in Munich in 1972, had been hijacked by the Palestine Liberation Organization (PLO), which murdered eleven Israeli athletes. The RCMP feared terrorists might strike again at the Montreal Games, and so the Security Service began investigating the extent of the international terrorist presence in Canada. The Olympics went off without a hitch, but the RCMP soon uncovered a network of Armenian terrorist groups that were using the country as a base for supporting their campaign for an independent homeland. The leading concern was the Armenian Secret Army for the Liberation of Armenia (ASALA), formed in 1975 to avenge the Armenian genocide of 1915, which resulted in more than a million deaths. Based in Beirut, ASALA was radical, violent and aided by Syria and Libya. Its philosophy was Marxist-Leninist, like that of the Popular Front for the Liberation of Palestine, with which it was closely aligned. ASALA attacks targeted the Turkish government.

One branch of ASALA consisted of five known operatives who had met through Armenian cultural organizations in Toronto. At their meetings, they would drink coffee and talk about the hated Turks who had stolen their family land. They were angry and vengeful and fancied themselves as revolutionaries. Harout Kevork, their leader, traveled to Beirut to meet with the ASALA leadership, and when he returned, the group began plotting a terrorist attack against a Turkish target in Canada. They obtained a copy of a government handbook listing the foreign diplomats posted in Canada, flipped to the section on the Turkish embassy, and chose a few names. Then they drove to Ottawa to scout the homes of their targets. The first address they found was the Riverside Drive apartment of Kani Gungor, the Turkish commercial attaché. His assassination was planned for March 24, 1982.

The RCMP Security Service happened to be monitoring Kevork's gang. They were listening in on their phone calls and watching the home of Raffic Balian, one of Kevork's men. But, as they would soon learn, it is not easy to stop a terrorist attack. On April 8, 1982, it was minus seven degrees when Kani Gungor left for work at 9:30 a.m. He walked to the parking garage below his apartment building and stepped into a burst of gunfire. Two bullets hit him from different directions. One struck his leg and another nicked his spine. A car that had been stolen from Balian's neighborhood in Scarborough, in Metropolitan Toronto, was found abandoned near the scene. Two days later, the youngest member of the group, seventeen-year-old Haig Gharakhanian of Toronto, who had helped scout the targets in Ottawa weeks earlier, delivered a letter to the Los Angeles office of United Press International taking credit for the shooting on behalf of ASALA.

The attack was the first major international terrorist incident in Canada, but it was somewhat amateurish and the RCMP quickly focused their investigation on Kevork and his gang. The ASALA members were brought in for questioning on several occasions, but it was two years before Kevork, Balian and Gharakhanian were arrested and formally charged. Gharakhanian's first thought upon being cuffed by the Mounties was: "What took you so long?" Three weeks into the proceedings, all three pleaded guilty to conspiracy to commit murder. The judge had harsh words for the terrorists: "When a minority of persons in the name of liberation assume the power of life and death over other human beings on Canadian soil, they are playing God when in fact, in my view, they are simply bandits and criminals. The members of ASALA were never liberators. They are assassins and murderers. There is no freedom there."

The judge was no doubt aware that four months after the assassination attempt, Armenian terrorists had struck again. When Colonel Atilla Altikat, the Turkish military attaché, had stopped at a red light while heading to work along Ottawa River Parkway, a gunman approached his passenger window and fired ten bullets into his head and chest. The Justice Commandos of the Armenian Genocide called news outlets in Montreal and Paris to take credit. In 1985, there was yet another attack in Ottawa. Three men stormed the residence of the Turkish ambassador in Ottawa and killed a thirty-one-year-old security guard, Claude Brunelle. The gunmen held the ambassador and his family hostage for four hours before surrendering. (Ironically, Brunelle's brother was a friend of Kevork's.)

Although prosecutors described the Gungor shooting as "a deliberate and cold-blooded conspiracy," the judge imposed sentences considerably less than the maximum fourteen years. Balian was sentenced to eight years while Kevork got nine, but when it came time to impose a sentence on Gharakhanian, the judge was more sympathetic, calling him a "misguided youth." Gharakhanian was the grandson of an Armenian woman who had survived the genocide and fled to Iran, still clutching the deed to the property she would never reclaim. He had a privileged middle-class upbringing in Iran. His father worked for Swiss Air, which permitted him to travel throughout Europe. In the buildup to the Islamic revolution in Tehran, his parents sent his older brother to Toronto and, in 1981, they sent Haig as well. Gharakhanian quickly fell in with the ASALA crowd and took part in the assassination plot from the beginning, helping scout Gungor's residence in Ottawa. He also participated in an insurance fraud scheme with Kevork to raise money for the group. But the judge described him as "a victim" and imposed a sentence of two years less a day. While the sentence was light for an act of terrorism, Gharakhanian was still facing the prospect of deportation because he was not a Canadian and could be expelled for his involvement in terrorism.

After he was paroled nine months into his sentence, Gharakhanian applied for refugee status. He obtained a Canadian government business loan so he could start a printing company. When the recession hit in the early 1990s, his business closed and his equipment was repossessed. He applied for welfare, became a shiatsu therapist and married a filmmaker. They had a daughter. A deportation order was issued in 1991, but Gharakhanian successfully fought it by appealing to the Immigration and Refugee Board (IRB). The *Ottawa Citizen* stepped into the debate over Gharakhanian's fate in a 1992 editorial that declared "it's time to stop punishing ... [Gungor] can't forget, but we can forgive." The eight-page decision of the IRB adjudicator, handed down in 1996, mentioned that Gharakhanian had "generally participated in plans to kill a Turkish diplomat in Canada." The victim was described as "paraplegic." It did not mention that Kani Gungor would live out his life in a wheelchair, did not have the use his hands, and could not even hold up his head. He would have to visit the hospital each day of his difficult life.

In contrast, Gharakhanian's achievements were described in detail. The IRB noted that he had completed his high school education. Gharakhanian had been in Canada for only a year before trying to assassinate a man, but the adjudicator said his roots were in Canada. The IRB adjudicator said Gharakhanian had "demonstrated significant rehabilitation" and was remorseful. "He lives a quiet, family-oriented and law-abiding life. I find that he poses little future risk to the public." The adjudicator overturned the deportation order and Gharakhanian was allowed to stay in Canada.

When I met Gharakhanian in a coffee shop in Toronto's Little Italy in September 2003, he said he had renounced violence and wanted to put that part of his life behind him. He is a slender man with a shaved head, and spoke articulately about karma and the inevitability of death. He was working as a musician, writing songs and playing guitar in a band. He said he had applied for Canadian citizenship.

Nicoghas Moumdjian, a former member of an Armenian militia in Lebanon and an associate of Gharakhanian and the other ASALA members convicted for Gungor's shooting, was later arrested as a national security threat. Although he was not involved in the shooting plot, CSIS said he had purchased materials necessary to make an explosive device and "believes in the indiscriminate use of violence in furtherance of political ends." But when Canada tried to deport him, he appealed to the courts and the Canadian Civil Liberties Association (CCLA) intervened on his behalf, arguing it was unconstitutional to deport someone because of his membership in an organization. The CCLA complained that Canada was deporting him simply for "alleged fraternization with an Armenian nationalist group." The court rejected the arguments and he was ordered to leave Canada, but by December 2003 he still had not left and the intervention was yet another indication that Canadians did not grasp the emerging terrorist threat. ASALA was the first to bring international terrorism to Canada, and it was treated not with resolve but with sympathy. Canada's handling of these early terrorists would set the stage for the decades to come.

As the world's ethnic nationalist wars began to spill over, flooding across borders into countries to establish sizable refugee and immigrant communities, police began to find signs that other terrorist organizations were taking root in Canada. After discovering ASALA, the RCMP found that the Irish Republican Army (IRA) was also fundraising in Canada, but authorities at first did nothing because collecting cash was considered a nonviolent pursuit that was not a threat to Canada. The British government, however, put pressure on Ottawa to take action, since the money raised in Canada was financing the purchase of weapons. Canadian-made detonators were turning up inside IRA bombs. The Canadian government eventually relented and the RCMP pulled some of its officers off the Armenian desk and reassigned them to spy on the IRA.

By that time, the RCMP was preparing to hand responsibility for terrorist-hunting to a new agency called CSIS. During the Front de Libération du Québec (FLQ) crisis, prime minister Pierre Trudeau told the RCMP to take care of the FLQ, and it did, but the Mounties were later taken to task over their aggressive, sometimes illegal, tactics. In 1969, the Mackenzie Commission found that a civilian agency was needed to handle the sensitive matter of security intelligence, and the McDonald Commission of Inquiry made the same recommendation in 1981. Bill C-157, "an Act to Establish the Canadian Security Intelligence Service," was drafted in 1981. It envisioned a department whose mandate would be to investigate threats to Canadian security, everything from espionage, sabotage and foreign influence to terrorism and subversion. CSIS was not to be a law-enforcement agency. Its agents could not make arrests. Its role was to investigate and to report its findings to the government. The bill was condemned by opposition groups who imagined it would give spies overly broad powers to investigate peaceful political movements. It was replaced by a watered-down version called Bill C-9, which was approved by the House of Commons on June 21, 1984. It was the last law passed by then–prime minister Pierre Trudeau.

CSIS was thrown at once into the various homeland conflicts spilling over into Canada. The initial targets of its counterterrorism desk were the IRA, Middle Eastern groups and Sikh extremists. The first CSIS agents were not unfamiliar with the Sikh problem. RCMP Security Service members, many of whom joined CSIS at its launch, had for a decade been aware of such groups as the Khalistan Commando Movement, whose leader Dr. Jagjit Singh Chauhan declared unilateral independence for Punjab in 1969 and set up Khalistan "consulates" in Vancouver, Winnipeg and Toronto. The Mounties were not overly concerned about Sikh militancy, however. In December 1981, the head of the Security Service wrote that "although this situation has potential for diplomatic embarrassment, there is no perceived threat to national security from Sikh activities in Canada."

The "Consul-General of Khalistan" in Vancouver was Talwinder Singh Parmar, a Sikh priest with a bright saffron turban. Parmar was born into a farming family in India's Punjab and was employed as a social worker before moving to Canada. He was not active in the Khalistan movement in India; that came only after he was firmly rooted in Canada. Parmar returned to India in July 1981 with his family, ostensibly to preach, but he disappeared and his family became concerned about his well-being. He resurfaced in Canada on May 1, 1982—just days after the Indian government asked for his extradition; he was wanted in connection with the November 19, 1981, murder of two police officers in Punjab state. On a trip to the Netherlands, Parmar tried to enter West Germany, but border authorities were alerted that he was wanted in India and arrested him. He was still in custody when Indian troops stormed the Golden Temple. Germany, however, refused to extradite him, and he was released.

Parmar arrived back in Canada on July 6, 1984, just as Sikhs were organizing mass protests across the country. A videotape shot at the Toronto airport upon his return shows dozens of Sikhs standing, with swords raised, shouting: "Death to Indira Gandhi!" The raid at Amritsar had generated unparalleled support for the Punjab separatist campaign that Parmar had long promoted. He stepped right into the middle of it, establishing himself as the leading Sikh holy man, and one who was not afraid to fight. He displayed photos of himself armed to the hilt. "Until we hand the heads of those sinners on the tips of our swords, we will not rest," Parmar told a Hamilton temple congregation on July 21. Bagri began referring to Parmar as "the Sikh nation's living martyr leader," and said the Babbar Khalsa leader's return from Germany was an act of God. "This is my belief," Bagri said in a speech, "that the true Emperor Lord has released that warrior, that Babbar, from prison for the cause, telling him, 'Go Babbar! Go dear son of your guru. Go, my son, take revenge and get even. Take young men with you and raze

Delhi to the ground." The RCMP had by this time revised its assessment of the potential for Sikh violence in Canada and had started to issue warnings that violence was now a serious threat. New Sikh extremist groups were popping up in Canada, first the Sikh youth group ISYF, then the Dashmesh Regiment, which had allegedly compiled a hit list of moderate Sikhs.

The Indian government certainly thought that violence was possible. There had already been a few minor incidents. India's acting high commissioner, K.P. Fabian, was pelted with eggs in Winnipeg in July. A Vancouver man who had sponsored an interview with Indian president Zail Singh on a Punjabi-language radio show was held at gunpoint by two turbaned men who threatened him with a *kirpan*, a ceremonial dagger. The high commissioner told the Department of External Affairs he feared that Babbar Khalsa members such as Parmar might return to Indian to carry out attacks. *He also thought that Air India planes could be attacked.* There was a feeling in the Sikh community that something big was about to happen. And so, on August 17, 1984, the newly formed CSIS launched its first large-scale counterterrorism investigation. The target: Sikh extremism.

CSIS at first put minimal resources into the Sikh investigation, but the agents were soon able to identify the main groups working in Canada and their key members. The climate took a turn for the worse that fall. On October 31, Indira Gandhi was assassinated by her Sikh bodyguards, setting off retaliatory attacks by Hindus and leading to "serious animosity between the two groups in Canada." Reports that attacks were imminent began to trickle in from various sources. Most proved false, but one was confirmed. It concerned four Sikhs who had approached Frank Camper, who ran the Reconnaissance Commando School near Birmingham, Alabama. The men, who had recently been in Toronto and were said to be acting on orders from Vancouver, said they wanted to learn about kidnapping, bomb-building and assassination.

From the start, Parmar was the focus of the Sikh investigation, and in the fall of 1984, CSIS applied for a warrant so it could begin intercepting his phone calls. Legal difficulties delayed the warrant. At the time, the Official Secrets Act was being replaced by the CSIS

Act. The solicitor general expressed some unspecified concerns about the Parmar warrant and it was withdrawn. It was not resubmitted until the following spring. The warrant allowed intercepts to begin on March 14, 1985. They did not begin until March 27. The wiretaps confirmed that Parmar was in contact with Babbar Khalsa members in the United States, Europe and elsewhere, but exactly what was being said in these calls CSIS could not say because it did not have a Punjabi translator. Even once it hired one, there was such a backlog of recorded conversations that he could not keep up. Then there were the code words. CSIS was aware that Parmar and his contacts probably spoke in code, but they did not break the code until it was too late. Only later did they discern that all the talk about "bows and arrows" they were hearing was referring to an attack on an airplane. "If they talked about 'shooting the arrow,' we had no idea they might mean blowing up a plane," one former intelligence official told me.

Parmar further drew attention to himself on May 2, 1985, when he warned at a news conference in Vancouver that the Indian government "will pay a price for attacking the temple." CSIS expected Sikh extremist activity to spike as the first anniversary of the Amritsar massacre approached. Sikhs were holding a Black Week vigil to mark the occasion and, on top of that, Indian prime minister Rajiv Gandhi would be visiting the United States from June 11 to 16. The threat assessments produced by CSIS warned about the possibility of an attack on Air India, and mentioned the use of bombs concealed inside transistor radios. "The government of India warned Canada on a number of occasions that Air India operations were about to be attacked or its aircraft hijacked," the Security Intelligence Review Committee (SIRC) later wrote. But CSIS felt the biggest danger to the airline was a hijacking rather than a bombing. As a result, there were impressive safeguards against a hijacking in place, but little was done to prevent a bomb from being planted on board an aircraft.

At the same time that CSIS was listening to Parmar's phone calls, agents were also conducting physical surveillance, monitoring his movements and keeping track of those he was meeting in British Columbia. On June 4, CSIS followed Parmar as he and his son drove to Horseshoe Bay with a Sikh named Surjan Singh Gill. They walked aboard the 3 p.m. ferry and sailed across the Strait of Georgia to Nanaimo, where they were met by another man, who brought them to the home of Inderjit Singh Reyat, a director of the Vancouver Island Sikh Cultural Society. The agents observed as Reyat drove his guests in his Mercury to Auto Marine Electric, where he worked, and then to a logging road deep in the bush. Parmar and Reyat were seen taking something out of the trunk and walking into the forest, where the spies lost sight of them. Parmar's son returned to the car and closed the door. A few minutes later, there was an explosion. "It scared the hell out of me," one of the CSIS agents said later. The agents thought someone was shooting at them and took cover behind a tree. Parmar and Reyat got back into the car and drove off.

The agents reported the incident to CSIS headquarters in Ottawa the next day. They knew Reyat owned a handgun and thought that was what they had heard. "We didn't know what it was at the time," said Jim Francis, the head of the counterterrorism unit in the B.C. regional office of CSIS. A government review would later determine that "the significance of the incident does not appear to have been realized at the time and we saw nothing in CSIS files to indicate if any comprehensive analysis of the incident was immediately undertaken." Francis wishes they had figured it out. "This is something we are constantly looking for. We would have loved to have it happen. I mean, this is the whole purpose of the exercise, is to catch Parmar with his goddamn hands in the cookie jar and so there is a constant vigil just waiting for him to make the wrong move."

An airplane bombing was not foremost in everyone's mind. The consensus was that if there was to be an attack, it would come during Rajiv Gandhi's visit to the United States, and would take the form of an attack against an Indian diplomatic mission in Canada or the Indian leader himself. The FBI had uncovered a plot to kill Gandhi during his trip, and that became the focus for Canadian investigators. When Gandhi's tour ended on June 16, there was a collective sigh of relief. It had passed without incident, as had the anniversary of the Golden Temple attack. Physical surveillance of

Parmar was suspended. A Russian intelligence officer was coming to Vancouver and he needed to be watched. On June 18, CSIS said the Sikh extremist threat in Canada had dropped as a consequence of these two developments, but only slightly. There was no indication, CSIS said, of any imminent threat to Air India.

On June 19, a man who identified himself only as Mr. Singh called the Canadian Pacific Airlines reservations line and said he needed two tickets out of Vancouver, one going east, the other going west. The ticket agent offered several options but the man insisted that both flights had to connect with Air India. They settled on two routes: Vancouver/Tokyo/New Delhi and Vancouver/Toronto/Montreal/London. Mr. Singh said the tickets were for Mohinderbel Singh and Jaswant Singh. The next day, he called back to change the names on the tickets to L. Singh and M. Singh. He paid in cash. "M. Singh" came to the check-in counter on the day of the flight and tried to check his bag through to New Delhi, but the airline agent said he could not because he was only wait-listed for the Vancouver to Toronto leg. He insisted. "My brother knows I'm confirmed," he said. "I'll go get my brother." It was a vague but plausible explanation, and one that the agent accepted. She checked the bag through to New Delhi. L. Singh also checked one bag for his flight. Neither of the men boarded his plane.

The bombs went off within an hour of each other.

At 6:19 a.m. GMT on June 23, 1985, a baggage crew at Narita Airport in Japan was transferring the luggage from Canadian Pacific Flight 003 from Vancouver onto an Air India flight when a suitcase exploded in a baggage cart. Two men were killed and four more wounded.

Air India Flight 182, inbound to London from Montreal, was approaching the coast of Ireland when the crew contacted air traffic control at 7:05 a.m. GMT with a cheery "good morning." Nine minutes later the plane vanished off the radar screen. Air traffic controller Michael Quinn hailed the plane a dozen times but got no response. He asked the other planes in the area if they could see the Boeing 747. A TWA flight soaring 1,200 meters higher said it could see only a vapor trail. By the time the Royal Air Force search and rescue helicopter arrived, the bodies were rising up from the depths. The sea was all wreckage and corpses.

When word reached Canadian authorities, they knew immediately it was an act of terrorism. It was indeed the worst terrorist attack in modern history. Three hundred and thirty-one lives taken in two symbolic acts of vengeance. (The record would stand for over sixteen years, until Al Qaeda attacked the World Trade Center and Pentagon.) Suspicion fell immediately upon British Columbia's Sikh extremists, and Parmar in particular. Within hours, CSIS had notified the RCMP that it believed Parmar and his adherents might have been behind the attack. Proving it, however, was another matter altogether.

CSIS had not been watching Parmar for the week preceding the attack, and it had not yet translated dozens of tapes from the wiretaps. It would be two months before the backlog was cleared. Worse still, CSIS had destroyed all but fifty of the tapes, believing they held nothing of intelligence value. The RCMP could not go back and listen to the wiretaps with the knowledge that a bombing may have been discussed. The Air India tragedy laid bare the difficulties inherent in having separate police and intelligence services. Since the bombings were a criminal investigation, the RCMP took the lead. But it was CSIS that had been monitoring Sikh extremists before the attacks. The spies had information that would surely help the police, but since CSIS was new, it was not entirely clear how the two departments should work together under such circumstances. The RCMP investigation would in all likelihood come across intelligence that CSIS would want. But how was CSIS to "plug in" to the RCMP? And tensions already existed between the police and the spies.

The RCMP thought that CSIS was holding back information, while CSIS accused the RCMP of not understanding its limited role as an intelligence-gathering agency. The biggest conflict was over the CSIS wiretap tapes. In 1985, CSIS did not yet have its own policies governing how wiretap tapes were to be handled. Instead it relied on the RCMP's *Technical Aids Policies and Procedures (TAPP) Manual,* which said tapes should be kept for ten working days after they had been sent for transcription. The maximum time a tape could be held was one month, and tapes considered "non-relevant" were to be erased at once. In addition, the CSIS transition team had drafted a memo stating that since CSIS was not a law-enforcement agency, it would not collect evidence, meaning it would not make or retain tapes for the purposes of a criminal trial. The tragic result was that of the 210 conversations of Parmar recorded before the Air India disaster and a week afterward, 156 were erased. "CSIS policies governing the handling, retention and erasure of audiotapes existing at the time of the Air India disaster were seriously deficient," SIRC wrote in its 1992 study of the case. The tapes were recorded and reviewed, but there was no solid policy for retaining them, so in most cases they were just erased, and that decision was often left to the lowest-ranking agents in CSIS.

Nonetheless, by the end of October, the RCMP believed it had the case figured out. An RCMP explosive ordnance disposal team returned to the secluded Vancouver Island road where the CSIS agents had followed Reyat and Parmar a month earlier. They found a blasting cap wire shunt and paper tape bundle, devices used to set off explosives. Then a man came forward claiming that, before the bombing, Reyat had approached him about getting explosives "for dissident means in India." The Woolworth's department store in Duncan confirmed that on June 5 it had sold a $129 Sanyo tuner similar to the one used to conceal the bomb in the Narita Airport explosion. The invoice gave Reyat's name and number.

The RCMP obtained a search warrant on November 4 and arrested Reyat at his workplace, charging him with six counts related to the bombing. "No, no," Reyat said as he was taken away. "What are you talking about?" At the police station, the officers tried to get him to confess by pretending to sympathize with the Sikh cause, and downplaying Reyat's role in the attacks. "Maybe the plane was supposed to blow up on the ground," one officer said. He described the bombing as "sort of self-defence ... you've gotta do what you can." When the investigators suggested that Reyat was not the ringleader but had only helped Parmar build the bomb, Reyat seemed to agree, saying he was trying to build something for Parmar for "a big job in India" such as blowing up a car or bridge. But it was not clear if he meant what he said or if he was simply trying to go along with the RCMP officer's suggestion that he was only a bit player in the plot. The Air India charges were soon dropped and he was convicted of a minor explosives charge. He was fined $2,000. Parmar was arrested at the same time but the case similarly fell apart and the charges were dropped. The RCMP and CSIS blamed one another for problems with the investigation into Parmar and the Sikh extremist movement. "There's enough blame to go around for Air India," a former CSIS official told me.

Sikh violence did not end with Air India. According to CSIS reports, Parmar's Babbar Khalsa was also involved in a plot to bomb the Indian parliament buildings, a plot to kidnap the children of an Indian MP, and plans to bomb trains and an oil refinery. Parmar was arrested again in 1986 and accused of plotting more attacks, but again the charges were dropped, this time because the evidence was obtained illegally.

Extremists continued their campaign of intimidation against those they considered traitors to the cause, such as Vancouver lawyer (and later B.C. premier) Ujjal Dosanjh, who was badly beaten for his stand against violence. "We know how to shut him up, you tell him," said a note delivered to his wife. In January 1986, a bomb was left on the steps of the moderate *Indo-Canadian Times* in Surrey, B.C. The newspaper's editor, Tara Singh Hayer, was eventually murdered. During a visit to Vancouver Island, Punjabi cabinet minister Malkiat Singh Sidhu was forced off the road by four men and shot in the arm. Four Sikh extremists, two of them ISYF members, were convicted of attempted murder. Two Sikhs in Montreal hatched a plot to bomb a second airliner. The conspiracy fell apart when one of them tried to buy explosives from a Quebec police informant.

Parmar returned to India in 1988 and leadership of the Babbar Khalsa in Canada fell to Bagri. But Parmar remained active in Sikh militancy and tried to purchase heavy weapons such as missiles for "a presentation to the Rajiv government from the Babbars to prove that the Babbars are still alive." A British publication quoted

Parmar in March 1989 as saying that Gandhi "will be paying for all his crimes. He will not live beyond 1990." India grew increasingly alarmed at the assassination rhetoric coming out of Canada. On April 17, 1989, the Indian consul general in Vancouver reported that Bagri had given a speech at a parade two days earlier in which he had said: "Oh Rajiv, your mother was killed and now it is your turn."

Sukhdev Singh Babbar took over the Babbar Khalsa International, which coordinated the BK's worldwide activities, and made Parmar his second-in-command. But the Canadian was forced out in a power struggle in 1992 and formed his own group, the Azad Khalistan Babbar Khalsa Force, also known as the BK Parmar faction. On October 15, 1992, Indian authorities finally caught up to Parmar and shot him dead during what CSIS called a "police encounter" in the city of Jalandhar, Punjab.

With Parmar's death, Bagri became the official leader of the BK Parmar faction, which CSIS had by now connected to a string of terror plots. The BK International is a separate organization but it has close ties to the Parmar group. "In Canada, the group tries to project itself as a charitable organization," a CSIS report says. "In fact, it remains determined to revive militancy in the Punjab and to that end is actively engaged in fundraising, procurement of sophisticated weapons and equipment, building up its cadres and arranging training for its members. The BKI has been responsible for a large number of killings and acts of terrorist violence in Punjab."

Support for the Khalistan movement faded through the 1990s and has all but died, mostly as a result of the aggressive policing in India, although there are still extremist elements in Canada that fervently believe in the cause. "Khalistan died because nobody wanted Khalistan," an Indian government official told me. "The people who wanted Khalistan were sitting in Canada and the U.K."

In October 2000, the RCMP at last laid murder charges against Bagri, Reyat and Ripudaman Singh Malik. The indictment named all 329 victims of the Air India disaster. Reyat was convicted of manslaughter for the Narita bombing; he later pleaded guilty to manslaughter for his role in the Air India bombing. Parmar continued to deny he was behind the bombing up until his death. On

March 16, 2005, Bagri and Malik were found not guilty. In rendering his decision, the judge concurred with the Crown's theory that the bombs were put on the plane in Vancouver.

The failure to bring to justice the terrorists behind such a high-profile attack within a reasonable time frame cemented Canada's international reputation as a safe haven. Brian Mulroney's Conservatives, and then the Liberals that replaced them, compounded the problem by failing to recognize that Air India and the Armenian attacks beforehand were not isolated incidents, but rather the opening shots of a new era that would see the world's major ethnic, religious and political conflicts spill across Canada's borders.

Air India was Canada's 9/11. Proportional to Canada's population, the death toll was equal to that of the attacks of September 11. Air India should have prompted the government to pass antiterrorism legislation and commit to security and intelligence. Instead, it opened the door for other extremist groups to set up bases inside Canada and export their terror abroad. Canadian politicians did virtually nothing about terrorism after Air India, and there was no public groundswell to force them to do anything, probably because, once again, the victims were mostly Indo-Canadians, which made it easy to portray the attack as targeting an isolated segment of Canadian society rather than a more fundamental assault on Canada, its security and its value systems. Security and intelligence budgets were reduced on the false assumption that the end of the Cold War had made them unnecessary. The government did not even revoke the charitable status of the Babbar Khalsa until 1996. And even then, proposals to crack down against charities fronting for terror were rejected by the Liberal cabinet. Only in 2003 did the cabinet at last outlaw the Babbar Khalsa, BKI and ISYF.

In the days of the FLQ, Canadian security and intelligence agents were taken to task for going too far to stop the domestic terrorist threat. With Air India, it was the opposite. They were accused of not doing enough to stop the international terrorist threat. But while there were serious problems with the investigation, that was not the main lesson of the Air India disaster. The first lesson of Air India was that when terrorists harness their cause to religion, there are no limits. CSIS thought that if Sikh extremists were going to attack Air India, they would hijack a plane. They thought that way because they viewed Khalistan as a political movement. Hijacking is a political act; terrorists seize an airplane full of passengers and make a series of demands, gaining publicity for the cause and concessions such as the release of an imprisoned terrorist leader.

As Bagri's Madison Square Garden speech showed, however, Khalistan had become a religious extremist movement. The intention was, after all, to gain independence for followers of the Sikh faith. The enemy, in Bagri's words, was not India, but the Hindus. The leaders of the movement were called priests; their cause was holy, and sanctioned by none other than God. The same trend surfaced in Canada once again on October 3, 1991, when four members of Jama'at ul Fuqra, a Pakistan-based Muslim sect, were caught at the Rainbow Bridge border crossing. Robert Junior Wesley, Caba Jose Harris and Tyrone Junior Cole were later convicted of plotting to explode pipe bombs at the Vishnu Mandir Hindu Temple north of Toronto and the India Centre movie theater in Toronto. They were deported in 2006 to their countries of origin, Dominican Republic and Trinidad. The Fuqras, also known as Muslims of the Americas, have at least six known communities in North America, including one in Barry's Bay, Ontario. "Over the past decade this Fuqra compound has continued to expand within Canada," says a 2006 intelligence report by the Integrated Threat Assessment Centre. "Fuqra members frequently travel to Pakistan for religious indoctrination and paramilitary training … Law enforcement officials suspect that paramilitary training takes place within their North American compounds."

Clearly not all homeland terrorist groups in Canada are motivated by religious zeal. The Mujahedin-e Khalq, for example, is driven by the desire to depose religious regime—the Shiite Mullahs who have controlled Iran since 1979. Regardless, the MEK has proven itself a menace to Canada. During the 1990s, the MEK recruited Iranian-Canadian teenagers and sent them to a base camp in Iraq to fight the Iranians. A brother and sister from Toronto, Mohamed and Somiyah Mohamedy were among them. Both were 16 when they left Canada for the guerrilla life. Mohamed returned in 2004. Somiyah may never return. The MEK is made up of revolutionaries, not religious extremists.

But when a cause such as Khalistan or the Fuqra's quest to defend Islam from its imagined enemies is portrayed as the will of God, there is no room for measured response. There is just violence, and the more blood that is shed, the more one is meeting the expectations of God. It is the same mindset that would surface again and again in terrorist groups throughout the 1980s and on—Hezbollah, Hamas, Al Qaeda. The failure of Air India (and, for that matter, the failure of 9/11 as well) was not realizing just how evil terrorism had become, that it was war without limits, killing for the glory of God.

When all else is stripped away—the ideologies, the dogmas and the hatreds—what is left is one fundamental question: how can terrorists indiscriminately kill others to promote their cause? Terrorism is not a crime of passion, it is coldly calculated. Air India was planned well in advance. Hamas suicide bombers do not just blow themselves up in a rage; they prepare weeks ahead of time.

How can they do it? It is not an easy question to answer, but from what I have seen it has to do with hiding behind the sanctity of the cause. When you listen to terrorists talking about what they have done, they sound like Nazi war criminals, who defend themselves by claiming they were only following orders. Terrorists, whether Islamic or Sikh, say they are only following God's command. Seconds before they carry out their attacks, Islamic terrorists often utter the words: "*Allahu Akhbar*." God is great!

And when someone believes they are merely acting out the orders of God, it is ironically easier to carry out the awful deeds of terror. They are not responsible for blowing up a bus full of civilians because they were just doing what God wanted. It is a safe retreat from responsibility, from human guilt and doubt.

There was another lesson to come out of Air India, but this one was for the terrorists. The world's terrorist organizations might have different causes, they might kill for different gods, but they do not work in isolation from one another. They train together, buy weapons from one another and learn from each other's mistakes. The terrorist groups working inside Canada learned a valuable lesson from the early spillover wars. That lesson was: the fastest way to put yourself out of business is to kill Canadians. The Sikh extremist organizations survived the aftermath of Air India, and indeed the chief suspects lived freely for a decade and a half until they were charged. But the disaster put Sikh militancy under a microscope, tarnished the cause and gave the Sikh community in Canada the momentum it needed to push the extremists aside.

The mistake of the extremist Doukhobors, Armenians and Sikhs was to commit acts of violence within Canada. On the other hand, as long as you don't bomb any department stores in British Columbia, shoot any Ottawa embassy guards or blow up planes filled with Canadians, the government will leave you alone and you are free to preach all the hatred you want and raise limitless sums of money to pay for war, terror and insurgency overseas. Canada deplores the import of terror to its peaceable kingdom, but appears indifferent to the export of terror. The money raised in Canada might pay for weapons and explosives that kill thousands of civilians in far-off lands, or it might finance an attack next door in Los Angeles, but the victims will safely be viewed as only Turks or Indians or Americans or Israelis. As long as the killing occurs outside Canada's borders, Canada is your playground. It is your safe haven.

And nobody learned that lesson better than the Tamil Tigers.

2

THE SNOW TIGERS

THE EVENING curfew in Jaffna has barely begun when the fighting starts up again. The barrage of long-range artillery unleashed by the army at Pilally soars over the saltwater lagoon toward the Tamil Tigers, who reply from their jungle hideouts with bursts of mortar rounds.

I am lying on a cot, shrouded in mosquito netting, unable to sleep, listening to the earsplitting discourse of war. The tropical night is so loud. Monkeys chatter, birds shriek like lunatics, and the civil war booms above it all. A dog-eared crime novel rests on the bedside table, and a dim flashlight, but reading is impossible with such a racket outside. There is nothing to do but lie there, floating in sweat.

There are two windows in my room in the United Nations guest house. Beneath one is a stretch of dirt road where the rebels planted a remote-control claymore mine a few weeks ago, detonating it just as a Sri Lanka Army convoy drove past. The other window overlooks the backyard of the guest house, where a bomb shelter made of stacked sandbags swells the ground beneath the jackfruit trees. The aid workers say the bunker is strong enough to withstand a direct hit—whether from an air force bomber or a rebel mortar rocket, they do not say.

Throughout the night, the war rumbles at the edge of the city, but not close enough to rouse panic on its streets. Curfew lifts at 4 a.m., the shelling subsides and the church bells clang, ringing in another hot day in Jaffna City.

Outside in the tropical garden, the morning sun is already heavy in the sky and the streets are filling up with students in starched white uniforms riding bicycles and women walking in saris the colors of exotic spices. There are not many men. Those who are not fighting have fled, fearing they might be rounded up by the rebels or arrested by the army on the grounds of "suspicion."

These are people used to war, and they carry on in its presence. For a visitor, however, nights of shelling and days spent under the constant gaze of nervous-looking soldiers are not easy to get used to. Even the bright promise of morning cannot suppress the self-examination: Just what am I doing here? What am I doing in this part of the world, an island where the latest convulsions of warfare are discussed the same way people at home talk about the weather? There is no good answer, except that sometimes we have to go far from home to find answers.

The Jaffna peninsula is the epicenter of a guerrilla and terrorist war that has killed more than 62,000 people and left one of Britain's most promising former colonies locked in a ruinous ethnic stand-off. The Sinhalese who make up more than three-quarters of the population and the Tamils, who are the minority, have been at war since 1983.

The fighting is intense—four thousand people were killed in the year 2000 alone—and has spread from the northern jungles to the cities, where Tamil terrorist squads wearing vests packed with explosives are routinely sent on suicide missions. Such attacks have made the Liberation Tigers of Tamil Eelam (known by locals as the LTTE or Tamil Tigers) one of the world's deadliest terrorist groups and the only one to have assassinated two world leaders, Rajiv Gandhi of India and Sri Lankan president Ranasinghe Premadasa.

To understand the war, one has only to look at a map of South Asia. The Tamils are the minority in Sri Lanka, making up just 15 percent of the population, but the island lies only thirty kilometers off the coast of India's Tamil Nadu state, so the Sinhalese are the minority within the wider region. The island's ethnic mix also includes Moors, who are descendents of Arab traders, as well as Burghers, who can trace at least part of their lineage to European settlers. But it is the Sinhalese and the Tamils who dominate the island politically, culturally and militarily.

It is the same formula that has fueled the conflict in the Middle East. Both ethnic groups here feel outnumbered, threatened and fully justified in their violent intransigence. Sri Lanka is the only Sinhalese homeland; its culture exists nowhere outside Sri Lanka. And there is a religious divide as well: Tamils are mostly Hindus while the Sinhalese are Buddhists. And each group speaks a distinct language, Tamil and Sinhala. Sri Lanka dispatches its army to conduct counterinsurgency operations. The Tamils have adopted the suicide bombing tactics of the Palestinians. Each group has its own version of history. Each claims moral superiority. Each insists its descendents inhabited the island before the other.

To call the Sri Lankan conflict a forgotten war would be to imply that anyone outside the region had ever paid it much attention. In reality, it is not so much a war the world has forgotten as one the world has ignored. Even though it involves a member of the Commonwealth and has been among the deadliest battles of the late-twentieth and early twenty-first centuries, Western powers seem hardly to have noticed. They might occasionally denounce the latest LTTE suicide bombing, but Sri Lanka is not considered strategically important enough to merit much beyond that. The Tiger rebels have benefited greatly from this indifference. They have set up a sophisticated overseas support structure that uses crime, front organizations and front companies to keep the fighting units supplied, and the most important of these offshore bases is Canada.

The Snow Tigers, as the Canadian branch of the LTTE is known, fundraise for weapons right under the nose of government. "Canada is their bank," says Rohan Gunaratna, a leading world expert on the LTTE. Indeed, the LTTE's chief accountant, Ponniah Anandarajah, lived in Canada for many years. When it comes to fundraising, the Tamil Tigers are unrivaled. They have used every conceivable tactic—government grants, front companies, fraud of every type, migrant smuggling and drugs. One CSIS report estimates that $2 million a year in collections is funneled to the Tigers from Canada to support the war effort. Another CSIS study puts the figure at $1 million per month. Millions more in crime proceeds also swell the war chest. "Canada is the LTTE's largest foreign base of operations," Canadian intelligence agents wrote in a May 1999 report. "Its main activities in Canada focus on fundraising and propaganda." To put it bluntly, Canada is the support base for a terrorist organization that has killed more than one hundred politicians, assassinated the leaders of two countries—India and Sri Lanka—and carried out more suicide bombings than any other militant group in the world.

To imagine how Sri Lankans feel about this scenario, imagine if Quebec separatists were raising money in some far-off land to finance suicide bombings in Montreal and Ottawa. And then imagine that the government of this country did not care enough to do anything about it. That is not, however, something Canada is eager to talk about. In December 2000, I was given access to a secret Canadian intelligence report that explained the Tigers' vast clandestine moneymaking empire in Canada, and how it was underwriting terrorism half a world away. The result was astonishing. The RCMP, which at the time had only a single officer investigating the LTTE in his spare time, assigned two officers to investigate my supposed breach of the Official Secrets Act. In the confused days before 9/11, it was not illegal for terrorists to use Canada to bankroll bus bombings in Sri Lanka, but for a journalist to write about it was considered a crime.

A stage fit for an outdoor rock concert has been assembled on the grass at Queen's Park, the grounds in front of the brown Victorian-style buildings of Ontario's provincial parliament in Toronto. There are stacks of loudspeakers and a backdrop of exotic color. On the stage, a troupe of South Asian dancers sway to the music beneath a fifteen-meter-high cutout of a chubby man dressed in striped jungle camouflage. A gun holster is fastened to his belt.

He is unrecognizable to the Saturday shoppers passing by in downtown Toronto, but those arriving by the busload and streaming into the park know him instantly. He is Velupillai Prabhakaran, or Prabha, the Supremo, the Sun God—the assassin who commands the Tamil Tigers. Over his right shoulder flies the LTTE flag: a yellow roaring tiger's head ringed by bullets and two crossed rifles. By the afternoon, several thousand men, women and children, some wearing Western clothes, others swathed in saris, have gathered in front of the stage, waving small Tamil Tiger flags, cheering on the giant likeness of the man they consider their national leader and hero.

Protests are hardly a rare occurrence at Queen's Park. Antipoverty groups, environmental activists and unions regularly converge on the lawns outside the legislature to wave placards and shout slogans. But the provincial parliament buildings have rarely seen a demonstration like the one brewing on this day—a rally in support of a distant terrorist campaign responsible for tens of thousands of deaths.

The Canadian branch of the Tamil Tigers, which organized the event, is in a mood to celebrate because the LTTE has just won a major victory in its separatist war against the Sri Lankan state security forces. Catching the army unaware, the Tigers stormed the military base at Elephant Pass, a slim land bridge that joins Sri Lanka with the northern Jaffna Peninsula. The victory has emboldened the Tamil independence movement, giving the impression that the rebels are poised to recapture the entire north which ethnic Tamils claim as their historic homeland.

The demonstration has been advertised as a "Victory Celebration" and the crowd behaves accordingly, cheering on the rebels as if the Tamil Tigers were a soccer club rather than a band of heavily armed killers. While this is a celebration of sorts, total victory is still not at hand, and the lengthy speeches focus on the march forward toward a homeland that Tamil separatists call Eelam.

The event officially begins when the Tamil Tigers' flag is raised by the mother of a "martyr"—an LTTE fighter killed in action. Shirtless men with big bellies take the stage to dance. Women dressed in the red and gold of the LTTE also dance, swaying with their palms pressed together above their heads. Videos showing the Tigers in battle are on sale, as well as CDs of Prabhakaran's revolutionary speeches.

Then a pudgy white-haired man wearing a gray suit raises the Canadian flag. He is Jim Karygiannis, the Liberal MP for the Ontario riding of Scarborough–Agincourt. "You understand that FACT [the Federation of Associations of Canadian Tamils] officers are situated in my riding and they probably have the largest Tamil community— if not the largest, one of the largest [sic] in my riding ... I've got an interest; these are constituents. It's not supporting one side or the other side," said Karygiannis, when questioned about his appearance at the rally.

The guest speaker, a member of India's parliament named P. Nedumaran (like most Tamils he uses only an initial for his given name), eventually takes the stage and, speaking in Tamil, cheers on the Tigers for more than an hour, justifying their violent campaign as a liberation struggle by an oppressed people. The Tigers are righting the wrongs of a thousand years, he says. He rejoices that they now have "the latest weapons" and he ends by imploring the audience to support the LTTE. And support it they do. A box covered with the Tamil Tigers' logo is brought out and the demonstrators line up to stuff money inside.

The speeches are delivered mostly in Tamil, so passersby and even the few television crews that show up to cover the event for local newscasts have no idea that what is going on is the justification of violence, the glorification of martyrdom and the nurturing of ethnic hatred that represents a truly shocking assault on Canadian values. That such an event could take place within Canada, openly and without consequence, seems to defy common sense. How is it that an organization that Canada's intelligence agency has long considered a front for terrorists could be allowed to hold a fundraising rally, on the steps of the provincial legislature no less, with an MP from Canada's ruling party as a speaker?

Politics in Ceylon was already split along rigid ethnic lines when the British formally handed the colony its independence on

February 4, 1948. As with so many other decolonized states, the island appeared to be heading unavoidably for a bitter fight. The Tamils in the north worried they would suffer under the rule of the Sinhalese majority. For their part, the Sinhalese wanted to redress what they saw as 150 years of British rule that had favored Tamils. Elected prime minister in 1956, S.W.R.D. Bandaranaike pursued an aggressive pro-Sinhalese agenda, passing the Sinhala Only Act, which made Sinhala the only official language. Tamils saw their worst fears coming true and ethnic riots erupted.

Bandaranaike backed down and negotiated a compromise pact, but the agreement was abrogated due to political pressure and he was assassinated in 1959 by a Sinhalese extremist. Bandaranaike's widow, Sirimavo, replaced her husband in 1960, becoming the world's first female prime minister. Barely a year into her term, Tamils formed the Federal Party and began a campaign of strikes and civil disobedience in the north that ignited further ethnic rioting. She lost control of parliament in 1965 and the new regime negotiated yet another pact with the Tamil political leadership, but again it failed over pressure from hard-line Sinhalese.

Mrs. Bandaranaike returned to office in 1970, just as a new faction called the Janatha Vimukthi Peramuna (JVP; People's Liberation Front) began an uprising that combined Sinhalese nationalism with Marxist-Leninist philosophy. Confrontations between the Sinhalese and Tamils claimed more than six thousand lives. In 1972, Ceylon became a republic and adopted the name Sri Lanka, which means "Resplendent Land." The change coincided with the emergence of organized militancy in the Tamil heartland of Jaffna, led by students angered that merit-based university admissions had been replaced by a regional quota system favoring the Sinhalese. The Tamil New Tigers (or TNT) formed in 1972, and, after a few random attacks, became the Liberation Tigers of Tamil Eelam in 1976. By 1977, Tamil militants were training in the Middle East with the Palestine Liberation Organization.

The opening shot in the civil war came on July 23, 1983, when the LTTE killed 13 Sri Lankan soldiers. In response, Sinhalese mobs rampaged in Colombo, attacking Tamils and their businesses. With the ethnic divide at its nadir, the government adopted a law on August 5 banning political parties that advocated separatism. Mass migration to India and Western Europe quickly followed, as the country found itself in a state of emergency. India felt threatened by the prospect of Western military aid flowing to Sri Lanka and began supporting the Tigers, who already had sympathy in Tamil Nadu due to the ethnic link. With India's aid, the LTTE tried to wrest control of the north and east by attacking police and military posts, as well as Sinhalese villages. Sixty-two Sinhalese were slaughtered in one attack, prompting government troops to kill sixty-three Tamils in a symbolic act of one-upmanship. The ancient Sinhalese capital of Anuradhapura was attacked by the LTTE on May 14, 1985, a week before Buddhist celebrations. One hundred and twenty people were killed.

Sri Lanka was trapped in a self-defeating cycle of violence—guerrilla attacks followed by government retaliation that led only to more guerrilla attacks. Desperate, the government tried aerial bombardments, helicopter attacks and shelling, but civilian casualties were heavy and that only added fuel to the rebel war machinery. The LTTE brought the fighting to the capital for the first time in the summer of 1986, bombing the national airport and the central telegraph office. The Resplendent Land was at war.

The fighting set off a migration of Tamils to safe havens such as Europe and especially Canada, which had more accommodating refugee laws. The year 1986 saw the first wave of Sri Lankan migration. Some 1,800 became permanent residents that year, more than double the 800 the year before. The figure then more than doubled again to 4,300 in 1987. By 1992, the annual influx had jumped to almost 13,000. Faced with a huge backlog of refugee cases in the early 1990s, the government began expediting claims from the major refugee-producing countries such as Sri Lanka. While the speeded-up process helped the Immigration and Refugee Board (IRB) improve its numbers, it had one major drawback. "With appropriate coaching, a concocted story and fake documents, almost anyone can meet the criteria for refugee status without ever being challenged," says Bill Bauer, a former IRB judge.

To make matters worse, in 1994 the board issued a set of guidelines indicating which claims were to be fast-tracked. They included "young Tamil males aged 10 to 40 or 45 from the north and east" of Sri Lanka and "young Tamil females aged 13 to 30." As Bauer points out, this perfectly fit the profile of former LTTE guerrillas, who quickly learned to exploit the system by fabricating an identity and a past to hide their involvement in the war.

Tamil migration has been aided by a sophisticated human smuggling industry that emerged to profit from the refugee flow and to redirect the money back to the Tigers. Agents in Colombo arrange passage for a fee ranging as high as US$30,000. I met one such agent in Colombo, a member of one of the Tamil political parties, who told me he had helped many Tamil guerrillas get to Canada. Later in Bangkok, I met one of the passport forgers who provide the bogus documents. He offered to provide a Canadian passport and to insert the photo of the person I wanted to smuggle. When I asked to see proof that he could do the job, he disappeared into his apartment and emerged with a handful of blank Canadian citizenship cards. He offered to throw one in for free. Police told me that some Tamils in Canada will also "rent" their passports to smugglers, who use them to bring more Tamils into Canada.

The RCMP immigration and passport branch became extensively involved in the investigation of Tamil migrant smugglers and document forgers, and the LTTE members they have brought to Canada. To aid this probe, the RCMP hired a Tamil translator named Kumaravelu Vignarajah. But a police informant recognized "Vic" as a high-ranking member of the Tamil Tigers and tipped off the RCMP. Photos of the translator posing with the corpses of Indian peacekeepers in Sri Lanka later surfaced. Police determined their translator was actually an LTTE intelligence officer, sent by the Tigers to get deep inside the RCMP. He had even written the RCMP entrance exam, hoping to become a regular member of the force. "They targeted us," a police source told me. The translator was arrested and the Mounties realized they had a serious problem: the Tamil Tigers had not only infiltrated Canada—they had infiltrated the RCMP.

Estimates of the number of Sri Lankan Tamils now in Canada vary widely. Lobby groups peg the number as high as 225,000. Although a few are Sinhalese or Muslims, the vast majority are Tamils, and most live in the Toronto area, creating a vulnerable exile community with money, freedom and a political system seemingly incapable of fighting terror—just what the LTTE needed. Canada soon had the largest population of Sri Lankan Tamils outside South Asia. With so many migrants arriving so quickly, it has proven a relatively simple task for current and former Tigers, as well as their supporters and members of their international war machine, to slip into Canada undetected. The RCMP and Toronto police believe that as many as 8,000 Tamil guerrillas with military weapons training are now living in the Toronto area alone.

Sergeant Fred Bowen, the top RCMP expert on the LTTE, believes that most of them are "in the retired category" but that a few remain active. Some have returned to Sri Lanka to fight. An RCMP search warrant executed in Toronto in 1998 says there are "a number of high-ranking present and past leaders of the LTTE in Canada," including ex-RCMP translator Vignarajah; passport forger Loganathan Sabanayagam, who showed up to his bail hearing wearing a T-shirt with a tiger on it; Selvarajah Kanagaratnam; and Manickavasagam Suresh.

Canadian intelligence began trying to infiltrate the Tamil community, and recruited the highest-ranking Tiger on the RCMP list, Thalayasingam Sivakumar, alias Major Anton, who had joined the LTTE in 1978 and twice served on its central committee before becoming one of Prabhakaran's top advisers. He started out as a student leader at the University of Jaffna, where he was treasurer of the Tamil Sangam, a cultural organization, and editor of the pro-LTTE newspaper *Unnarvu*. His activism attracted the attention of the army, and soldiers searched his home and campus. A 50,000-rupee reward was offered for information leading to his arrest, forcing him to flee to India.

In 1983, the Tigers made Sivakumar their liaison with India's external intelligence division, the Research and Analysis Wing (RAW). He represented the LTTE at Indian-sponsored peace talks in 1985, and in 1987 was appointed chief of the LTTE's planning and intelligence division. When fighting broke out in Jaffna between the Tigers and the Indian Peacekeeping Forces, Prabhakaran made Sivakumar commander-in-chief of the LTTE offensive. A month into the Battle of Jaffna, Sivakumar began to doubt the wisdom of a protracted war against India and advocated a strategy of negotiations. He entered into talks with the RAW the following year, but they soon broke down and the fighting resumed. Sivakumar put the blame on Prabhakaran's inflexibility and accused the rebel leader of lacking any meaningful policies or ideas. He also opposed attacks on nonmilitary targets. He was promptly expelled from the Tigers.

He left India in January 1989 and made his way across the globe, arriving in Canada on June 16, 1989 and filing a refugee claim five days later. He was awaiting a decision on his claim when he got a call from Al Treddenick, an agent in the CSIS counterterrorism branch. Treddenick told Sivakumar that CSIS knew about his LTTE past and that he was being investigated as a possible security threat to Canada. According to Sivakumar, the CSIS agent told him that unless he cooperated, his chances of obtaining refugee status could be in jeopardy. Sivakumar agreed to talk to Treddenick about his involvement with the LTTE. Two days later, Treddenick called again and they met at a restaurant in Scarborough. The questions were general, about the operations of the LTTE and specific incidents. The meetings became weekly after that.

By September, a second CSIS agent, Dann Martel, had taken over as head of the Sri Lanka desk and Treddenick faded from the picture. Martel met Sivakumar every two weeks, sometimes along with another agent, Allen Wells. At one meeting, in January 1990, Martel proposed that Sivakumar work for CSIS and infiltrate LTTE operations in Canada. Sivakumar said he did not want to get involved in politics again and would not spy because it was too dangerous. But he agreed to provide information within his existing knowledge. Sivakumar said Martel told him that "CSIS was of the belief that hundreds of LTTE members had entered Canada by lying about their involvement with the LTTE and that some of them continued to work for the movement from Canada."

Three months later, Martel again asked Sivakumar to work for CSIS and handed him an envelope. Inside it was $200 in cash. Sivakumar said he did not want to work for CSIS and did not want the money. All he wanted was to finalize his refugee claim and bring his wife and child to Canada. Sivakumar claims the CSIS agent assured him his claim would be dealt with, and that he would not be sent back to Sri Lanka. With those assurances, Sivakumar agreed to become a paid informant. He took the money.

He met monthly with Martel at a room at the Inn on the Park in Toronto, answering questions about LTTE agents in Canada as well as the group's overseas operations. At one point, Sivakumar heard that a friend, an LTTE operative in the United States, would be sending a diskette of information to Tigers leader Prabhakaran through Canada. Sivakumar tipped off CSIS and the package was intercepted. Although it was an intelligence coup, it exposed Sivakumar. The LTTE accused him of informing.

Martel was replaced by Gerald Baker in April 1994 and the meetings continued, even when Sivakumar's refugee claim was rejected and deportation arrangements were being prepared by the immigration department. Sivakumar eventually sued the Canadian government for reneging on what he had understood was a deal to secure his refugee status in exchange for his help cracking the Tigers' Canadian network. He remained in Canada under uncertain status, unable to return home, wanted by both the Sri Lankan government and the Tigers.

"I am a marked man," he says.

While his days as an informer are over, Sivakumar handed invaluable information to the government in the early 1990s that should have given Canada a decided edge against the Tigers. Sivakumar says he gave CSIS details of the LTTE's "overseas fund collection and who controlled the fund, where it went, names of key men in arms purchasing for the LTTE and how the arms are purchased." This early infiltration of the LTTE movement let CSIS quickly establish that money was being collected in Canada and secretly moved out of the country to, among others, Prabhakaran himself. From time to time, CSIS agents would bring Sivakumar lists of names and photos, and ask if he could identify them. After the assassination of Rajiv Gandhi, Martel brought photos of the suspects and asked Sivakumar to name them. They discussed the Black Tigers, the suicide unit of the LTTE. And Sivakumar says they sometimes spoke about "covert LTTE offices in Canada and their activities."

The shops at the Birkdale Plaza strip mall in Scarborough sell South Asian jewelry, saris and fish. There is a bookstore that doubles as a money-transfer outfit; a Sri Lankan grocer; and a restaurant called the Madras Palace. The conversations are mostly in Tamil. So are the shop signs. A yellow and red banner draped from a window with an air conditioner hanging out of it says Student Organization of the World Tamil Movement and bears a distinctive emblem: the head of a roaring tiger. It is the only indication that the office in the eastern reaches of the City of Toronto is affiliated with a war taking place half a world away.

The World Tamil Movement (WTM) is the main Tamil Tigers front organization in Canada. A secret list of LTTE front organizations in Canada compiled by CSIS lists the WTM at the top, complete with the Ellesmere Road address of the strip mall, as well as seven other groups in Toronto, Ottawa, Montreal and Vancouver: the Federation of Associations of Canadian Tamils (FACT), Tamil Rehabilitation Organization (TRO), Tamil Coordinating Committee, Eelam Tamil Association of British Columbia, World Tamil Movement (Montreal), Eelam Tamil Association of Quebec and Tamil Eelam Society of Canada, which has been getting about $2 million a year in federal government funding.

"The LTTE operates in Canada under the guise of several front organizations," Canadian intelligence agents wrote in a 1999 report. "These organizations perform legitimate cultural and humanitarian functions within the Tamil community, however, a portion of the money they raise is sent back to Sri Lanka in support of the LTTE's terrorist activities." The international LTTE network "operates like a multinational corporation," CSIS wrote in a report. "This network consists of commercial companies and small businesses set up in Malaysia, Singapore, Bangladesh, China and some Western countries." It includes "political offices, pro-curement offices, and humanitarian organizations located in at least 40 countries worldwide." The global support structure is so complex, so well organized, it is sometimes called Tamil Tigers International or Tigers Inc.

The Tigers realized early on that they could not achieve independence without a strong international support network. The Tiger fighters could easily cause havoc in the jungles of Wanni and in downtown Colombo, but they could not achieve outright military victory on their own. They were too few in number, too ill equipped. They needed weapons. They needed a propaganda campaign to legitimize their violence and convince the world that Tamils are an oppressed people, that the LTTE was the African National Congress of South Asia and that the Sinhalese were bloodthirsty racists, Buddhist fanatics incapable of living in harmony with a minority culture. Above all, they needed money. The mass resettlement of Tamil refugees held great potential for the Tigers, creating large expatriate communi-ties earning salaries unheard of in Sri Lanka, with the freedom to do as they pleased without having to worry about the Sri Lankan security forces. The Tigers began to organize Tamils who lived overseas and to seize control of institutions, turning them into fronts that would work closely with the LTTE leadership. Tiger sympathizers quickly gained control of Tamil organizations that had begun forming in the 1980s to accommodate the influx of refugees from Sri Lanka. The LTTE also began dispatching loyal members abroad disguised as refugees to serve as point men in the international network.

In 1990, the Tigers sent one of its veteran operatives to Toronto to run the Canadian branch of the LTTE. Manickavasagam Suresh was born in 1955, the son of a railway station master in Battilacoa on Sri Lanka's northeast coast. His mother was a school teacher. Suresh was an early LTTE member, joining in 1978. He was later assigned to help with the expanding international support network, at first in the Netherlands and then Toronto. Suresh lied about his past to Canadian immigration authorities and was accepted as a refugee on April 11, 1991. He soon took over as coordinator of FACT, an alleged umbrella organization for all the major LTTE fronts in Canada, and the World Tamil Movement.

The WTM is a registered nonprofit society in Canada. In its incorporation papers it lists its mandate as serving the needs of Tamils, lobbying government and raising funds "for charitable organizations serving the Sri Lankan Tamils, particularly destitute refugees." The WTM has never concealed its support for the Tigers. Suresh admitted "there is no doubt that the WTM has close contacts with the LTTE" and that "fundraising for the LTTE was done publicly by the WTM." Even so, the group managed to secure a $19,000 grant from the Ontario government in the early 1990s to hire a "volunteer coordinator." A Tamil business directory published by the WTM contains an endorsement by then-Ontario premier Mike Harris, immediately next to a statement from Prabhakaran. "Greetings from the premier, World Tamil Movement," Harris wrote. Mel Lastman, the former mayor of Toronto, also wrote a greeting for the directory.

Only later did Harris and Lastman learn that the WTM was not just another multicultural organization, but a crucial part of the international network set up to harness political and economic support for the LTTE. Of all the world's terrorist organizations, few have mastered the art of fundraising as well as the Tamil Tigers. The RCMP reports that "new Tamil refugees in Canada are traditionally contacted by Tamil Tiger front organizations [that] promote LTTE interests and collect funds ... LTTE sympathizers in Canada are under pressure to provide funding to the Tigers in Sri Lanka. All Tamils are encouraged to donate 50 cents a day to the LTTE."

Avid supporters of the LTTE go door to door in Tamil neighborhoods soliciting donations. Those who decline to hand over money are sometimes threatened. Their homes or cars might be vandalized. While some donate freely because they support the independence drive, others do so out of fear that they or their families will be harmed. "WTM henchmen were tapping at every door to collect money and forced people to offer money in large amounts," a Scarborough man told me. "People in Toronto have to give without demur for fear of reprisal on the streets of Toronto or [against] their relatives in the villages of Jaffna. There are so many Tamils like me who want to live a peaceful, honest, violence-free life in our adopted country. But things are going from bad to worse."

I have heard similar accounts from many Tamils, but the fronts deny extorting money. A telephone survey commissioned in Canada by the WTM, and conducted by the polling firm Small World Communications, asked respondents whether they had ever been subjected to "extortion attempts or any other form of intimidation by WTM." Most said no, but 3.4 percent answered in the affirmative. The WTM released the figures as proof that they were the victims of "false and misleading statements." Looked at another way, if there are in excess of 200,000 Tamils in Canada, as the front groups claim, then 7,000 of them have been extorted by the WTM. And that assumes that all those who did not complain of pressure were being truthful, when logic dictates they would be unlikely to tell pollsters working for the organization responsible that they were being extorted.

Following a resurgence of aggressive money-collection efforts in Toronto in late 2005, Human Rights Watch sent an investigator, Jo Becker, to make inquiries. Her report, released in February 2006, concluded that the LTTE was using high-pressure tactics tantamount to extortion to raise money for a "final war" to secure Tamil independence from Sri Lanka. "The LTTE and groups linked to it such as the World Tamil Movement repeatedly call and visit Tamil families seeking funds," the report says. "Some families have received as many as three visits in a single week. Fundraisers may refuse to leave the house without a pledge of money, and have told individuals who claim not to have funds available to borrow money, to place contributions on their credit cards, or even to re-mortgage their homes." The WTM vehemently denied the report's conclusions.

The report highlighted another form of LTTE fundraising. Several Canadian Tamils have complained that when they return home to Sri Lanka to visit their families, they are forced to pay a tax to the Tigers. One woman told Human Rights Watch that when she went through a Tigers checkpoint in 2005 to visit her parents she was told to report to the LTTE administrative office within three days. When she did, she was asked how long she had lived in Canada and how much she had contributed to the rebels. She explained that she had children and had been living on welfare, and had nothing to give. The Tigers let her go, but made her sign a pledge form promising to pay forty dollars a month to the WTM, she said. When she got back to Toronto, a WTM activist called asking for the money. "They left three or four messages, but I didn't pick up the phone," she said. "If my children answered, they told them I was at work." Eventually, a man came to the door. He had all the details she had given the Tigers in Sri Lanka— her name, her children's names, her address and passport number. "He said, 'I'm from the World Tamil Movement. You said in Sri Lanka that you would give money. I am here to collect it.'"

Fundraising has also taken place at rallies held in Canadian cities. Organizers approach boards of education and ask to use schools for Tamil cultural events. The fronts charge a $10 admission fee and sell LTTE battlefield videos, books, CDs and cassettes of Prabhakaran's speeches, as well as T-shirts and flags bearing the Tamil Tigers logo. The events begin with a parade by men who wear military uniforms and carry replica rifles. This is typically followed by a video presentation, showing war casualties, and a speech by a keynote speaker. A box wrapped in the Tamil Tigers flag is then passed around and audience members stuff cash inside. One intelligence officer described the sequence as: "Get them sympathetic, work them up and get them to make a donation."

Law-enforcement officials who monitor such events told me the money goes to LTTE fronts. Intelligence agents have shown me photographs of rallies held at schools in the Toronto area. In the photos, armed "soldiers" wearing LTTE uniforms can be seen in front of a large map of Sri Lanka that shows the areas under Tiger control. "To carry replica guns in a school and sell rebel flags and videos is not appropriate," one officer told me. Added another: "It's not good to have a display of armed conflict in schools. To use a school for that type of cause is a little bit immoral." But for Canadian politicians it is a chance to secure ethnic votes by showing they sympathize with the LTTE cause.

Law-enforcement and intelligence officials told me they often see Liberal members of Parliament at these militaristic rallies. One such event was held at a Montreal school in 2000. Photos published on a pro-LTTE Internet site show children at Royal Vale High School wearing military camouflage uniforms, carrying fake weapons and hoisting a casket draped in the LTTE flag. When I called the school board to inquire about the event, officials were completely unaware of what had taken place. I directed them to the photos on the Internet and they were shocked. They immediately tightened their policy on the use of schools for after-hours events.

The Montreal chapter of the World Tamil Movement, which staged the rally, admitted money was collected. "They were passing the hat," said a representative. "That is done very commonly at these events." He admitted his organization supports the LTTE. "That's right," he said. "Some countries they say we are terrorists but we are not terrorists. We don't believe in terrorism; we are [for] freedom, we want to get back our country, that's all." I asked him what happened to the money that was collected at the school and he told me it went to humanitarian projects. "Those people who are voluntarily giving we are taking this to feed the people, you see ... So many children are dying without getting good food."

One of the boldest moves by Tamil activists was their foray into the world of philately. Canada Post had just introduced a vanity stamp program that allowed Canadians to submit photos of themselves and their loved ones. For a fee, Canada Post would produce stamps using the photos. A Toronto man sent in a photo of Kumar Ponnambalam, a lawyer assassinated in Sri Lanka who is revered by Tamil separatists. Canada Post printed a large run of the stamps, which were sold at an auction in Toronto. When I asked postal officials about the matter, they told me they were about to print another similar stamp showing a man with a moustache. I sent them a photo of Prabhakaran and they confirmed his was the likeness on the photos. The print run was canceled. Had it gone ahead it would have served the Tigers splendidly, allowing them to mail letters with stamps bearing the image of their commander and giving the impression that the Canadian government not only supported him, but had honored him with his own stamp.

Money is also collected at the Hindu temples that have emerged around Toronto. In September 2001, I discreetly wandered into the Ganesh Hindu temple in Richmond Hill, north of Toronto, along with thousands of others celebrating the completion of renovations. Buses and cars were lined up along the shoulder of the highway outside as worshipers wearing a mix of Western and South Asian clothing arrived in a steady procession. As I entered the temple grounds, I was greeted not by a priest but by eager youths selling LTTE flags. Photos of Prabhakaran, CDs of his speeches, and battle videos were laid out for sale on tables. "This is our national leader," a youth selling the photos told me. "This is our national flag." I bought a flag for $5 to prove what I had witnessed but later I wondered if I had done the right thing, since even my meager contribution might end up in the hands of the Tigers. Men nearby waved collection jars, soliciting money for the Tamil Rehabilitation Organization, one of the groups CSIS claims is a Tigers front. "Money for the refugees," they shouted.

I also found LTTE symbols at the Ayyappan Temple in Scarborough. The Tiger logo was affixed to the door of a hut on the temple grounds. The hut was painted in red and gold, the LTTE colors. Inside, I could see a poster of Prabhakaran draped over a desk. Extremist groups often target religious institutions because they "afford the ability to move around and circulate without initial interference from security and intelligence organizations, which traditionally have been very wary about putting foot into a temple," said David Harris, a former CSIS agent. A movement to keep the LTTE out of Toronto temples emerged but was quickly suppressed. Board members who spoke out against mixing religion with the LTTE got death threats at home. A few had their windows smashed. "The other four guys also got phone calls and they called their wives," one of them told me. "The women, they were afraid. They said, 'Resign, resign, we don't need the temple.' And they resigned. They said, 'Don't go to the police. If you go to the police they will send the gangs and they will harm us.' The government, they do not take proper action against this." He complained to police, but the cellphone from which the threats were made had already been disconnected.

One Hindu priest tried to start a new temple that would resist intrusion by the LTTE. The day before his temple opened, he got a call from the WTM, which said it wanted to set up tables at the event. "That is a criminal offence," he said. "This is a challenge to the government. The people came here to live in peace but these people, they collect money," he complained. "The people are giving money, but the people don't know what they do [with it]."

The director of a Toronto temple told me that late in 2005, he was instructed to make a $1-million contribution to the Tigers.

While those making donations may believe their contributions are paying for food and medicine, CSIS claims in a secret report that "most funds raised under the banner of humanitarian organizations such as the TRO are channeled instead to fund the LTTE war effort." Accusations of Tamil Tiger fundraising in Canada are met with outright denials by Tamil organizations. They may be raising money to send to Sri Lanka, but it is for aid, not weapons, they claim. "You see our community is not very rich. We are fairly poor compared to other communities, not like the Jews at all who are well established," FACT said through a spokesman, Sita Sittampalam. "A lot of our people are on welfare, they are on government assistance. A lot of our people are working in factories for small pay you see, and they're living on a very, very meager income. We are not flush with money to be throwing about for big fundraising for arms and all that. That's not the situation.

"I don't know what the Canadian intelligence service is about on this matter. We are trying to fight for a cause which we feel is legitimate. We have been oppressed for a long time, fifty years they have been peacefully demonstrating. We are appealing peacefully in Parliament. That is what Canadian values are. That is what we look for. Democracy. And you must appeal to people, at least to government. Our representatives have spoken thousands of words. We have decided to live in that country together in independence, but when we found that things were going badly after all the peaceful means of trying to get some hearing for our cause, the international community was silent. The army was sent and we found that there was no way out. That was probably what compelled the young people to take up arms to fight, as a last resort, and which is legitimate and I think which anybody can accept."

While activists try to discredit evidence of Tiger fundraising in Canada, calling it the result of Sri Lankan government propaganda, every federal security agency that has independently studied the matter has concluded that Tamil fronts are indeed financing the purchase of LTTE arms. Much of the money collected for so-called humanitarian projects goes to the Tamil Rehabilitation Organization. The TRO was registered as a nonprofit society in Ontario in 1995. Its first president was Elagu Elaguppillai, a prominent Liberal party supporter and nuclear scientist who worked for Atomic Energy Canada. He told me he quit the TRO after one year, when CSIS officers told him it was considered a front for the LTTE. In 1996, Anton Sinnarasa became a director of the TRO. Two years later, when he was working for Ontario MPP Jim Brown, he was named on RCMP search warrant as a member of the LTTE. Although named in the warrant, Sinnarasa denied having any involvement. He has never been charged and no evidence has been presented of any role. In 2003, the Liberal party made him a delegate for the leadership convention that would choose Canada's next prime minister.

The Immigration and Refugee Board, ruling in the case of a Sri Lankan refugee claimant who had worked as a TRO fundraiser in Switzerland, later concluded that the TRO was a Tamil Tigers front. The board said it had seen "reliable evidence from three sources that affirm or strongly suggest [that] the TRO is the rehabilitation wing of the LTTE; the funds it collects are used for both rehabilitation and weapons procurement. It is part of the LTTE modus operandi to siphon off funds that are intended for rehabilitation programs in Sri Lanka."

Tellingly, CSIS has found that money-collection efforts fluctuate according to the intensity of the war in Sri Lanka. During a drive to recapture the A-9 Highway, Sri Lanka's main north-south artery, the LTTE asked Tamils in Canada for $1,000 per family. When fighting resumed in November 1999 after a lull, the Tigers collected $1.6 million in Toronto in a single day. After the Tigers captured Elephant Pass in April 2000, raising hopes that the LTTE was poised to conquer Jaffna, fundraising reached frantic levels in Toronto. The LTTE directed the WTM to come up with an additional $10 million in 1999 and 2000, according to CSIS.

The money raised in Canada makes its way to the Tamil Tigers through a series of secret bank accounts and front companies. The LTTE's chief arms buyer, Tharmalingam Shanmugham, who uses the alias Kumaran Pathmanathan, or KP, runs a food supply company in Thailand that serves as a cover for weapons dealing. The arms acquisition wing is known as the KP department, after its boss, who has a degree from the University of Jaffna and is described in the CSIS report as the senior "arms procurer" for the LTTE, "known to operate a highly-secretive network of companies and businesses around the world. He is directly involved in the purchase of weapons and materials for the LTTE in Sri Lanka." The CSIS report claims Kumaran set up two import-export companies in Toronto to launder money raised by the WTM and other fronts.

Kumaran has "extensive links" with the two companies, which are "operated by known LTTE supporters," the report says. "The businesses were set up at the request of Kumaran and receive most of the inventory from Kumaran's company in Thailand. One of these individuals is responsible for raising and distributing funds on behalf of the WTM, and the second individual is a close friend of Kumaran's. It is believed that the LTTE currently derives revenue from two import/export businesses, but there could be as many as five companies operating in Canada providing funds to the LTTE. Although there are no official profit figures available for these companies, there is some indication that they are highly lucrative and the LTTE are becoming increasingly dependent on these types of ventures to supply their war coffers."

The money transfers are concealed using a price-fixing scheme. The Toronto companies import goods from Kumaran's company at hugely inflated prices. For example, the front company in Canada might pay $100 for a head of lettuce that cost Kumaran 10 cents. Kumaran pockets the markup and puts it toward arms purchases. "The laundered amounts would most likely be the funds raised by the WTM and/or profits generated by the front companies," the CSIS report says. Invoices sent by Kumaran are paid up immediately, which "may indicate that these funds are destined for more urgent requirements than day-to-day business transactions." Kumaran sends unusually pricey invoices just before Black July, when Tamil Tigers honor their dead rebels and the LTTE traditionally steps up its military campaign. "This amount is significantly higher than invoices received during the rest of the year from Kumaran, possibly indicating that the money is used to fund the LTTE activities in Black July and not businesses enterprises," CSIS wrote.

The heart of the KP department is its shipping network. With the help of a Bombay shipping tycoon, KP has built an LTTE-owned and operated shipping operation that has allowed the Tigers to cease their reliance on commercial freight companies whose trustworthiness and willingness to turn a blind eye to arms smuggling could not be guaranteed. The fleet numbers somewhere between ten and fifteen freighters, some of them heavily armed. They travel under Panamanian, Honduran and Liberian flags of convenience. With his fleet ready to transport his purchases, and his pockets flush with cash provided by the Canadian fronts, Kumaran travels throughout Asia and the former Soviet Union, making weapons deals that keep the Tigers equipped. Sometimes he travels on a forged Canadian passport supplied by the Snow Tigers.

The Tamil Tigers are a relatively small guerrilla force of about 5,000 to 7,000 hardcore fighters, and another 10,000 who play support roles, but by the late 1990s they had amassed some 10,000 automatic rifles, as well as tanks, jet boats, land earth satellites and a submarine. It is the need for missiles, artillery and ammunition, however, that drives the weapons procurement machine. The Tigers got their hands on more than 32,000 mortar bombs in 1997 by hijacking a shipload of arms destined for the Sri Lankan government. The Sri Lankan Defense Ministry had arranged to purchase them from Zimbabwe through an Israeli subcontractor, but the LTTE used bribery to take possession of the arms and loaded them onto one of KP's vessels instead. By the time the government learned of the heist, the bombs had already been delivered to the Mullaituvu coast of Sri Lanka. The U.S. embassy in Colombo received a fax reading: "We, the Tamil Tigers, inform you by the present that on 11 July 1997 we have hijacked a vessel carrying arms destined for Colombo ... The cargo [is] confiscated. We make known and warn that we will take action against all persons participating in the supply of military equipment used against the legitimate rights of the Tamil people and will severely punish those concerned."

Missiles in particular have been a high priority, especially since the Sri Lanka Air Force improved its size and strength, and started using air strikes to take out rebel bases. The rebels have been building up an arsenal of Soviet-made SAM-7 surface-to-air missiles bought from Cambodia and more potent Stingers left over from the Soviet war in Afghanistan. The quest for more sophisticated weapons has added urgency to international fundraising efforts. A message reading "Urgent Appeal for Money for Missiles—Contribute Generously to LTTE" was posted on Carleton University's FreeNet Internet service in 1996. The LTTE chief accountant, who at one time lived in Canada (though not any more), was involved in the purchase of Soviet SA-14 missiles.

Of all the weapons the LTTE has amassed, it is the explosives that have most defined the war. Civil war was formally declared in 1983 when the Tigers set off a remote-control bomb on a road as a government convoy was passing by, but it was the first suicide bombing four years later that set the tone of the conflict. Suicide bombings were then a relatively unusual occurrence in world terrorism, since they require a rare level of zeal. They are not only a weapon but also a statement of total commitment to the cause.

Such attacks emerged in Lebanon in the 1980s and the Tigers borrowed the technique and refined it. Suicide operations are extremely difficult to stop because the bomber is not worried about being captured and needs no escape route. If the mission succeeds, the bomber is killed and therefore cannot reveal his or her accomplices. The components of a suicide bomb—explosives, steel ball bearings, nuts, bolts, batteries, wires and a switch—can be acquired easily. As government security measures were tightened in Sri Lanka, and the LTTE found it more difficult to cause the kind of damage needed to keep the country off balance, it began outfitting conscripts with suicide vests and sending them into crowds in

Colombo, bringing the war to the capital like never before. As police became more adept at spotting potential bombers, the rebels began using women and children for suicide missions, knowing they were less likely to be searched.

Kumaran pulled off what may be the largest-ever purchase of explosives by a terrorist organization. On September 22, 1993, the sum of $990,987 was wired from an HSBC Bank account in Vancouver to an LTTE procurement account overseas. The Vancouver account was in the name of B. Thambirajah, but it was controlled by the LTTE's senior leadership in Canada. Eight months later, Kumaran used the Canadian money to pull off a deadly arms deal. Carlton Trading, an LTTE front company in Dhaka, used forged Bangladeshi military certificates to arrange the purchase of sixty tonnes of RDX and TNT from the Rubezone chemical plant in Ukraine. The LTTE freighter *MV Swene* took delivery of the cargo at the port of Nikolayev and, guarded by Sea Tigers speedboats, cruised to Sri Lanka's northeast coast, where the explosives were offloaded and taken to secret jungle bases. From there the explosives were parceled out for use in land mines, booby traps and suicide bombs. The Black Tigers suicide squad got their hands on a large portion of the deadly cargo.

The results would prove devastating.

Late in the 1990s, Toronto police began noticing a spike in violent crimes in which the common denominator was that both the victims and the criminals were of Sri Lankan origin. They suspected a new organized crime group was emerging, bringing with it the same problems police had encountered when Asian-based crime came to Canada in the 1980s. Motives, witnesses and suspects were elusive. Language and cultural barriers were frustrating investigations. In response, the Toronto Police Services launched a pilot project called the Tamil Task Force, a branch of the intelligence unit that would work closely with the RCMP and Citizenship and Immigration Canada.

The task force soon discovered that organized crime involving people in Canada of Sri Lankan origin had its roots far away. The key players, rival gangs called the VVT and AK Kannan, were aligned with warring Tamil factions in Sri Lanka. AK Kannan, which has an estimated three hundred members in Canada, derives its name from the AK-47 military assault rifle, the weapon of choice for Tamil fighters. Police say the gang is headed by Jothiravi Sittampalam, also known as Kannan or Ravi, a former member of the Tamil Eelam Liberation Organization, which battled the Tigers for leadership of the Tamil rebellion.

"He hates the Tigers," Sergeant Bowen testified at an immigration hearing. Sittampalam's father, a school principal in Kariveti, Sri Lanka, was kidnapped and tortured by the LTTE.

"He has sworn revenge," Bowen said. "He is very prone to violence. He has got a number of criminal convictions."

The VVT, AK Kannan's main rival, is the most powerful pro-LTTE gang in Canada, with a strength of 350 to 500. VVT is short for Valvedditurai, the birthplace of the LTTE and its leader, Prabhakaran. The gang's leaders are suspected current or former Tiger guerrillas and remain loyal to the cause, serving as money collectors and street muscle in Tamil neighborhoods. Even AK Kannan, which violently opposes the Tigers, has LTTE ties; a former LTTE guerrilla gave weapons training to the gang members in Toronto.

The gangs use brutal violence to suppress dissent within the Tamil community. A Tamil video store owner who stayed opened during the Black July day of remembrance was threatened by a gang that later set fire to the business. As with any society, Tamil Canadians are divided in their views about the Tamil Tigers. A degree of ruthlessness is therefore required to maintain the fiction of a unified front and prevent community institutions from splitting between pro-LTTE and anti-LTTE factions, which would send a mixed message to the outside world. The gangs use strong-arm tactics and intimidation to convince Tamils to support the cause. "Members of the VVT will act as enforcers for the political representatives of the LTTE in Canada," the Tamil Task Force said in its 1998 report. "Extensive links and associations between the VVT and LTTE are common knowledge in the Tamil community." The officer in charge of the RCMP's immigration and passport section in Milton, Ontario, said the "Tamil Tigers control every aspect of Tamil gang life in Toronto."

One of the top-ranked VVT leaders is a Sri Lankan named Niranjan Claude Fabian, who has been identified by Toronto police as a former LTTE assassin. Fabian joined the gang shortly after arriving in Canada in 1990. Another high-ranking VVT leader, Sri Ranjan Rasa, also arrived that year and made a refugee claim in which he said he had been abducted and tortured by Indian peacekeeping troops and the Sri Lankan military. The Immigration and Refugee Board accepted his claim on July 8, 1991. During a subsequent police search of his apartment, investigators found photos of Rasa wearing camouflage, carrying weapons and standing in front of the LTTE flag. In addition to the two main gangs, there are a number of smaller ones including the Jane Finch Gang, Kipling Gang, Sooran Gang, Seelapul Gang, Mississauga Gang and the Gilder Tigers, all pro-LTTE factions loyal to the VVT. Three gangs, Udupiddy, Tuxedo Boys and Silver Springs, are against the Tigers and pledge their loyalty to AK Kannan. Sergeant Bowen has referred over two hundred Tamil gang members to the immigration department for deportation. All told, there are about a thousand gang members in Toronto, often drawing their ranks from former Tamil guerrillas who "are known to have had extensive paramilitary training in the use of automatic weapons, hand to hand combat, Russian RPGs and other offensive weapons and substances," the Tamil Task Force reported. "Many of these have been used in the Greater Toronto Area to carry out their projects."

Gangs have been a longstanding feature of Tamil political extremism. Sri Lanka had an extensive smuggling and extortion underworld well before the current civil war. Prabhakaran was a gang member in the 1970s before he struck off to help launch the Tamil New Tigers. After TNT leader Chetti Thanabalasingham was killed, Prabhakaran took over. He rose to prominence by assassinating the mayor of Jaffna and then boasting openly about it. His reputation for sudden and decisive violence cemented, Prabhakaran changed the name of the organization to the Tamil Tigers and launched his violent drive for independence. The Tigers were thrust into a power struggle with five other Tamil factions, mainly the Tamil Eelam Liberation Organization and the People's Liberation Organization of Tamil Eelam, which were supported by India in an attempt to undermine the LTTE. Desperate to be the sole revolutionary organization, the Tigers embarked on a campaign to systematically eliminate their rivals, which they did ruthlessly and effectively. The bitterness between the Tamil factions survives to this day, and the gang violence in Canada between the VVT and AK Kannan mirrors these old grievances.

Gang extortion rackets, in which pro-LTTE crime groups collect "donations" from Tamil homes and businesses, are also rooted in the homeland, where the Tigers have imposed a taxation system on families, businesses and criminal enterprises in the areas under their control. The LTTE used the same tactics in Europe. Ten people were arrested in Germany for extorting 50 Deutschmarks per month from Tamil families. The same thing took place in Britain, France and Switzerland. Aside from extortion, the LTTE's Canadian gangs are involved in home invasions, kidnappings, murder, attempted murder, passport theft, counterfeiting, credit and debit card fraud, bank fraud and auto theft. The gangs take turns attacking each other's hangouts in drive-by shootings using sawed-off shotguns; it's a deadly turf war that has begun to turn parts of Toronto into a shooting gallery.

With so many bullets flying it was only a matter of time before innocents were caught in the crossfire. "They're not very good shots and somebody else is going to get hurt," a police officer told the *Toronto Sun* in February 1997. Ten months later, nineteen-year-old University of Waterloo student Kapilan Palasanthiran was sitting with two friends at a window table at Cross Country Donut Shop in Scarborough when four men wearing dark clothes and hoods stopped outside. Without warning, they opened fire at the window. All three friends were hit by the hail of bullets, one in the chest. Palasanthiran was struck in the back, and pronounced dead at Sunnybrook Hospital. Police believe the shooting was the work of gang members who mistook the victims for their rivals.

The gangs have formidable firepower. During one investigation into gang activity, police stumbled across a weapons cache hidden in a snowbank behind a Scarborough gas station. A 9-mm submachine gun, a Beretta 12-gauge shotgun, a Winchester 12 gauge and two semiautomatic pistols were recovered. Two of the weapons had been stolen in break-and-enters in Toronto and Montreal. Officers from Toronto's 14 Division seized an Uzi submachine gun from a man at a Tamil Co-op apartment where gang members were holding their meetings. VVT members smuggled an AK-47 into Canada, as well as armor-piercing bullets.

Gang members have told police about possessing M-16s. An AK Kannan member was driving through the Toronto suburb of Scarborough at 10 p.m. on January 24, 1998, when he was attacked by VVT members with bats and beer bottles. He fled and his Chrysler Daytona, which was loaded with firearms, was stolen. The VVT ransacked the car, took the weapons and blew it up with a "napalm" bomb made of gasoline, soap and Drano, an explosive mix used commonly by the Tamil Tigers.

Early in 1998, VVT leader Niranjan Fabian was convicted of conspiracy to forge a Canadian passport, conspiracy to commit assault causing bodily harm, and attempting to obstruct justice. The judge said Fabian "was prepared in order to protect his interest in the illicit trade of passports to go so far as to resort to violence, in which innocent third parties could have been harmed. The full extent of his criminal activities and his criminal mindset discloses very little respect for the law." Fabian was declared a danger to the public and ordered deported. However, at the end of 2003 he was still appealing his case and living in Toronto.

Sri Ranjan Rasa, was convicted of conspiracy to commit assault causing bodily harm on March 3, 1998, and sentenced to seven months in jail. On the same day, he was convicted of conspiracy to use a forged credit card, and possession of a restricted weapon. The judge rebuked the VVT for its bloodthirsty tactics. "What I find to be the most alarming feature of the group's organization is the fact that they were all too willing to resort to violence and the use of prohibited weapons in order to preserve their criminal enterprise from any encroachment," he said. Rasa was deemed a danger to the public and processed for deportation, but has been appealing through the courts.

As LTTE gang violence reached ridiculous proportions in Toronto, the Tamil Tigers' leadership became concerned that the gangs were giving the Tamil independence movement a bad name. The Tigers feared a government crackdown that would interrupt the flow of money from Canada. Prabhakaran dispatched an assassin named Shukla from France to impose a truce. The WTM and Tamil Eelam Society invited him to read Prabhakaran's warning to the gang leadership. An initial peacemaking attempt failed, but in May 1998 a few hundred AK Kannan and VVT members assembled at a Hindu temple in Richmond Hill, Ontario, and, with the blessing of a priest and elders, renounced violence.

The truce did not last. Within six months violence had resumed and by early 1999 was spiraling out of control once again. In June 1999, a VVT member and two friends were driving on Ellesmere Road in Scarborough at night when AK Kannan members pulled up behind them and started firing. The car fled but the attackers pursued them, firing as they went, leaving a trail of shell casings scattered along a one-kilometer stretch of road. The VVT gangster was killed by a gunshot wound to the back. Two days later, another bystander was killed. A sixteen-year-old girl was chatting with friends in a Burger King parking lot when a black Lincoln Navigator pulled up. The passenger rolled down the window and fired a shotgun blast that hit the teen in the back. Police believe the gunman was trying to kill another man who was present, an associate of a Tamil gang. Police estimate there were at least fifty Tamil gang shootings that fall.

Police had little success tackling the gangs. A "bond of silence"—a tacit agreement that neither side will go to the police—means many crimes are never even reported. Witnesses were too frightened to testify. One gang circulated a flyer in the Tamil language offering a reward for information on Crown witnesses. On the few occasions that witnesses have testified, gangsters have sat in the courtroom holding up photos of the witnesses' children and relatives. "Many of the Tamils in the Greater Toronto Area live in fear of the gangs and the various extremist groups living in their communities and few will testify or complain to police," according to an RCMP report. The Canadian immigration system has also proven ineffective at getting rid of gangsters. On October 18, 2001, hundreds of police and immigration officers in Ontario rounded up more than fifty Tamil gang members for deportation. Unable to lock them up for their crimes, police decided the solution was to just deport them. But it proved more difficult than anyone had imagined, and two years later few had actually been deported and almost all were back on the street.

The consistent pattern of Tamil gang activity has been its use of violence and coercion to get money. "The gangs are doing anything for money," Sergeant Bowen said. And the money is making its way into the LTTE coffers. An RCMP intelligence study "found strong connections between the LTTE and organized crime, specifically street gangs, in Toronto and Montreal. There is clear evidence to support the relationship and that the money involved is being funneled to the LTTE for extremist purposes in Sri Lanka." The RCMP study "backs up the connections and indicates large numbers of LTTE members have a presence in Canada and connections to the criminal gangs ... for monetary and enforcement purposes." The RCMP also found evidence that gang members were being recruited in Sri Lanka to conduct gang activities in Canada, and reported ties between Tamil gangs and the LTTE front organizations.

When Manickavasagam Suresh took over as the Canadian leader of the LTTE, intelligence agents began to keep a close watch on him. The Tigers did not make it easy. When the Canadian LTTE leadership wanted to meet, they would travel in separate cars and then randomly select a house. They would ask the occupants to leave and then take over the house for a few hours. That way there was no way CSIS could bug their meeting places. With so many foreign extremists working in Canada, and the bill for deportation proceedings reaching $1 million each, CSIS had decided that instead of going after them all, it would selectively target those in leadership positions and use them as examples. Suresh appeared to fit the bill.

After Suresh applied to become a landed immigrant, CSIS put together an intelligence file summarizing his past and his activities in Canada. The report said that Suresh was a high-ranking member of the Tamil Tigers, which "operates in Canada under the auspices of a front organization, the WTM, for the purpose of fundraising, propaganda and procurement of materiel." Suresh had been in contact with the LTTE's international leadership and had not only raised money for the Tigers but also had purchased equipment with military uses, it said. As such, Suresh was not permitted to remain in the country because the Immigration Act stipulates that members of terrorist organizations are inadmissible to Canada. CSIS took its file to the solicitor general and minister of immigration, who signed a certificate declaring Suresh a threat to national security. He was arrested on October 18, 1995.

Even after his arrest, Suresh remained in charge of the Canadian LTTE network. Despite his imprisonment at Toronto's Don Jail, he continued to communicate with members of the WTM. He provided advice and guidance by telephone and was still considered by Tamil extremists to be the Canadian LTTE leader. Using a telephone transfer system, he was able to speak with senior international members of the LTTE. (Suresh let a fellow prisoner use the same system. Mansour Ahani, a secret agent in the Iranian foreign assassinations branch, used it to call Iran.)

The Snow Tigers responded to the arrest by organizing a Free Suresh campaign. In letters, demonstrations and political lobbying, the Federation of Associations of Canadian Tamils portrayed Suresh as a political prisoner. The Tigers were not a terrorist group, they argued. They were a liberation army acting in self-defense of the Tamil people. Likewise, Suresh was not a terrorist leader; he was a "community activist" and a "human rights" worker. Suresh himself wrote that he was being detained "because of my lawful political activities." Should Suresh be deported, the campaigners argued, he would be tortured and killed. Eight hundred and fifty people demonstrated outside the House of Commons demanding that Canada suspend deportation proceedings against Suresh. "The Tamil Canadians are rightly indignant that Suresh has been treated as a common criminal and unreasonably incarcerated," FACT said in a statement. "This act of the Minister of Immigration is an affront against the Tamil Canadian community."

The Free Suresh campaign emphasized that Suresh had never been charged with a crime, "not even a traffic violation," but the slogan also served to highlight the glaring void in Canadian criminal law that allowed agents of foreign terrorist groups to openly fundraise to promote political and ethnic violence. The United States, on the other hand, brought in legislation in 1996 that made it illegal to provide material support to foreign terrorist groups. Penalties range as high as ten years' imprisonment. "Foreign organizations that engage in terrorist activity are so tainted by their criminal conduct that any contribution to such an organization facilitates that conduct," the U.S. Congress noted. The first list of organizations banned under the law was released in October 8, 1997. More than two dozen groups were designated as terrorist groups, including the Tamil Tigers; the World Tamil Movement and FACT were listed as "known front organizations." The legislation had a crippling effect on LTTE fundraising in the United States. The Tigers' supporters challenged the designation in the courts but lost the case. Fundraising was quickly curtailed, making Canada the North American base of operations by default. The ruling was also a blow to Tiger propaganda efforts, which had sought to convince the world that the LTTE were liberators, not terrorists. Now the world's most powerful country had branded the Tigers as terrorists. It was the price the Tigers would have to pay for committing such atrocities as the Rajiv Gandhi assassination and the mounting toll of suicide bombings in Colombo.

The case of Manickavasagam Suresh was heard by Justice Max Teitelbaum of the Federal Court of Canada, who heard fifty days of testimony before ruling that the CSIS evidence was solid and reasonable. The judge ruled that Suresh was "a dedicated and trusted member, in a leadership position with the LTTE," which he said had engaged in terrorism. He said the WTM was "part of the LTTE organization or is, at the very least, an organization that strongly supports the activities of the LTTE." He further ruled that Suresh had obtained refugee status "by willful misrepresentation of facts" and said Suresh should be removed from Canada as quickly as possible.

But Suresh's Toronto lawyers had other plans. They went to the Ontario Court of Justice, which ordered that he could not be deported until all his avenues of appeal had been exhausted. With no end in sight for his court proceedings, he was released from jail. His next appeal failed as well. The Federal Court upheld his deportation, saying he had not established his case. Terrorist fundraising was not a form of expression protected by the Charter of Rights and Freedoms, the court ruled.

Suresh then took his case to the Federal Court of Appeal. Its decision in January 2000 was as hard-hitting a ruling as a Canadian court has ever written on terrorism. Judge J.A. Robertson upheld the deportation of Suresh, saying his activities had put the security of Canada at risk. The judge had harsh words for agents such as Suresh. "Those who freely choose to raise funds to sustain terrorist organizations bear the same guilt and responsibility as those who actually carry out the terrorist acts."

The ruling was a defeat for the Snow Tigers, but they soon got a big boost. FACT staged a dinner in Toronto in May 2000 to celebrate the Sri Lankan New Year. Invitations were issued to local, provincial and federal politicians, including two members of the federal cabinet, Maria Minna, then minister of international cooperation, and Paul Martin, then minister of finance, who was the guest of honor. When a source in the Toronto Tamil community phoned to tell me about the event, at first I could not believe that cabinet ministers would attend an event for an organization considered by CSIS to be an LTTE front, so I called their offices and their aides confirmed that they would indeed be attending. I later obtained documents showing the ministers were warned about the event. "Further to Signet message, referencing possible attendance by Minister Minna at a FACT-sponsored 'Tamil New Year Event' on Saturday, May 6, the following should be taken into consideration: the recently released US Annual Report on Terrorism continues to name FACT as a 'front organization' for the LTTE," stated an e-mail message sent by the Canadian High Commission in Colombo to the Department of Foreign Affairs on May 4. A front-page article in the *National Post* on the morning of May 6 also cautioned that the ministers were planning to attend an event for a group considered by many to be a Tigers front.

CSIS, it turns out, also told the ministers not to go. "We told them, look you're being used," a former high-ranking intelligence official said. The ministers' position was that FACT was a community organization and it should not be punished because of the actions of a few extreme members. CSIS officials responded by pointing out that if that was what the government wanted, it should give counterterrorism agents the tools they need to deal with the extremists. The ministers went to the dinner anyway, but they did nothing to help CSIS deal with the Tamil Tigers' support network. "It's all about votes," the intelligence official shrugged.

Minna was no stranger to the Tamil Tigers. As far back as March 4, 1994, she had written a letter to a Sri Lankan government minister on her House of Commons letterhead on behalf of her Tamil constituents, whom she said "have expressed to me their desire to see a legitimate workable peace plan put in place." Foreign Minister Bill Graham wrote to the same minister on March 8 saying that he had "many constituents of Tamil descent" and that "all are seriously concerned about the situation prevailing in Sri Lanka." Both letters invited the Sri Lankan minister to Canada. The similarities in the letters and their timing strongly suggest the politicians were responding to lobbying. Unfortunately, they were addressed to the wrong side of the conflict. The month after they were sent, the LTTE shot a man in Paris to prevent him from publishing a book critical of the Tamil Tigers. The Sri Lankan government did enter into peace talks at the time, but the LTTE only used the ceasefire to rearm. When fighting erupted again in 1995, it was even more ferocious than before.

The attendance of Martin and Minna at the FACT dinner was a propaganda coup for the LTTE, which used the event to give the impression that senior levels of the Canadian government supported the Tamil Tigers. But it also backfired, generating intense debate in the press and Parliament about the acceptability of terrorist support activity in Canada. The LTTE support network went into high gear, accusing the media and the Canadian Alliance opposition of racism. The Liberals fell right into the trap. "To condemn these people, to call them terrorists, is anti-Canadian," Martin told the House of Commons on May 30. "I will tell you, Mr. Speaker, there is Irish blood coursing through my veins, and I am not a member of the IRA."

His response was illogical, but it perfectly served the interests of the LTTE support groups, which had long deflected criticism by claiming that any condemnation of the LTTE was an attack on all Tamils. The Tigers' skilled propaganda wing could not have crafted a more perfect reply. Minna called the opposition questioning "pure racism." The Alliance continued to attack the Liberals on the matter, handing the file to Monte Solberg, the foreign affairs critic, who said that "FACT is a fundraising organization for the Tamil Tigers. That's well established. Yet even though our own security agency has made that very clear, the Finance Minister and other ministers go to these sorts of events and put money into that organization." Asked why he had attended a function for a group that the U.S. State Department had designated an LTTE front, Martin responded: "This Minister and this government do not take orders from the U.S. State Department." He neglected to mention that CSIS had published a paper only weeks earlier listing FACT as a front. The issue was still surfacing in the House in the fall of 2000, and the Liberals continued to respond with accusations of racism rather than informed discussion of policy. "Let me simply say that the leader of the opposition says that he is the new sheriff in town," Martin said. "It sounds to me like he is trying to organize a lynch mob." The Liberal strategy was to equate counterterrorism with the Ku Klux Klan. How politically convenient, and how utterly damaging for Canada.

Suresh, meanwhile, was trying a new approach to beat Canadian authorities. "I fear that I will be detained, tortured and ultimately murdered in Sri Lanka," he said. He appealed to the Supreme Court of Canada on the grounds that deportation would be a death sentence. Ten lobby groups asked the court's permission to intervene. Seven were allowed to take part, including FACT, the Canadian Arab Federation, Canadian Council for Refugees, Amnesty International, Canadian Council of Churches, the Centre for Constitutional Rights and the United Nations High Commissioner for Refugees. All argued that Suresh should not be deported. "The right to be free from torture is an absolute human right that applies to all people in all circumstances," said Alex Neve, who heads Amnesty's Canadian chapter. "We're concerned that no country, including Canada, start to carve out exceptions, limitations and restrictions to that right." The Canadian Bar Association was later added as an intervenor, also on the side of Suresh.

When the government lawyers appeared before the country's top justices, they would be facing not only Suresh's lawyers, but also a row of powerful interest groups. A more one-sided fight would be hard to find. The federal lawyers were blunt about what was at stake. "This case will determine whether Canada will become a haven for terrorists," the government legal team said in its submission to the court. "The elimination of terrorism requires the elimination of the funds which fuel violence. To preserve the security of Canada and the integrity of Canada's refugee determination system, Canada must not be a haven and a fundraising base camp for terrorists." The government's "Statement of Facts" went on to describe the LTTE as an organization that promotes its agenda "by directing terror at civilians." Suicide bombings, land mines, murders, ethnic cleansing, kidnapping and forced conscription of child soldiers were attributed to the LTTE and its "cult-sacrificial death culture and rejection of democratic institutions ... These examples of brute force and contempt for human rights require money. The LTTE raises money through drug trafficking. It also raises money by relying upon the willing and unwilling expatriate communities abroad, such as the large number of Tamil refugees in Canada."

The World Tamil Movement and Federation of Associations of Canadian Tamils were named as "examples of political and benevolent front organizations which support the LTTE." The lawyer representing FACT countered that fundraising was a constitutionally protected form of expression and that there was no evidence that FACT or its members, including Suresh, had committed any crimes or were responsible for terrorist violence. "The federal government is constitutionally justified in addressing a terrorist presence in Canada, but only through means that are proportional. Placing individuals at risk of deportation for engaging in associational and expressive activities is a particularly deleterious consequence for members of a community who legitimately fear mistreatment, persecution and even torture upon returning to Sri Lanka."

The court decision sealed Canada's fate as a haven for terrorists, ruling that if terrorists caught in Canada were at risk of being tortured in their homelands, the government could not deport them except in rare circumstances, where their presence in Canada poses such a great public danger that they have to be removed. Suresh's case was sent back to the immigration department for another look. In October 2005, on the tenth anniversary of his arrest, Suresh was living in a suburban home near the Toronto airport. I caught up with him as he was waiting at a bus stop, on his way to work. He looked like any other office-bound commuter, wearing loose jeans and a hooded winter bomber jacket. "You are bothering me," he muttered. He was still living freely in Toronto at the time of this writing. "If we can't get rid of Suresh," a former high-ranking intelligence official told me, "whom can we get rid of?"

The global support network established by the LTTE is so successful that there are legitimate fears it could become a template for other terrorist and insurgent forces. If the Tigers can make use of this kind of system, so can anyone intent on causing mayhem. What is unique about the Tigers is that by behaving in turn like an international corporation and an organized crime syndicate, they have been able to build a frighteningly potent war machine. And they have done so almost completely on their own, without the assistance of a benevolent state sponsor. Hezbollah has Iran to keep it financed and armed. The Tigers have done it alone—or have they? If not for Canada's willingness to tolerate LTTE activity without regard for the bloodshed it causes, the LTTE would be hard-pressed to maintain a fighting posture. Perhaps Canada is in effect the LTTE's state sponsor, and the Sri Lankan conflict is Canada's dirty little war.

The Canadian government finally outlawed the Tigers on April 6, 2006. "The decision to list the LTTE is long overdue and something the previous government did not take seriously enough to act upon," Public Safety Minister Stockwell Day said. Two days later, the RCMP raided the Montreal chapter of the World Tamil Movement. A week later, the RCMP backed a rented U-Haul truck into the parking lot of the WTM head office in Toronto and began carting away papers and computers as part of an investigation called Project OSALUKI. "The LTTE extorts and exploits large Tamil communities in North America, Europe and Asia to obtain funds and supplies for its fighters in Sri Lanka," said a search warrant executed by the RCMP at the Vancouver WTM office. "The WTM is an integral part of the LTTE strategy to raise funds for re-armament and to gain legitimacy. In Canada, the WTM is an LTTE front organization." No charges have been laid and the WTM denies the allegations.

After investigating the LTTE's tentacles in Canada, I wanted to see for myself the results of Canada's coddling of the Tigers. What happens to the blood money collected by the LTTE network in Toronto, Montreal and Vancouver? What do people in Sri Lankan think about it? Just what kind of war were the Canadian fronts financing anyway? In the spring of 2000, while I was on assignment in the region, I set off into Sri Lanka's northern jungle. I would be the last foreign journalist to make it out before the place blew up in a burst of factional violence.

The taxi clears the military checkpoint and pulls up outside the Ceylon Inter-Continental Hotel. A smartly uniformed concierge steps up to open the passenger door for Rafeek, a well-dressed young man with dark sunglasses and a telescopic cane. Rafeek does not seem at all uncomfortable to be back in this war-damaged sector of Colombo, just across the street from the bank where he was working as a manager four years earlier when a Tamil Tigers suicide squad attacked. A devout Muslim, he blames no one and explains away the bombing as God's will. "Who knows if you or I will even be alive tomorrow," he shrugs.

Rafeek was working at the American Express Bank when the first blast shattered the calm of morning. Initially, he thought nothing of it. There was construction next door and he dismissed the noise as the work of the building contractors. Then he heard three gunshots. He ran into the bank foyer. Panicked office workers were out on the streets, running and crying. The blasts were automatic-weapon fire from Tamil insurgents attacking the nearby Central Bank. Rafeek shepherded his employees out of harm's way, and then a powerful explosion blew him off his feet.

"I was about to return to my office, to my desk, where I worked, when the bomb went off. Immediately when I heard this noise I recited part of the Koran and I was just thrown out of the building," he says.

As the building began to collapse he got back on his feet, but then his vision faded. The explosion had embedded shards of glass all over his body, including in his eyeballs. "I was in terrible pain. My body was numb." It was ten or fifteen minutes before the debris settled. The surviving bank staff got him a chair and gathered around, crying, not sure what to do. Three employees had been killed, crushed beneath the debris of the ruined office tower: a security guard, a receptionist and a driver. One of Rafeek's eyes had come out of its socket, and the other was full of blood.

"My condition was very bad," he says. The doctors thought he would not survive. They operated until 4 a.m. Then his lungs failed. American Express tried to bring in a corporate jet to airlift him out for treatment, but there were problems and the plane had to be grounded. He was eventually taken to Madras, India, but during the flight the pressure change stung his ruptured eyes and he could barely tolerate the pain. "God really gave me a lot of courage and power," he says. Doctors thought he might regain sight in his left eye, but then they found a small piece of glass embedded in his pupil. "It had gone right into the eye and almost into the brain." His retina was destroyed while doctors removed the shard. He stayed at hospital in Madras for more than three months. His chin, partially blown off in the blast, started swelling later; doctors cut a piece of skin from his leg and grafted it on. That didn't work and the procedure was repeated two years later, this time successfully.

"Although I lost my vision, to me I lost nothing because God has helped me come through," he says. "Everything happens by God's will and things happen in life. The best thing is to forget about the past."

Although the bombing was carried out by local Tiger operatives, the plot originated in Toronto. Sri Lankan intelligence officials tell me they traced the explosives used in the bomb and found they had come from the Ukrainian shipment purchased two years earlier with money wired from British Columbia. CSIS agents flew to Colombo to assist with the investigation, but the trail tying the Snow Tigers to the bombing had gone cold. Among those killed in the bombing were two Canadians, a mother and her daughter visiting from Toronto.

The Tamil Tigers have carried out over 160 suicide bombings, more than all other insurgent and terrorist groups in the world combined. They have used the method to assassinate politicians, including Rajiv Gandhi, the former Indian prime minister who was killed by Tamil assassins in retaliation for his support for the Sri Lankan government. In July 1997, a female suicide bomber threw herself in front of a government motorcade, killing twenty-one and injuring fifty. A civilian passenger train was bombed a few days later, killing seventy civilians. Twenty more civilians were killed in October 1997 when a rebel suicide crew set off a truck bomb that damaged the World Trade Center of Colombo, the Sri Lankan Finance Ministry and Colombo's three top international hotels. The sacred Buddhist Temple of the Tooth in Kandy, Sri Lanka, was bombed in a suicide attack in January 1998, and in March 1999 three bomb attacks in Colombo—which targeted the train yard, a power transfer station and the state-owned bus terminal—resulted in one death and twelve injuries. The year 2000 saw a major resurgence in suicide attacks, many of them during national elections.

The suicide bombers are celebrated by the Tamil separatists, who refer to them as the "protective armor" of the Tamil people. Black July celebrations are held in their honor in countries such as Canada each July 5, the anniversary of the first attack in 1987, when a rebel known as Captain Miller drove a truck packed with explosives into the Nelliyadi army camp in Jaffna, killing thirty-nine soldiers. Rebel radio marks the occasion by reading out the names of the bombers killed in the previous year. In July 2000, forty-one suicide bombers were so honored. In rebel-held areas, shops are closed and public rallies and religious ceremonies are held.

The bombings have turned Colombo into another front line, ensuring its citizens, though far from Jaffna, are forever on alert, constantly terrified. To be Canadian in Colombo is also terrifying. It is truly disturbing to come face to face with the effects of the violence that is cheered on and financed by the LTTE's wing of supporters in Canada. It is bad enough that groups such as the LTTE have brought their wars to Canada. Here in Colombo, the war comes full circle: Canada brings war to Sri Lanka, because to the extent that this vicious terrorist violence is paid for by the Snow Tigers, and permitted to continue unchecked by Ottawa, this is a Canadian war.

For foreign travelers, the first sign of Sri Lanka's troubles is evident in the Thai capital, Bangkok. Despite a two-hour stopover when the flight from Hong Kong lands there, passengers going on to Colombo are not permitted to leave the plane, and the cabin undergoes a thorough security sweep. All the baggage stored in the overhead compartments is traced to its owners. Three hours later, the plane lands at Bandaranaike International Airport, which is guarded like a military compound. Young soldiers hold assault rifles at the ready, and elevated guard towers surround the complex, which is encircled by tall fences. In the hotel room, a travel guide rests on the desk, optimistically declaring: "2000 AD, dawn of a New Era, Let Us Resolve to Ensure Peace and Prosperity in Our Motherland Through Unity and Dedication."

The first few hours of a war assignment are the most difficult. There is a feeling of tumbling into a living nightmare as you kiss your family goodbye at the airport, jet through time zones and emerge in a daze at a darkened airport inhabited by uniformed men sporting automatic weapons. You are weary, desensitized by hours of travel, but you are also terrified, by the unknown, by your own laughable vulnerability and the dread that you will never return. A sensible person would flee. The journalist steps willingly into the unknown, in pursuit of nothing more tangible than a story.

Colombo is the political and commercial capital of Sri Lanka, a coastal port city of 500,000 with modern glass office towers, pungent slums and ancient Buddhist temples. There are lavishly decorated Hindu temples, Muslim mosques and Christian church-es, vestiges of early European traders. The winding beaches, lush tropical gardens and colonial buildings, not to mention the amiable demeanor of Sri Lankans, should make the city an earthly paradise. But the scars of two decades of war are not easily hidden.

In the downtown business district, the skeletons of what were once office buildings line the streets near the waterfront—empty memorials to a wave of deadly terrorist bombings. Although far from the frontlines to the north, Colombo still has the uneasy feel of a city at war. Military checkpoints slow traffic at intersections, outnumbering even the statues of Buddha. Armed soldiers hang from the rear doors of buses to deter rebels from planting bombs. Government buildings are guarded like fortresses, as are the homes of prominent politicians.

The hotel taxi driver, a gray-haired Sinhalese with a kindly, round face, points out the landmarks as he drives through Colombo. Concrete patches cover the section of the Hotel Galidari that was bombed in 1997 by rebels targeting the American servicemen stay-ing there. We head through the wild city traffic, toward the elegant Cinnamon Gardens district, with its colonial homes and shady, park-like properties. "There is the residence of the prime minister," the driver says, pointing to a large home. The brick and mortar wall in front of the house has been blasted away, leaving a crevice. "It was bombed last year and some security personnel were killed," he says.

Moments later, the driver points to the other side of the street, where a black statue marks the spot where the security minister was standing when he was blown apart by a suicide bomber. A lit-tle farther down, the cabby points again, this time to a building with white pillars and a dome roof. "The president, she was stand-ing on a stage right there," he says, "giving an election speech when a suicide bomber made an attempt on her life." The grass is still scorched on the spot where the bomb went off.

The LTTE keeps a hit list of assassination targets. President Chandrika Kumaratunga is at the top, but number two is Lakshman Kadirgamar, the foreign minister. Kadirgamar is an elo-quent statesman; his diplomatic skills have been honed by his years at the United Nations, and he uses them to lobby Western nations to help curb Tiger fundraising activities. The fact that he is an ethnic Tamil only makes him more hated by the rebels, who have systematically eliminated Tamil politicians advocating anything less than full independence for Eelam.

The streets surrounding Kadirgamar's home in Colombo are protected by soldiers in sandbag bunkers. High cement walls encircle his property and guards in elevated towers are posted at each corner. Even his gardeners wear military fatigues as they trim his grass and tend to the flowers—orange, red, purple and white—that sprout between the palms. The minister's home encapsulates the condition of Sri Lanka: a place of incredible beauty that is in perpetual fear of the unexpected blast of violence.

The minister sits in a bamboo chair on his porch, sipping lemon juice, and before long the conversation turns to his campaign against LTTE fundraising. "We are getting, I would say, a fair deal of international *moral* support," he says. "We're not getting any good support in terms of fundraising."

Expressions of sympathy and condemnations of terrorism only go so far. For Kadirgamar, the money that is collected at Tamil Tiger functions in Western cities such as Toronto is linked all too clearly to the dead civilians who are left lying among debris in the streets and the dead soldiers who are shipped home from the northern flank.

"It's well known that fundraising for terrorist purposes is one of the main reasons terrorism is continuing. If the funds did not come," he says, "the weapons would not be unloaded on our beaches."

On Friday August 12, 2005, Minister Kadirgamar, 73, had just finished his evening swim when he was struck in the head and chest with bullets fired by a sniper positioned in a neighboring home. The Tamil Tigers are suspected of carrying out the assassination.

Sri Lanka's three million ethnic Tamils have paid a high price for the LTTE independence drive. Terror attacks invariably create more internal refugees and trigger a backlash and security crackdowns. Police at checkpoints in Colombo wave through vans filled with Sinhalese, but those carrying Tamils are searched. The Tamil

slums of Colombo—a maze of roads, shops and ornate temples—
are watched closely by police charged with trying to stop the next
suicide bombing. Government emergency measures require that
Tamils who come to Colombo from the north and east of Sri Lanka
must register with police, who issue them a certificate. Hotels are
not allowed to rent rooms to Tamils unless the would-be guests
have registration papers, and police frequently raid the hotels,
known as lodges, in the Tamil district of Fort to enforce the policy. Fort consists of a maze of narrow streets, an unreal island of
small commerce, temporary shelter and illicit pursuits. The stench
of refuse and fish is so pervasive it permeates your clothes. Every
possible nook and cranny sprouts signs of human life—cooking
stoves, children, merchants and prostitutes. To walk through Fort's
streets is to have one's senses exhaustingly assaulted. Aggressive
taxi drivers pursue me, shouting in a way that suggests no one in
their right mind would walk in the city in such heat. The jewelers,
soft drink peddlers and textile merchants do not sit back and await
customers; they yell out at likely candidates, attempting to lure
them into the shops through loud argument.

It is no use visiting Colombo with Western expectations. I
have come with the addresses of places I am supposed to visit,
names of businesses and phone numbers. None of it has any
meaning here. Even the cab driver cannot find the addresses on
my list, although he is certain they exist. He stumbles across one,
but the slums are so confusing I don't know where I am and when
I try to return the next day, the street is nowhere to be found. I
wander for hours, but it has vanished. I eventually lean against a
building, attempting to regain my bearings and lose the dizziness
in my head. A cab slows and the driver shouts that I should get
into his disheveled machine. An old woman walking by stops,
parts her legs, and urinates through her sari.

Island Lodge, one of the largest low-rent lodges, or hotels, in
Fort district, with forty-two tiny rooms, was shut down by police for
three and a half years but has now reopened. "They didn't give any
reason," says Joseph, the manager. The lodges are part refugee
camps, part holding areas for those waiting to leave the country to
join relatives. They are also a smugglers' den, where shadowy

agents lurk in search of customers willing to pay thousands of dollars for fake documents that will ensure their passage to the West.

The halls of Island Lodge are crammed with Tamils, mostly women and children whose husbands have gone to Switzerland, Norway and Canada to make refugee claims. If they are accepted, they will sponsor their families to join them. If not, they will come home and try again somewhere else. An old man explains how the war split apart his family: his daughter is in Germany, another daughter is in Switzerland and his son is in Ontario. "His son is sending some money," Joseph says. At the front counter, Joseph shows the book he is forced to keep under the security measures. Inside it are the registration papers of his Tamil lodgers, along with their photos. Police frequently come by to check the papers, he says. At one lodge, a woman from Jaffna longs for "a normal life" but doubts that is possible. "No one is going to win or lose this war," she says. "The fighting is going to go on and on."

I arrange to meet Rafeek for dinner and we travel in his car to the Colombo waterfront. There, the driver helps Rafeek cross a set of railroad tracks to a restaurant, where the owner greets him warmly. We take a table on the beach, and for a moment this could be California or Vancouver, but the conversation turns invariably to the war. "In my neighborhood," says the owner, "Sinhalese, Tamils, Muslims, they all live together like family, no problem." If only, he says, it could be that way in the rest of the country.

The Central Bank bombing that took Rafeek's office colleagues and his eyesight may not have dulled his faith, but it has robbed him of the opportunity to see the remarkable beauty of this evening as the sun flares and crashes into the Indian Ocean. Perhaps it is the knowledge of what he is missing that causes his optimism to slip momentarily.

He confides that he misses driving. In his old job at American Express, he would travel all over Sri Lanka by car, from the ports to the east to the southern resort towns, stopping at quiet teahouses and ancient ruins. Now he must ride in the back seat, sitting in darkness, hiding his demolished eyes behind sunglasses.

"Let's pray that these types of things will come to an end," he says. "We want that to come very soon."

The war has divided Sri Lanka into what the military calls "cleared" areas (those under government control) and "uncleared" ones in the north and east. Jaffna, the capital of the Tamil homeland and the city at the heart of the war, is at the very northern tip of the island, which is technically a cleared area but is cut off from the rest of Sri Lanka by the rebel-held Wanni jungle to the south. Getting to Jaffna by road therefore means cutting through the heart of rebel territory.

As Mohan, the taxi driver, drives north from Colombo, the chaotic city traffic gives way to rural roads bookended by lush green hills that could have been transplanted from the coasts of West Africa. By noon, Mohan is no longer talkative and seems to be intensely focused on merely keeping awake, resisting with all his will the narcoleptic powers of the midday sun. He stops for "petrol" in Anuradhapura, but once behind the wheel again begins to slide toward lethargy. Falling asleep at the wheel is a major cause of death and injury in Sri Lanka, so much so that overtired truck drivers will sometimes stop and lie on the road in front of their trucks to sleep, bathed in the glow of their headlights.

Perhaps it is not that drivers here are more prone to sleep but simply that the tropical drowsiness, twisting narrow roads and impatient relentless pace of traffic make for a deadly combination. Mohan at last surrenders and suggests I might like to see the temple at Mihintale while he closes his eyes for a moment. "I worked so late last night," he apologizes.

Mihintale is a mountaintop shrine, accessible by 1,840 steps carved neatly into the rock. The steps are small and you mount them two or three at a time, passing slow-moving families making weekend pilgrimages. The stairs come to an end at a plateau, a broad amphitheater enclosed by peaks. It was like standing inside a volcano. "No shoes are permitted in the sacred areas," says an old man. He gestures to a rack of shoes beside him. "You must leave your shoes here." I tuck my runners into a cubbyhole and hand the man a few rupees which he accepts with a nod.

The shrine is a wonder, an open-air church. The Indian emperor Asoka sent his son, the priest Mahinda, to Sri Lanka in the third century BCE to introduce his friend, the Sinhalese king

Devanampiyatissa, to Buddhism. It was at Mihintale that they met, and where Buddhism first took root in Sri Lanka. Set among the palms and ochre-colored dirt is a giant statue of Buddha, in all his calm reflection; a dome-shaped temple; and at the center of it all, a craggy old tree. A guide attaches himself to me, without being asked, and follows me, giving his well-practised tour. Ancient headless statues surround the tree. The guide tut-tuts and shakes his head. "Vandals!" he says. "They come at night to ravish the symbols of Buddha."

He leads me up a steep path cut into the rock. We follow a procession of worshipers to the peak known as Meditation Rock, and he scrambles to the peak. Before us lies the lush green of the banana groves and palms below, and a shimmering lake to the east. The guide points to the banana farm where he works during the week. On weekends he climbs to Mihintale to show visitors around, in the hope of a tip. It is as if we are floating above the fertile paradise of fruit trees, the polished white symbols of religion making our lookout feel all the more lofty. "Yesterday," the guide says, pointing to the white dome of the temple, "somebody threw two hand grenades inside the temple, during a visit by the minister of sport."

The closer I creep to northern LTTE territory, the more I run into soldiers and roadblocks, until eventually the troops line the roadway in an unbroken procession. They are facing the forests, with their backs to the highway and their rifles held at the ready in anticipation of a new assault from the dark jungles. Vavunya, the northernmost city under government control, is in a state of military occupation, all drab green jeeps and open trucks packed with troops heading off to war.

The soldiers are very young, and their faces look alternately cocky and terrified. Their equipment is a joke, as if inherited from a century ago. The newspapers in Colombo are filled with tributes to youths killed in battle. Eighteen, nineteen, twenty years of age. At lunch a young ex-military officer mentions that he recently watched the video taken at his wedding seven years earlier. Of the male guests captured on film, half had since been killed in the war.

The army is a deadly career choice. Many enlist for a steady income, others out of ideology, even hatred perhaps. The battlefield is fierce and desertions are common. The government regularly holds amnesties to invite AWOL soldiers to return to their units without penalty. Some of the troops here look almost too young. The Sri Lankan government has been criticized in the past for using soldiers under eighteen, and it has vowed to end the practice. The Tigers have always used child soldiers. Reports from the rebel areas indicate that children are forcibly recruited by the LTTE. Families are expected to give up one child for the cause, a cruel form of taxation. The army regularly captures Tiger soldiers as young as twelve, and finds young bodies strewn across the battlefields. The puzzle of war is that the longer it continues, the more a nation's youth grow up without knowing peace, and the harder it is to bring the violence to a lasting conclusion. War feeds on itself; if allowed to continue for too long, it becomes not a temporary state of depravity, an upheaval needed to move into a more enlightened condition, but a way of life.

Mohan is reluctant to go any farther north, but I push him on until we reach a hut made of sandbags and corrugated tin. It is another hundred meters to the sentry who guards the last checkpoint before the crossing into the rebel zone. I flash my press card and government media accreditation card. The soldier looks the ID over and disappears into a bunkhouse. He emerges followed by a soldier dressed in a T-shirt and camouflage pants. He is bigger and older than the others, and appears to be in charge.

"This is the end," he says. "You can go no farther."

"But I am a journalist. I want to continue."

He points up the road.

"From here, it is Tiger country."

It is no use arguing. These are hardened soldiers who spend their days staring down the enemy. They are not sympathetic. Best to retreat to Mohan's car. This is as far north as I am going to get by land. The only way to Jaffna will be by air.

Calculated risk is the only wise philosophy in a war zone. Few journalists live dangerously; adrenaline junkies who live for the sound of gunfire are rare. But sometimes it is necessary to take risks to get a worthwhile story. The most frightening times are in airplanes. That is when you feel most vulnerable, that your fate is entirely in someone else's hands. In the hands of a pilot you do not know. In the hands of a rebel with a surface-to-air missile. In the hands of God. On the ground, you can chart your own course and turn back when you sense danger. Not in an airplane. The government gives you the option of flying with the military on a Soviet Antonov transport carrier, or taking the civilian passenger flight operated by the air force. The latter seems a better choice. Maybe the LTTE would not open fire on a civilian flight.

"Is it safe?" I ask the foreign ministry spokesman.

"Were you safe in the Balkans?" he responds. In other words, there is a war going on; there are no guarantees, not for anyone, anytime, but those who tread cautiously may be rewarded with survival.

At the air force base north of Colombo, I wait in a hangar canteen with soldiers who are watching television. Palm trees and bright tropical flowers fill the spaces between the olive-green guard towers. The plane is owned by Crimea Air and the captain and crew are Ukrainians working on contract for the air force. Once everyone is on board, a man in a military uniform walks down the aisle spraying disinfectant from an aerosol can above the passengers.

Clouds of steam billow inside the sweltering cabin and the passengers fan themselves with their flight-sickness bags. As we climb over the ocean, the air conditioning kicks in and the cabin becomes so foggy I can hardly see the Norwegian diplomat sitting across the aisle. The flight attendant is a Sri Lankan soldier in camouflage fatigues with decorations over his left pocket. He sleeps the eighty minutes until our plane suddenly plummets and we pass over burned-out homes and a Catholic church, a remnant from the island's early days as a Portuguese colony. The man sitting in front of me cups his hands over his ears and rocks, grimacing in the pain induced by our rapid descent.

It is raining when the plane lands at the Pilally Air Base. A jeep carries me to the Security Forces Headquarters, and I am led into an office where Brigadier Parakrama Pannipitiya is talking on the phone beside a "Secret Deployment Map" on the wall. He hangs up and, using a red laser light, he points to where his fighting regiments are stationed and reminds me of the 9:30 p.m. to 4 a.m. curfew. Sounding like a travel guide, he rattles off statistics about Jaffna: 140,000 square kilometers, monsoons from October to January, income derived from agriculture, livestock and fishing. Then the statistics become more stark. Between January 1998 and December 1999, 601 government troops killed, 737 missing in action and 3,156 wounded. During the same period, 1,524 LTTE "cadres" confirmed dead, according to radio messages intercepted from the Tigers. But the government estimates the actual figure is higher, about 1,900.

The general tells me the Jaffna population supports the army, which recaptured the peninsula from the rebels in 1996. Civilian casualties are common, but he attributes them to poorly aimed rebel mortar fire. "The normal public is with us," he says, adding that the locals fear the Tigers and bring information about them to the military. The army recently shot an LTTE leader who had been collecting money for the rebels through threats, he says. "We were lucky enough to ambush him and kill him."

In his estimation, such measures have helped endear the local population to the army. "They have clearly understood that the government security forces are helping them to exist." Another officer enters the room and introduces himself as Lieutenant Colonel W.A.R. Gunawardhana. "You can call me 'War,'" he says. True, prices are higher in Jaffna, he says, but that is because it is so difficult to transport goods into the war zone. The way he describes it, everyone is carrying on their lives as best they can. The schools are open. In fact, Jaffna students recently won first and second place in nationwide math contests, he says.

I board a bus at the airport and the driver waves me to the front. A soldier also rides up front for security, and I press deep into my seat to avoid being in the sights of his rifle. The driver plays wild Indian music so loudly that the elderly man behind me complains, but to no avail. School has finished and the kids are riding their bikes home in their white uniforms. Some hold umbrellas in one hand and grasp their handlebars with the other.

Jaffna is like a frontier town. The streets are rough and filled with small buses and three-wheeled taxis. Small shops sell bread, cloth, shoes and the gold jewelry cherished by Sri Lankans.

There are military patrols and checkpoints everywhere in Jaffna. At the UN headquarters, safety precautions are outlined on photocopied sheets. "When moving in vehicles, flak jackets and helmets sufficient for all occupants should be carried ... DO NOT run to or from checkpoints ... All residences should have a designated safe room or bunker ... MINES and BOOBY TRAPS are a very real danger and may be encountered anywhere." A second sheet of do's and don'ts says: "Do not—collect war souvenirs such as shells, weapons, etc. Do not—try to be a hero!"

The Sri Lanka Army lists the Jaffna population at almost 500,000, down from its estimate of 738,000 in 1989, but close to the 515,062 in 1995, just before it was recaptured by the government forces. While the numbers may be growing by the military's estimate, the locals seem preoccupied with getting out. Almost everyone hopes to send their children to live with relatives in the West, or at least to Colombo.

"For youngsters, when some incident takes place, they will round them up," one man tells me. "It's risky to keep kids. If you have contacts abroad, you will send them." The shadowy agents who arrange for fake documents and passage abroad charge 800,000 to 1.2 million rupees, he says. "They don't tell you to which country they will send you. Those who have money have already left. Those that are here, they have no means." The man has to pass through eight military checkpoints each morning to reach his job at a foreign-aid agency. His plans to send his own son, age nineteen, as soon as possible. "He's in a very vulnerable stage; I am saving every cent I get." Another man describes the situation in Jaffna as "very, very unpredictable. I would say it's a stalemate still. Even if one Tiger is left, he can make problems. So they have to negotiate. Life is difficult here. Things are very expensive. Here the youths they have no future."

A UN worker explains how humanitarian efforts are having little impact because of the military restrictions, which have closed the Jaffna economy. Everything brought to Jaffna must be approved by the military. Vehicles bought a year earlier are still in Colombo awaiting transport. Goods are "routinely" held for months. Nongovernmental organizations are not allowed to partner up with local organizations. Perishable goods cannot survive the delays, so export is out of the question. The economy is subsistence- and relief-based. "It is becoming clear that [the aid agency] cannot deliver, either cost effectively or quickly," says a report by a major international aid agency. The computers at the aid agency's office are ancient, and attempts to import new ones into Jaffna have met with military resistance. "All this because the technology can be used by the LTTE. Well, these are 386 machines, several years old, and so technologically out of date that their only contribution to the conflict would come if someone threw them out of an office window."

Behind the colonial-era villas that make up the UN compound, the bomb shelter stands at the ready, a bunker under a hummock of sandbags. In the courtyard, the staff use the casing of an old claymore mine for an ashtray. Jaffna is one of the most heavily mined areas in the world. The government security forces have encircled their positions with Pakistani and Japanese land mines, while the Tamil rebels have laid their homemade "Johnny" mines in a nuisance pattern—around wells, houses, anywhere soldiers might gather. "They're far more difficult to deal with," says one of the international relief workers.

The college has been mined, even the elementary school. At least once a week, a civilian steps on a mine, sometimes fatally but more often resulting in the loss of the lower leg. The known minefields are identified with red pins on a map at the UN de-mining office. The UN has been trying to remove the mines, but with little success. "The obvious problem is there's still an ongoing conflict," the worker says. He opens a locker and pulls out a homemade mine, a wooden box with a simple pressure trigger. Painted along the bottom are the words "Made in Tamil Eelam." The mines are crude but effective, as the latest batch of amputees in the hospital can attest.

Mohan Tharmalingam sits on cot 21, resting the bandaged stump of his right leg on an embroidered pillow, waiting to be fitted with a prosthetic limb. The thirty-year-old broom-maker was crossing a rice field early one Saturday morning near the village of Alaveddy Kambalai, collecting sticks for his trade, when a muffled blast erupted beneath his feet. "First I could hear the sound of the explosion, but I didn't know what had happened to me," he says. "I suddenly turned back to see what had happened."

As he toppled over, he knew he had stepped on a mine. He worries that, as an invalid amid war and poverty, he may not be able to support his wife and two children, a three-year-old and a one-month-old. With so many mines strewn across Jaffna and so little that can be done about them, aid workers focus on mine awareness. A mine safety message has been inserted as a trailer on rental videos; newspaper and radio ads, and even a drama group, are helping spread the word. But education can go only so far. Tharmalingam says he knew there were mines around the rice fields near his village, but he believed he wasn't in any danger because he was familiar with the area and thought he knew a safe path. "I used the same route as always," he says.

After the mine blew off most of his foot, Tharmalingam shouted for help, but his fellow villagers feared that they too might set off a pressure mine. Bleeding heavily from his mangled leg, he was forced to crawl out of the field. He was taken to the nearest hospital within half an hour and then transferred to Jaffna. But the damage was too great to save his leg; doctors had to amputate just below the knee. He is the perfect metaphor for his country: desperately poor, but maimed by war and so unable to do anything about it.

As night falls, the heat of day eases and the birds in the jack-fruit trees resume their wild screeching. Foreign-aid workers relax on the porch of a colonial-style house, sipping wine and eating lobster tails bought from local fishermen. A Swiss aid worker seems surprised that I was able to reach Jaffna by plane. She says her agency takes the twenty-two-hour boat ride from Colombo rather than risk the ninety-minute flight. She points her index finger at a forty-five-degree angle and raises it like a shooting projectile. "Because of the missiles." At 9:15 p.m. sharp, the American host stands to announce that curfew approaches. There is a dash for cars and bikes as the young staff of the UN, the

International Committee of the Red Cross and other relief groups scurry to their compounds.

The sun seems bigger in the north. It is more intense, and heavier. There is also no hiding from it. Not like in the city, with its prolific shade. The landscape seems more arid as well, the dust more pervasive. This is Sri Lanka's dry zone. The monsoons that batter the south aren't as strong this far north. Farming is more difficult here, the trees more stunted. The terrain is flat. Jaffna looks and feels different from the lush, mountainous south, a geographic anomaly that can only add to the sense of uniqueness, of nationalism.

The tension is palpable, the troops ever-present, nervous and angry. The military vehicles rule the roads and the people live cautiously, exploiting each lull in fighting to prepare for the inevitable next round, when supplies and freedoms will again become scarce.

Getting to Jaffna wasn't easy, but leaving proves nearly impossible. The UN driver drops me off outside the army office, where hundreds of people are lined up awaiting permission to leave the peninsula, umbrellas in hand to shade them from the high midday sun. I sheepishly skirt the line and am escorted by soldiers to a man sitting behind a desk who examines my papers. He hands me a pencil and dictates a letter attesting to how grateful I am to the military and how well I have been treated.

He sends me to a more senior officer, who signs and stamps my letter. Papers in order, I am permitted to leave, except I have already missed the bus to the air force base. I walk toward the center of town in search of a cab. Dozens of taxis are lined up along the road, but they look like junkyard heaps and appear to have been abandoned. The city is decades behind the capital to the south, as if frozen in time at the outbreak of war. Rusted old vehicles, crumbling buildings, obsolete technology. Bicycles are the main mode of transportation. Jaffna Teaching Hospital is old and full of the sick, pregnant and war-wounded. Running out of time, I rouse an elderly man sleeping in the front seat of a cab that must have been built in the 1950s.

The rain begins as we drive north through the bombed-out homes, past land-mine victims hobbling on prosthetic limbs that jut out of their sarongs, and soldiers with their backs to the roads. At the air base, soldiers lead the air passengers to an outdoor holding area, where we must wait for the flight to Colombo. A merchant is selling lemonade and tea from a stall.

Suddenly the travelers are jolted by a deafening blast. Not one hundred meters away, the army is firing off artillery rounds. The soldiers search the luggage closely. Another soldier appears and steers the passengers into a closet-sized room for a body search. A bus takes us to the airstrip and we walk past an ancient armored vehicle with a gun turret, and duck as a military helicopter swoops low overhead. We climb into an old Soviet-built plane that takes off to the north and then ascends sharply in a series of tight concentric circles until it has reached cruising altitude. In the jungle below, the LTTE has such an array of weaponry, courtesy of Canada's Snow Tigers, that the plane must make defensive maneuvers. "The pilot must climb quickly to avoid the surface-to-air missiles," a soldier sitting next to me says, as we soar over lemonade-colored sea.

3

PARTISANS OF GOD

THE ISRAELI military intelligence officer, a wiry man with short black hair, sits in his cramped upstairs office in a government building in Tel Aviv. His hands are clasped in front of him on a desk cluttered with files stamped "Secret". Behind him, a sheet of plastic covers the window. The Americans have just launched their assault on Baghdad, and Israel is bracing for the worst. Israelis have been instructed to seal their windows in case Saddam Hussein tosses a chemical or biological warhead this way. "Everyone is dealing right now with Iraq; no one has time for the Iranian side," the officer tells me. "They are in the shade right now."

He is talking about the long-term strategic threat posed by Iran, which he believes has aspirations of becoming a regional nuclear power so it can dominate the Middle East, blackmail the West into abandoning Israel, and then capture Jerusalem for the Muslims. Until then, Iran is preparing the ground for the coming confrontation, waging a low-intensity battle using its proxy force, Hezbollah, the extremist group that sporadically shells northern Israeli cities and sends undercover operatives around the world, including into Israel itself.

"Fauzi is part of this process," he says.

Fauzi Ayub is a father of three from Toronto, with an impeccably groomed black beard. He was captured by Israel's Shin Beit security service while the House of Commons in Ottawa was debating whether Hezbollah was best described as a terrorist organization or a collective of Lebanese farmers and teachers. Ayub's mission remains somewhat of a mystery, but Israeli security officials believe he is a known member of Hezbollah's elite international operations squad. Canadian officials told me that Ayub confirmed the truth of the allegations.

"Fauzi Ayub is a very important guy for them," the Israeli official says. "We have good information that he is connected to this apparatus. There are not many guys like that." Ayub is being held as an "enemy combatant" and can be detained indefinitely. He is in prison as a threat to Israeli security.

As a teen, Ayub, a Lebanese Shia Muslim, joined the Amal militia in 1975. He said he needed to protect his family during the Civil War. During the day, he went to school, and at night he would pull out his grenades, Kalashnikovs, M-16s, rocket launchers and explosives, take cover behind a stack of sandbags, and open fire on the Christian militias. "The Christians oppressed us," Ayub explained in his testimony in a Tel Aviv court. The brutality of the fighting and the sight of a city being wrenched apart by war led him to the conclusion that it was his religious duty to protect the oppressed. "I saw dead people, women and children. It affected me. I saw that the miserable ones have to be protected."

In 1983, he left Amal and joined the more radical Hezbollah, which was just emerging as a force in Lebanon. After three years, he was sent on a mission to Romania to hijack an Iraqi airliner. Iraq had imprisoned several Shia Muslim clerics. Hezbollah wanted to negotiate their release in exchange for the airline passengers. Two teams of hijackers were sent to perform the task.

Sh'alan, the point man in Ayub's group, went first, and arrived a few days before the others. "Sh'alan was supposed to meet us and give us weapons, a small handgun," Ayub said. But Sh'alan was caught and confessed. Ayub was arrested as soon as he arrived at the airport in Bucharest. The second team, however, succeeded: the day after Ayub was arrested, the Hezbollah operatives hijacked a plane. It crashed in Saudi Arabia. Sixty-two died.

"The Romanians told me the next day," he said. "I didn't know that people will die," he added. "When I found out, I sat and cried."

Ayub was sentenced to seven years in prison but Hezbollah sent an agent to pay off the Romanians and he was released after just ten months. He decided to leave the Middle East. "I had an opportunity to go to Canada," he said. An uncle sponsored him to immigrate under a special government program that offered refuge to Lebanese displaced by the 1975–91 civil war. He arrived in 1988.

"Did you tell the Canadians that you were involved in Romania?" an Israeli judge would ask him later.

"No," he replied.

"Why?"

"They didn't ask me."

"They didn't ask if you have a criminal background?"

"No, they didn't."

It was not the first time that Canadian authorities had slipped up and allowed a known Middle Eastern terrorist to enter the country. The previous year, Mahmoud Mohammad Issa Mohammad, a member of the Popular Front for the Liberation of Palestine (PFLP) who was known as Triple M, had somehow slipped through the CSIS security firewall and settled in Ontario with his family, despite having taken part in a deadly assault on an El Al passenger plane in Athens in 1968, as well as numerous other attacks. Although he had been sentenced to seventeen years' imprisonment by a Greek court in 1970, he was freed a year later after the PFLP hijacked a Greek airliner and demanded his release. Canada's immigration department ordered his deportation in 1988, but Mohammad made a refugee claim and launched a series of appeals that continue to this day.

Although the Mohammad case received widespread publicity, Ayub managed to stay below the radar. Not even CSIS knew who he really was. He led a normal life in Canada and married a woman from Detroit. He worked at a supermarket and studied in the evenings. "I tried to forget everything that happened in Beirut." But it was not so easy. Israeli officials claim that even in Canada he was active in Hezbollah, although Canadian officials did not confirm this. "It's very easy for a guy like Fauzi to live inside Europe, to live inside Canada, and do things that are not exactly legal," the Israeli intelligence official tells me.

Ayub became a Canadian citizen in 1992, but his marriage fell apart over the matter of children. He wanted a family but his wife didn't. He left her in 1994 and married a woman from Lebanon. A son, Abbas, was born in 1995. Mohamed came two years later. Ayub worked for a computer company, but his new spouse wanted to return to Beirut so they started saving their money. "My wife didn't like the life in Canada," he said. They moved back to Lebanon in 2000 and he bought a bakery and ran a building supplies business that soon went deep into debt. It was around this time, the Israelis say, that Ayub was contacted by high-ranking Hezbollah members he had known since his early days with the movement. They needed someone with a Western passport to carry out a sensitive mission.

The assignment: infiltrate Israel.

Hezbollah's headquarters in Haret Hareiq, Beirut's maze-like Shia neighborhood, is not easy to find. There is no sign hanging outside, just a gated entrance leading into a dark cave of a stairwell plastered with posters emblazoned with Arabic slogans and the Hezbollah logo—a raised fist clutching a Kalashnikov. Photographing the entrance is forbidden, a reflection of the security paranoia within the militant organization. Up three flights of stairs, I am ushered into a room and invited to wait on a worn couch opposite a giant portrait of the Ayatollah Khomeini. Heavy curtains cover the windows.

The door opens. Ghaleb Abu Zeinab appears, dressed in a black turban and gown, and sits in an armchair beside the yellow and green Hezbollah flag. He has a heavy black beard and a countenance that teeters between divine serenity and wild-eyed rage. A servant enters and sets down a tray holding cups of Turkish coffee. "As far as we are concerned," says Zeinab, a member of Hezbollah's political council, drawing a sip from his tiny coffee cup, "the Canadian people are a friendly people and enjoy respect among Lebanese people, and there are very strong ties between Lebanon and Canada."

There are equally strong ties between Canada and Hezbollah, but that is not something Zeinab and his leader, Sheik Hassan Nasrallah, nor the government of Canada, will admit. Hezbollah has skillfully learned to exploit Canada, which it has turned into a critical offshore base. Hezbollah uses Canada as a safe haven for agents who need to hide before and after attacks. It has also sent sleeper agents to Canada, and it gets significant sums of money from Canada, as well as the equipment needed by its military fighters, not to mention the stolen luxury vehicles that its high-ranking leaders drive.

In 1998, Ward Elcock, the CSIS director, admitted for the first time that Hezbollah and other Shi'ite Islamic terrorist organizations were active in Canada and being watched by his counterterrorism agents. CSIS has had a long-standing investigation into Hezbollah, and since the late 1990s it has known that money was flowing to the organization from Canada. The difficulty was that because Canada had no law against terrorist financing, the only way to bring criminal charges against the fundraisers was to prove that a donation was used for a specific act of terrorism. But terrorist organizations such as Hezbollah are smart. All monies are deposited in a central fund, which finances humanitarian and political causes, as well as terrorist activity. There is no way to trace whether a $500 contribution from a Canadian was used to pay for school textbooks for a Shia neighborhood in Lebanon or C4 explosives. "We believed a certain amount of that went to support terrorist activity," a former high-ranking intelligence official told me. "Being able to prove it was difficult." The RCMP has also repeatedly reported since the late 1990s on the inventive money-making schemes employed by the Canadian branch of Hezbollah. "Canada has an enormous infrastructure of Hezbollah inside the country," a senior Israeli security official told me.

"This is funny," Zeinab responds when I put this to him. "An organization cannot depend on car theft for its funding. This is a Hollywood-style story. Hezbollah does not need these various ways to acquire funding and doesn't adopt these methods because it is against religious principles. This is called stealing. Moreover, we are not in need of this money. We are accused of stealing from here and from there to fund ourselves. This is an attempt to distort the image and to say that Hezbollah has an external wing which does these activities."

The leaders of Hezbollah have told this lie for many years now, that it is just a political movement dedicated to improving the lives of Shia Muslims and aiding Palestinians. It admits to having an armed wing but says its purpose is limited to resistance against Israeli "aggression." But Hezbollah is so much more than a political party backed by a militia; it is an international network with international objectives that include, in the short term, the destruction of Israel and, in the long term, the worldwide spread of Islamic rule. Its preferred tactic is martyrdom.

Hezbollah operates internationally much like Al Qaeda, but in some ways Hezbollah is more dangerous than bin Laden's band of holy warriors: it has decades of experience fighting the Israeli military; it has the backing of three states, Iran, Syria and its host Lebanon; and it has its own political infrastructure, which includes elected representatives such as my interview subject Zeinab. It also has long-range radical Islamic revolutionary objectives. For these reasons, American politicians call Hezbollah the A-team of terrorism.

One of the tools that Hezbollah uses to advance its aims is an élite unit called the Islamic Jihad, controlled by Imad Fayez Mugniyah, one of the world's most wanted terrorists. Mugniyah began his terrorist career with Yasser Arafat's Fatah, then joined the Amal movement, which eventually became Hezbollah. "Mugniyah established ties with Iran through Iran's ambassador to Syria," a Hezbollah agent told Canadian intelligence agents during a 1993 interview. "When he joined Hezbollah—by the way, he is a very fierce fighter—they carried out many bombings and assassinations. Imad Mugniyah's group operates in great secrecy; he commands a number of men."

The Islamic Jihad is a clandestine branch that recruits and trains operatives and dispatches them around the world to serve as sleeper agents who maintain a low profile until they are activated for martyrdom duty. This unit is distinct from the Islamic Resistance branch of Hezbollah, the militia based in South Lebanon—although both report to the Supreme Council of

Hezbollah, headed by Hassan Nasrallah, and ultimately to Iran, which uses Hezbollah as its proxy force and provides it with weapons and two-thirds of its $1-billion annual budget.

In secret apartments in the Lebanese capital, Ayub underwent intensive training and learned to handle explosives. But more importantly, he learned the art of deception. He was taught how to remove any traces of his Lebanese origins. Imad Mugniyah, the Hezbollah mastermind, is thought to have done some of the training himself. "The training included briefings on rigorous rules of behavior for his stay in Israel, which included using the English language exclusively and denying his Arab identity," according to an Israeli intelligence document.

After months of preparation, Ayub traveled to Europe on his Canadian passport. There he became a new man. He got rid of his personal effects and bought new ones. He discarded his Canadian passport and met an agent who gave him a counterfeit American passport. He was no longer Fauzi Ayub; he was now Frank Bushy. He went to Greece and traveled by boat to Haifa, Israel, in October 2000. "Then I did what I was told to do. I went to Jerusalem, I stayed in hotels, and I bought a cellphone and called and said I was in Jerusalem."

The Israelis claim he began scouting for arms drops in the city and spent a lot of time in an area of the capital that houses many government buildings. In December 2000, another suspected member of the Hezbollah network entered Israel, a British Lebanese citizen named Jihad Shuman. A month after his arrival, Shuman was caught, allegedly as he was preparing an attack. Police searched his hotel room and found a large stash of money, a timer, three mobile phones and a *kippa*, a skullcap worn by Jews. He was caught just three hundred meters from the prime minister's residence.

"Partisans of God," as the name Hezbollah translates from Arabic, was formed in response to the Israeli invasion of Lebanon in 1982. Following the Six Day War of 1967, Yasser Arafat moved the Palestine Liberation Organization (PLO) to Jordan, but he was chased out by King Hussein and fled to Lebanon. As Palestinian terrorist attacks mounted, including an attempted assassination of the Israeli ambassador in London, the Israelis clashed at the border with the PLO and then launched a ground assault—which quickly moved up to Beirut—to expel Arafat and his command.

Radical members of Amal (an acronym for the Arabic meaning of Legions of Lebanese Resistance) wanted a more hardline response from their leaders, and so broke away to form Hezbollah. The new organization rose quickly to prominence, in part by filling the power vacuum left by the PLO. Hezbollah is the leading terrorist group within the Shia branch of Islam, which split from the larger Sunnis' branch in the seventh century. It derives its inspiration from the 1979 Islamic revolution in Iran that brought Ayotollah Khomeini to power. Iran played a major role in Hezbollah's rise, providing training, money, spiritual guidance and funding for schools and clinics in the Shia community that facilitated recruitment. Hezbollah was also greatly aided by its association with Grand Ayatollah Fadlallah, head of the Council of Shia Religious Scholars.

Hezbollah has three objectives. The first is to drive Israel out of Lebanon. This was largely accomplished in 2000 when the Israelis withdrew from the southern strip of land they had held for defensive purposes. Second, it aims to destroy the state of Israel and turn it into an Islamic state, with Jerusalem as its capital. Finally, Hezbollah wants to rid Lebanon of all Western influences and turn the country into an Islamic nation modeled after Iran, whose clergy view Lebanon as an experiment in the export of Islamic revolutionary ideology.

The first large-scale Hezbollah strike came in April 1983, when it bombed the U.S. embassy in Beirut. Six months later, it struck again, this time at the U.S. Marines barracks. A truck bomb loaded with about a tonne of explosives exploded early in the morning of October 23, killing 241 American servicemen as they slept. That was followed in September 1984 by a blast at the American embassy annex. The following year, Imad Mugniyah is believed to have orchestrated the hijacking of a TWA flight. A U.S. Navy diver was killed, a crime that landed Mugniyah on the FBI's Most Wanted Terrorist list, which offers a US$25-million reward for information leading to his arrest, the same amount that was put on the head of bin Laden.

This kind of talk makes Zeinab wince. Hezbollah administers a social fund for orphans and the poor, he says. It is not involved in terrorism, nor does it redirect Canadian contributions for military purposes, he insists. "From a religious point of view, it is not acceptable to use it except for the purpose for which it was sent. So saying it is funding military activity is a great fallacy." He does admit, however, that some of the money goes to the families of so-called martyrs killed in action. Such financing encourages acts of terrorism by reassuring militants their families will be looked after upon their death.

"What we want is only to liberate our land," Zeinab says. "America's stance towards us we understand in the language of politics. The American administration is totally biased and blind-ed in favor of Israel." Canada, he says, should not follow the Americans. "What I hope is that Canadian opinion is not drawn after American opinion and that there be a reexamination of the position ... and to make a true distinction between resistance and terrorism and to maintain a good relationship with Arab and Muslim people."

Flight 414 from Frankfurt landed at Mirabel airport on August 6, 1991 and Mohamed Hussein Al Husseini, a Beirut-born construction worker with a double chin and thick eyebrows, walked off without a passport. He told the Canadian immigration officer he had left Lebanon by boat two months earlier, traveling to Cyprus and Italy, by train to Frankfurt and then to Canada by commercial airliner. He had destroyed his fake passport before landing. Upon his arrival, he claimed refugee status, saying he had been arrested by Syrian troops in 1990 because his father took part in a demonstration against Syria's occupation of Lebanon.

He said he had been held in a Beirut cell one meter by two meters and had been tortured with an electrical wire. He was only released after his uncle bribed a Syrian officer with a bottle of wine. After hiding in East Beirut, he boarded a ship on the Mediterranean, leaving his wife and two children behind. He said he came to Canada to "flee persecution" and to "live in peace" and emphasized that he does "not believe in violence for political purposes." It was a story that impressed Canada's refugee judges, who accepted his claim within months, but it was a lie.

Al Husseini was living on social assistance in Montreal and studying French when a CSIS agent called the home he shared with a Lebanese friend on July 9, 1992. The intelligence service contacted Al Husseini because they had found his Lebanese passport. A man had arrived at the airport and presented it as his own. Four days later, the agent met with Al Husseini, who stuck by the story he had told refugee officials. He said he disliked the Syrians for what they had done to him, but said he would not take revenge in Canada. "He added that one day there will be a settling of accounts in Lebanon," the CSIS agent wrote in his notes, "and that if he does not do it, his son will." As the meeting was drawing to a close, Al Husseini dangled a carrot before the agent: he would be willing to provide information to CSIS regarding the security of Canada.

The next clue that Al Husseini was not being up front came in August 1993, when he flew to Lebanon—the country that he had convinced the refugee board would persecute him should he return. He was back at work in Montreal a few weeks later. On September 17, he telephoned the CSIS agent to ask why his application to become a landed immigrant was taking so long. Another meeting was arranged, this time at the Peel Street offices of CSIS in Montreal. The agent said he had information suggesting that Al Husseini was a member of Hezbollah. "NO!" came the reply. Then the agent dropped a figurative bomb. CSIS knew that Al Husseini had taken part in Hezbollah's 1988 hijacking of Kuwait Airlines Flight KU422, an operation organized by Imad Mugniyah. The agent peppered Al Husseini with questions, tossing out names and asking if he recognized them and how. And then, realizing he was caught, Al Husseini leaned forward and, after a short silence, began to talk.

"There's one thing," he said. "Look, I'm lying. I can't deny it.

"I know what my problem is. You know it and I know it. But there's one thing—I can't say one word, and even you, you need me—I know you need me, but there's something important, I want a guarantee.

"I can tell you what you want to know. No one else can. I'm not confessing to anything, but there's one thing, if I don't see my wife, you'll get nothing from me. If I say one word, my life will be in danger. What guarantee can I have? I know you need me, I know that, and don't think I don't know who gave you this information. In Canada, I know everything about my situation. So what's my guarantee? I'll tell you everything, even how I was born."

Over the next ninety minutes, Al Husseini tried to negotiate a deal. He wanted CSIS to expedite his immigration application and bring his family to Canada. In exchange, he would talk. But CSIS would not bargain, which seemed to exasperate him. The agent would only guarantee that the information he provided would remain confidential. "For heaven's sake," he said. "I've told you I want to talk. I'll tell you what you want to know, but I have to get something in return. That's what maddens me. Okay, I'll give you what you want, that's right, whatever you want.

"Give me some assurance that in Lebanon my house won't be destroyed, my wife and children burned, and my parents abducted, and that I won't be killed here in Canada. I won't give you any answers, though, before I know this is going to work.

"I am a very stubborn person, but I have a good heart, and if you really help me, if you guarantee that no harm will come to me, I'll tell you everything. I won't lie, I'm ready to tell you everything. The person who gave you this information can't help you as much as I can. I can help you a million times more than he's helped you. That's why I'm here."

As Al Husseini continued to beg for a bargain, the agent resumed his questioning, asking about the hijacking. Al Husseini admitted he lived in the area where the hostages were held, but he kept steering the conversation back to his deal. He then offered a sample of the information he could provide, saying he knew who had hijacked a TWA flight in 1985. He offered their names, and said one was now living in Germany. He provided additional information about Imad Mugniyah and his group, and then he began describing the situation in Canada. He said he had information about cigarette and weapons smuggling, which he would provide "in good faith" if CSIS would agree to help him.

"Hezbollah has members in Montreal, Ottawa, Toronto—all of Canada," he said. "Hezbollah wants to collect information on Canada, on life in Canada, its roads and so on, in case there's a problem with Canada."

Hezbollah also had members across Canada who were not active "because Canada does not have a problem with Hezbollah or with Lebanon—unless you create a problem with me now. Then you'll have a problem with Hezbollah." According to the agent's notes, Al Husseini laughed after uttering these words.

"If the people in Canada are not really active in the organization," the agent asked, "does the organization send members here who carry out activities for a short time, then return to Lebanon?"

"This is how Hezbollah operates," Al Husseini replied. "Let me think for a bit about how I can explain it to you. OK. Hezbollah has a security service, just like you do. This security service is the most powerful in the Middle East. It could gather information even on its own members, who are scattered all over the world, it's true, to find out what's happening to them and what their situation is."

"You said 'could.' Have they done so in the past?" the agent asked.

"Maybe anyone traveling from here to Lebanon can give Hezbollah information about Canada, even about your own security service, and especially about you personally, for example, if you interview them."

He continued: "The intelligence service obtains information from persons abroad. For example, if Hezbollah wants to know something specific, it sends its own people, providing them with passports, visas, tickets and money. It takes care of everything and sends them over. And with photographs, cameras and videos,

Hezbollah can find out anything it wants, down to the smallest details. For example, if Hezbollah decided to get this building, it would get it, I mean it really would.

"The Hezbollah executive sends operatives to execute tasks, but the preparations are made here in Canada. In other words, if Hezbollah wanted to blow up this building, it would rely on the foreign intelligence service and on the executive."

Al Husseini explained that there was a division within the Montreal Shia community, with one group opposed to Hezbollah while the other, based at the Jamaa Islamique on Côte Ste-Catherine, was pro-Hezbollah. He then said Hezbollah had shot spy videos of Canada.

"I know that films have been shot here and sent back there," he said. "Video films ... they film roads, life, everything."

He went on to describe three armed units within Hezbollah, including the one headed by Mugniyah, but said they work closely together and all report to the Hezbollah leadership. "The orders for these units come from Iran, but final approval is obtained from Hassan Nasrallah and Sayed Fadlallah. Hassan Nasrallah has personal contact with these three units." Hezbollah is basically "Iran's weapon," he added. "The weapon with which Iran strikes is the Lebanese and these three units."

The CSIS agent asked the question he had started with three hours earlier. Was Al Husseini a member of Hezbollah? He replied that he would answer that later, but the agent persisted, saying Al Husseini must be a member to know as much as he did. "Yes, yes, I'm going to tell you that I am with Hezbollah, but with reservation, I tell you with reservation."

"You mentioned that when you lived in Lebanon, there were a lot of Hezbollahis who controlled your district," the agent asked. "Have you seen any of these people here in Montreal?"

"Yes."

"They were members of Hezbollah?"

"Yes, yes."

Al Husseini again returned to discussion about his deal, saying he would tell more if he could get his immigration papers. He promised information on hijackings of Iraqi and Jordanian planes, details about Beirut and a list of "all the members of Hezbollah in Montreal and Ottawa."

The agent thanked Al Husseini and the interview ended. It was 7 p.m., and CSIS had its first inside account of the Canadian Hezbollah network.

They met again two weeks later. Al Husseini kept asking for a deal but was more reticent, and backtracked. "I never said I was a member [of Hezbollah]," he said. "I said that I lived in the Hezbollah environment."

It was clear the interview was going nowhere. The agent asked if Al Husseini had any additional information about Hezbollah. He said no. Police arrested Al Husseini a short time later under the authority of a national security certificate declaring he was a threat to Canada because of his membership in Hezbollah. In January 1994, a Federal Court of Canada judge upheld his deportation. Why did CSIS pass up the chance to recruit Al Husseini as a source? An official told me he was uncooperative and unreliable. Agents checked out some of his leads and they did not seem to go anywhere. Maybe he was making it all up in a desperate attempt to stave off deportation. But in the years that followed, his claims that Hezbollah agents had penetrated Canada's major cities and were involved in crimes such as tobacco smuggling to raise money for the cause would prove entirely accurate.

By the time of Al Husseini's deportation, Hezbollah had evolved from a Lebanese resistance movement into an international terrorist force. In 1992, Hezbollah attacked the Israeli embassy in Argentina and two years later it bombed the Israeli cultural center in Buenos Aires—a plot that Argentine and Israeli investigators concluded was carried out with the cooperation of the Iranian embassy and senior government ministers in Tehran. (The families of 153 marines killed in the 1983 Beirut attack also claim Iran was behind the operation, and have launched a lawsuit for damages. Their lawyer cited intercepted communications that called for "spectacular action against the U.S. Marines.") Imad Mugniyah was the mastermind behind both attacks.

Another of Mugniyah's operations was the 1996 bombing of a U.S. military barracks in Saudi Arabia that killed 19 servicemen and injured 372. The bomb plot had begun in 1993 and was directed by the Iranian military, which funded the operation and selected the U.S. Air Force quarters at Khobar Towers in Dharhan from a list of possible targets. The explosives were brought in by truck from Lebanon. One of the men suspected of being involved in the attack was Hani Abd Rahim Al-Sayegh. A U.S. indictment calls him "a prominent member of the Saudi Hezbollah." He was actively involved in recruiting young Saudi Shiites to join Hezbollah, arranging for those men to undergo military training at Hezbollah camps in Lebanon and Iran; assisting in the surveillance of potential targets for attack by Hezbollah and carrying out terrorist attacks. U.S. prosecutors said Sayegh helped plan the attack and spent two weeks at a farm helping to convert a tanker truck into a massive bomb on wheels. He then served as a scout, directing the truck bomb to the target, which had been selected by Iran.

At 10 p.m. on June 25, 1996, a tanker truck loaded with two to three tons of plastic explosives lurched into the military base parking lot. Sentries noticed the truck and tried to evacuate the barracks but were unsuccessful. The bomb was twice as large as the one that destroyed the federal building in Oklahoma City in 1995. Following the bombing, Sayegh left Saudi Arabia using a fake passport. He traveled to Boston and then to Canada in August 1996. He made a refugee claim using a bogus name and settled in Ottawa. "Upon his arrival, Al-Sayegh attempted to integrate quietly into the community, studying English and working part-time," said a CSIS report that cited his case as an example of Canada's role as a safe place for terrorists. He was arrested on March 18, 1997, at an Ottawa convenience store.

A short time later, another Hezbollah agent turned up in Canada. The man, identified only as Mr. X in Immigration and Refugee Board files, admitted he had been a Hezbollah instructor who taught commando groups the intricacies of suicide attacks.

Then there was Omar El Sayed, who arrived in Edmonton in August 1998, using a fake Dutch passport. He worked illegally under the name "Mr. Rahyn," using a false social security number and fraudulent bank cards and made a refugee claim in which he "admitted to being part of Hezbollah, a terrorist organization in Lebanon," according to an RCMP affidavit filed at his extradition. A check of his fingerprints revealed he was wanted in Germany for trafficking in heroin and cocaine, selling firearms and threatening to kill an undercover police officer. The RCMP arrested the "foreign fugitive" in May 1999, for extradition to Germany.

An immigration official called El Sayed "a soldier for the Hezbollah" and "a willing participant in the training with respect to the Jihad or Holy War that Hezbollah was involved in." The immigration department wanted El Sayed detained until his deportation because he was a danger to the public. "He's been trained as a soldier for a terrorist organization, someone who trades in guns and drugs and threatens to kill people." Despite the concerns raised by the immigration department and El Sayed's admission of ties to Hezbollah, the judge said he was not convinced the man was a danger to Canadians and set him free. He has not been seen since.

It is said that nobody cares about a victimless crime. In Canada, one of the reasons that terrorists have been able to operate so freely for so long is the perception that their activities have no impact on ordinary Canadians. If Lebanese Canadians or Muslim Canadians want to send money to the Middle East to support Hezbollah, who are we to stop them? And so even as Hezbollah's strength grew in the 1990s, through both a campaign of horrific international terrorist attacks and a war of attrition against the Israelis, the Canadian government paid little attention—until Hezbollah started stealing cars.

By 1996, auto theft was costing the Canadian insurance industry $600 million a year. The RCMP mounted an intelligence operation to identify the organized crime groups involved. Project Sparkplug analyzed a half-dozen major investigations into car-theft rings operating mostly in Ontario and Quebec. The cars, often luxury vehicles, were stolen in cities such as Toronto, and within days were loaded onto container ships and sent to buyers overseas. The police analysts found that the groups behind the heists were mostly ethnic-based rings, primarily Asian, East Indian, African and East European.

Police determined that one of the most active groups, based in Quebec, was Lebanese. Its profits were traced to Hezbollah. A 1998 investigation called Project Mermaid, a collective probe by the RCMP, Canada Customs and Sûreté du Québec, uncovered a network that stole high-end vehicles such as Mercedes, Jaguars and Jeep Cherokees in Ontario and Quebec and exported them in cargo containers, three per container. Police seized fifty-five stolen cars worth $2.5 million. Shipping them cost $5,000, and they were sold for US$40,000, leaving a hefty profit margin, a tenth of which went to Hezbollah. Some of the luxury cars were also shipped to leading Hezbollah members in Lebanon.

The RCMP criminal intelligence branch reported in 1999 that "Middle East–based organized crime activity is on the increase in Canada. Most Middle East extremist groups have a presence in Canada to legally raise funds and recruit." The most prominent groups, it said, were Hezbollah and Hamas, the Palestinian organizations that pioneered suicide bombings. Their crimes ranged from "theft to smuggling ... Middle East-based criminal groups may also be supplying extremist groups with equipment obtained by criminal means."

Mohamad Hassan Dbouk's Vancouver acquaintances knew him as just a family man, a married father of two who had fled his home in Beirut and moved to Canada in 1998 to start a new life near his sister and her family, who lived in Burnaby, British Columbia. He would take his kids to Stanley Park, and to the movies, and was close to his sister's husband, Ali Amhaz. But a starkly different picture of the man emerged from the bug placed on his telephone by CSIS agents, who had started watching him closely in February 1999 after getting a tip about his suspected ties to a Middle Eastern terrorist cell.

The tip had come from the Americans. Bob Fromme, a detective in North Carolina's Iredell County, was moonlighting as a security guard at the JR Tobacco warehouse in Statesville when he saw a group of men he thought were Mexicans buying hundreds of cartons of cigarettes. As he observed them, he realized they were not speaking Spanish. They were speaking Arabic. He followed them as they loaded the cigarettes into a van and drove north on Highway I-77. "The only thing north of Statesville is Mount Airy, the home of Andy Griffith, and a state line," Robert Conrad, the U.S. attorney for the Western District of North Carolina, said later. "And once that van crosses a state line, a federal felony is committed." Fromme reported his hunch to state authorities, and then the Bureau of Alcohol, Tobacco and Firearms, which launched an investigation in July 1996 into what it soon discovered was a Lebanese cigarette-smuggling ring.

The scam was simple. The ring members would buy bulk cigarettes in North Carolina, truck them to Michigan, where tobacco taxes were much higher, and resell them at a huge profit. The smugglers were shipping three to four vans full of cigarettes to Detroit each week. During the course of the investigation, they bought US$8-million worth of cigarettes, which they resold at a profit of roughly $2 million. The ringleader was identified as Mohammad Youssef Hammoud, a Lebanese who flew to New York in 1992 from Venezuela using a fake visa he had purchased for US$200. The U.S. Department of Justice was about to lay charges when "the FBI walked in with news that they had, through their intelligence investigations, discovered a Hezbollah terrorist cell," according to Conrad. "And they showed us a series of pictures ... and what was interesting about this is that each of these people pictured, whom the FBI had identified as being involved in the terrorism financing cell, were also our cigarette smugglers. And this case ceased to be about cigarettes and became about Hezbollah."

The transcripts of wiretaps are closely guarded by intelligence services not only for the treasure trove of valuable secrets they reveal, but also because of the worthless, mundane, but highly invasive personal secrets contained within them. So it is rare to get a glimpse of wiretaps, but it can also be extremely informative. Even those engaged in the most outlandish deceptions seem to let down their guard on the phone. They speak candidly, unaware that agents are recording their calls, intercepting their mail and photographing their every move.

At about the same time the FBI's Charlotte office took over the cigarette case, CSIS agents in Vancouver began recording the conversations of Mohamad Dbouk. The two topics that surfaced again and again, particularly in calls with his brother-in-law Ali Amhaz, were Lebanon and money. Hiding money, moving money and making money. Some of Dbouk's fundraising schemes were outlandish. There was a $1-million project "building sunrooms." And a scam he called the "miracle strike," which involved taking out life insurance on people in Canada and faking their deaths in Lebanon.

On Sunday February 28, 1999, Hezbollah detonated two bombs beside an Israeli military convoy, killing a brigadier general, two sergeants and a reporter for Israel Radio. The Israeli military responded by launching air strikes on Hezbollah bases in South Lebanon. When the story hit the television news, Amhaz called Dbouk and said he "was watching the latest news on today's operation involving Hezbollah in southern Lebanon," the CSIS agent noted. "Amhaz congratulated Dbouk for Hezbollah's success and their improving ability which was making Israel retaliate for the attacks."

Just what Dbouk was doing to help Hezbollah became clearer a few days later, when Dbouk told his wife he had "visited a military supply warehouse and looked at some military supplies and instruments in Vancouver and [was] able to obtain some catalogues." Dbouk sent a fax to Lebanon on March 5 with the prices and specifications of the equipment, including the ITT Night Vision pocket scope, Night Quest 5000 Series night goggles, a night camera and two computers. Four days later, he called a Hezbollah purchasing agent in Lebanon, Hassan Laqis, who told him to go ahead and buy some of the gear, adding he wanted the night camera "on a rush basis."

Dbouk phoned Said Harb, a key member of the Charlotte-based cigarette cell, and invited him to Vancouver. But when Dbouk tried to discuss politics, Harb said he wanted "to be careful over the telephone," the CSIS agent noted. "Dbouk remarked that he did not care about anything and was committed to securing all the items for the brothers [the term used by Hezbollah members to refer to each other] at any cost. He was attempting to avoid going to hell and to secure a place in heaven by doing so. Dbouk continued that the only purpose for him to be in Canada was to accomplish something for the brothers and that he was happy because he felt that he was doing an important job. Dbouk added that he did not like living in Canada." Harb said he would send US$20,000.

Dbouk's calls revealed the existence of a cross-country Hezbollah terrorist procurement network, with operatives in Montreal, Toronto, Windsor and Vancouver. Harb flew to Seattle and Amhaz met him at Sea-Tac airport. They drove to Vancouver in a rented car. Harb's mission was to deliver to Dbouk a fraudulent credit card, a fake social security card and a series of forged checks that were to be used to purchase the gear requested by Hezbollah. CSIS agents trailed Harb in Vancouver, photographing him as he met Dbouk on the waterfront. The photos show them talking at a dark meeting point, their shoulders hunched and hands thrust deep into their winter coats against the cold. Later, they were photographed strolling across the Lynn Canyon Suspension Bridge, a tourist attraction in North Vancouver. Harb left Vancouver in April, but called Dbouk to tell him he would open a bank account in Dbouk's name with an initial deposit of US$10,000. The illicit cigarette money was at Dbouk's disposal.

Dbouk bought the equipment and sent it to Lebanon. Later, he followed up with a fax to the Hezbollah purchasing boss, in which he explained that in addition to the requested items, he had sent a "little gift," a pair of binoculars and a Palm Pilot. "I'm trying my best to do anything you want so please you must know that I'm ready to do anything you or the Father [Mugniyah] want me to do and I mean anything!!!" He signed the letter "your little brother."

It says something about a country when a terrorist organization decides to send one of its prized agents there to set up a base. Dbouk was just such an agent. He had applied five times for martyrdom duty, but each time he was turned down by the Hezbollah command, which decided he was too valuable to waste on a suicide mission. After three years in Vancouver, Dbouk desperately wanted to return to Lebanon. He hated Canada. But Hezbollah would not let him leave, saying he was more beneficial to them in Canada.

So Dbouk stayed and continued moving money and buying equipment, including tools that could make rocks explode, stun guns, mine detectors and sophisticated computers. At one point,

Laqis asked for a "nitrogen cutter." Dbouk tried to conceal his activities, depositing his cash in small sums to avoid arousing the suspicion of the banks. In one act of deception, he told Amhaz to wire money to his contact in Montreal. Then he flew to Montreal to pick it up. He began to plan credit-card frauds. He handled huge amounts of money, but was also miserly. Instead of buying plane tickets to fly his wife and son back to Lebanon, he planned to wait until they were deported so the Canadian government would have to pay the airfare.

There was intense fighting as Hezbollah tried to oust the Israeli-backed South Lebanon Army from the buffer zone established following the Israeli withdrawal from Beirut. Passions ran high among Lebanese, including those in Canada. Dbouk's uncle called one day asking for advice on sending $1,000 to the "brave people" in South Lebanon. Dbouk replied that it would be better to buy something and send it to Hezbollah. Then Dbouk made what amounted to a confession. He told his uncle that others had left money in Canada and Dbouk had used it to buy equipment for the "brave people."

Canadian intelligence agents watched Dbouk for four months before realizing just whom he was working for. Dbouk was talking to Amhaz on June 1, 1999 when his brother-in-law mentioned the name "Haj Imad." Dbouk called Imad "the whole story," which authorities interpreted to mean Imad was behind the procurement operation. Dbouk then admonished Amhaz: "What a terribly dangerous thing to say. Would anyone bring up Imad's name here or in any other country and stay alive?" U.S. officials believe the "Haj Imad" referred to in the wiretap is none other than Imad Mugniyah.

Dbouk finally got his wish to return to Lebanon in June 1999, but he continued running the Canadian procurement network from abroad. Said Harb returned to Vancouver in August and, together with Amhaz, bought electronic equipment including computers, a digital camera and a video camera for Hezbollah. CSIS agents followed him, and took photographs as he met on a sidewalk in downtown Vancouver with Amhaz and several other Lebanese men. Harb, wearing denim shorts, a T-shirt and running shoes, kissed the others as they arrived. CSIS was still watching

Amhaz in October when two men paid him a visit. "The three men had a very long discussion," the CSIS agent noted. The conversation touched on a lens that Amhaz had bought for Dbouk and planned to take to Lebanon. "They know that Dbouk is related to you," Amhaz was warned. "They are not stupid, and when you take lenses to Lebanon you are helping Hezbollah who would use them in operations." Amhaz was spooked by the encounter. Maybe CSIS was on to him?

Israeli troops withdrew from South Lebanon in May 2000, setting off celebrations among Hezbollah supporters. Amhaz got a call from a friend who "quoted the CBC as saying that no one humiliated Israel like Hezbollah by forcing it to quit Lebanon," according to the CSIS report on the intercepted conversations. Another friend called to say a party was planned at the Lebanese Islamic Centre in Montreal, which would be followed by a procession of cars waving flags. Amhaz called Dbouk in Lebanon "and congratulated him with a very jubilant voice, and went on to denounce ... the Canadians and the Zionists." Amhaz said he suspected there were spies among his group of contacts, and Dbouk urged his brother-in-law to be careful. "Kiss every fighter that you see on my behalf," Amhaz said.

On July 21, 2000, the U.S. Attorney's Office in North Carolina filed charges against eighteen suspects involved in the cigarette-smuggling ring, which they termed the Charlotte Hezbollah Cell. Among those charged were Hammoud, Harb and the two Canadian operatives, Amhaz and Dbouk, whom the charges called "a purchasing agent for Hezbollah" who "regularly purchased technical equipment in North America which was thereafter transported to Lebanon for Hezbollah." Dbouk had supplied the terrorist group with equipment and computers that aided Hezbollah military operations (officials said the cameras were used to record attacks for recruitment videos).

When FBI agents raided Hammoud's house, they found a collection of photos and videotapes. One picture showed Hammoud at age fifteen, posing at a Hezbollah center with an AK-47. In one of the videos, members of the Hezbollah Martyrs Squad swear their allegiance to the organization. "We will answer the call, and we will take an oath to detonate ourselves, to shake the grounds under our enemies, America and Israel," Hezbollah leader Hassan Nasrallah said. "We will answer your call Hezbollah, we will answer your call," the martyrs proclaimed. Another tape showed Nasrallah leading chants of "Death to America, death to Israel." But the most disturbing was a home movie of Hammoud's two nephews in Lebanon. "Tell them who you are," an adult voice tells the little boys standing in front of the camera. But the children do not respond, so they are slapped in the face. "Tell them who you are!" The younger of the boys, age three, murmurs: "Hezbollah."

All those arrested in the United States were convicted and sentenced, despite an attempt by Hammoud to arrange the assassination of Kenneth Bell, the chief prosecutor in the case, and blow up the office where the evidence was housed. Dbouk and Amhaz were charged but never convicted. Dbouk was untouchable in Lebanon, which has no extradition treaty with the United States. Amhaz was picked up by the RCMP for extradition to the United States to stand trial. But Canadian law allows the government to extradite suspects to another country only if they are charged with a crime that is also illegal in Canada. Dbouk was charged with terrorist fundraising, which was not against the law in Canada at the time. He was set free, although in the United States he remains a wanted man. He has at all times denied any involvement in the smuggling operation and still lives in B.C.

Later, testifying before the Senate Judiciary Committee in Washington, DC, in November 2002, Robert Conrad underlined the threat posed by Hezbollah: "You know, Senator," he said, "post-9/11, people tend to forget who Hezbollah are in the wake of the attention focused on Al Qaeda. But we didn't forget." He said all those involved in the Charlotte cell had met justice, except for four fugitives, including the two Canadians.

"It's pretty hard to extradite from Lebanon," Republican Senator Arlen Specter commented.

Conrad replied: "And Canada."

Hezbollah is just one of many Middle East terrorist organizations that operate in Canada. On a visit to Gaza City during the latest war in Iraq, I attended the funeral of a Hamas leader. Hundreds of people packed the streets waving the flags of their affiliated organizations. There was green for Hamas, black for Islamic Jihad, red for the Popular Front for the Liberation of Palestine and yellow for Fatah. "We have every color except white," a young Palestinian journalist told me. Every color except the color of surrender.

And all of the organizations have international support networks in Canada. Hamas raises money in Canada. According to intelligence documents, the primary Hamas front in Canada was the Jerusalem Fund for Human Services. Also, some mainstream Islamic organizations in Canada have solicited funds for the Holy Land Foundation for Relief and Development, a huge Texas-based charity that was shut down after September 11 because it was found to be funneling money to Hamas. Palestinian groups are not considered as great a threat to Canada as Hezbollah, because they are so intensely focused on Israel. However, they have committed international terrorism in the past and will likely do so again. In addition, the Islamist ideology of such groups as Hamas and Islamic Jihad make them potential threats well beyond the Israeli theater.

During a trip to Gaza in 2005, I visited a man named Iyad Aqel in the town of Nasariut. We discussed his cousin, Jamal Akkal, who had immigrated to Canada after finishing high school.

"He was eager to go there, to study, to have the language and to change his life. He didn't like the life or the style of life here," he said.

Jamal had moved to Windsor, Ontario. He hoped to get his degree at the University of Windsor. "He was so happy there," his cousin recalled. After a few years, he wanted to marry. He was 23. The family told him it would be better if he came home and found a Palestinian bride. And so, in the fall of 2003, he flew to Cairo and crossed the border into the Gaza Strip. He visited his extended family and met his cousin Shaima. They were soon engaged.

During his visit, however, Jamal met someone else, a wanted member of Hamas. His contact with the terrorist organization began with a man named Mohammed Bashir Abu Matar, also known as Abu Sahil. They spoke on the phone. The conversation

126

concerned one of Jamal's cousins, who had been killed by Israeli troops. Jamal was upset, but Abu Sahil told him: don't grieve, get revenge. Abu Sahil introduced Jamal to Ahmed Wahba, better known as Abu Osama. He declined to be interviewed, but an Israeli official said he is a recruiter for Hamas.

"He wasn't one of the leaders but he was a recruiter and he had authority to do whatever he did," Ofir Gendelman, Second Secretary at the Embassy of Israel in Ottawa, told me.

Abu Osama took Jamal to a farming area called the Mughraka and taught him how to shoot an M-16 rifle. They shot at targets 200 meters away. Eight bullets. The Israelis say Abu Osama was preparing Jamal for an assassination in North America.

"There was intelligence of his whereabouts and about his actions," Gendelman says. He would not explain what kind of intelligence but adds, "Our security services were aware of his whereabouts and of his plans.

"The idea was, for the first time, to carry out a terrorist attack by Hamas in North America," he says.

Abu Osama and his Canadian friend talked about a plot to kill Jewish community members and visiting Israeli dignitaries, the diplomat says. He claims that Hamas wanted to expand its war against Israel to Canada and the United States, and as a Canadian citizen, Akkal was their man.

"Two scenarios were involved," Gendelman says.

"One scenario was basically to booby trap a car or a house— the front door of a Jewish person here in Canada. The Jewish person was supposed to be identified by his clothing, whether he was wearing a yarmulke, an Orthodox dress and so forth. Another scenario that was discussed was to kill an Israeli VIP who would come to visit Canada or the U.S."

The Israelis were already on the alert for these types of attacks. Their security and intelligence agencies were telling them that terrorist groups were actively recruiting Arabs and Muslims from outside the Middle East. Just before Jamal came home to Gaza, two British Muslims had orchestrated a suicide bombing in Tel Aviv.

"Now, Jamal Akkal was interested in getting involved," Gendelman says. "He was interested in participating in that terrorist attack. He was instructed in how to use an M-16. He was instructed to make up homemade bombs in order to booby trap that car or that house.

"He was supposed to identify the Israeli VIP through the media. He was supposed to follow reports in the media about an Israeli minister or a dignitary who would come to visit the country and he was supposed to track him down and to shoot him."

Jamal was supposed to buy the gun from a gang in Detroit because he knew it was not so easy to get weapons in Canada, the Israeli diplomat says, citing the Canadians confession statements.

"He was interested in carrying out this attack. He was interested in getting the necessary training to do so and he was trained, and he has confessed to everything during his interrogation."

Jamal's lawyer, Jameel Khateeb, lives in Ara, a Palestinian village on the road between Nazareth and the Mediterranean coast. His law office is on the top floor of his family's textile business. He is also Jamal's cousin. He says the allegations of terrorist training are not true and that gunplay is common in Gaza, as is harmless talk about attacking Israelis.

"I believe to shoot eight bullets, it's not a kind of military training anyway. To shoot eight bullets will not make him a professional sniper as they claimed anyway. He never tried to shoot anyone."

At the end of October, 2003, Jamal said goodbye to his family, traveled to Rafah in southern Gaza and boarded a bus for the Egyptian border. As he was exiting Israel, he was detained. The Israelis say they already knew about his activities with Hamas.

"Our security services were suspicious of him and they had information about his plans, about his future involvement in terrorist activities in North America, and that's why he was arrested," Gendelman says.

Jamal was handed over to the General Security Service and interrogated. When his relatives found out, they couldn't believe it.

"I was shocked when I heard that because it's unbelievable," said his fiancée, Shaima. "Jamal, he is a calm person. Everybody loved Jamal and he never hate anybody." Said his cousin Iyad, "Okay, what is it, what's this, are we in a movie, is it a play that they are acting? It's hard to believe."

Following the arrest, Jamal's lawyer tried to visit him but was denied permission. He says the Israeli authorities tortured Jamal. "They tied his hands from the back and they seated him in a chair for a lot of time. They interrogated him for twenty hours a day. They didn't let him sleep and ... they threaten him that they will arrest his father, and his brother who is in Germany."

The Israelis do not deny using psychological pressure to convince Jamal to talk. But they say no physical violence was used. "Well, I don't think an interrogation is a pleasant experience," Gendelman says. "By no means. But no violence was applied. Psychological pressure? Yes. But no violence." Asked what constituted psychological pressure, he said, "Sleep deprivation. Loud music, at times. Heat, cold. Some psychological pressure."

The Israelis laid conspiracy charges against Jamal and in November 2004, a year after his arrest, he pleaded guilty. He was sentenced to four years in jail and fined 2,000 shekels, about $650.

His lawyer recommended that he take the plea.

"I believe that because we got this confession [and] his trial was in front of the military court, it was difficult to drop all these charges. And it was a good thing to do was to plead guilty and to get this deal," he says.

Later, I visited Jamal's family home in Nasariut. A Hamas flag fluttered on the roof. Hamas graffiti was spray-painted by the front door. A cousin led me upstairs to the martyr's room. The walls were covered with photographs of five family members killed in military and police confrontations. One shows Jamal's eldest brother Walid, an accused Hamas figure imprisoned by the Israelis for the past fifteen years. A replica of the Al Aqsa mosque in Jerusalem—whose dome forms part of the Hamas logo—hung on the wall, alongside portraits of Ahmed Yassin, the Hamas founder, and the late Hamas spokesman Abdal Aziz Rantissi, who were both killed in Israeli missile strikes.

Jamal's nephew kept the room in order, a shrine to the family martyrs. His most recent addition: a poster of Jamal, posing in prison with his brother Walid. The image of a military assault rifle has been pasted between them in the background.

"I already admitted in front of the court that a lot of his family are members of Hamas group, and these things are known for the Israeli authorities and for the Israeli intelligence also," the lawyer said.

But Jamal was not among those in his clan involved with Hamas, he insisted. His cousin Iyad believes it is an effort to turn Canadians against Palestinians. "Maybe it's a kind of incitement against Palestinians inside Canada so they want Canadians to go and attack Palestinians there."

It is possible that Jamal only dabbled in terrorism—and in Gaza, that is not a difficult thing to do. But meeting with terrorists, shooting off weapons and discussing plans for acts of terrorism would be enough to qualify, in many jurisdictions, as a criminal conspiracy. And after living through a barrage of horrific terrorist violence, the Israelis take such threats extremely seriously.

Hamas denies any knowledge of Jamal.

Jamal was imprisoned at the Nahfa Prison, in the baking Negev desert. He came to Canada to get away from Gaza, but in the end he found that was not such an easy thing to do. But according to his lawyer, he intends on returning to Canada once he is released

---

The potential for the spillover of violence from the Arab-Israeli conflict also became apparent on the morning of April 5, 2004, when the United Talmud Torahs School was firebombed in Montreal. As the Jewish school burned, investigators found a three-paragraph letter taped to the door calling the fire "the consequence of your crimes and your occupation. Here is the answer to your assassinations. Here is where the terrorist Ariel Sharon is leading you." The letter went on to say that while this time the target was an empty school, "If your crimes continue in the Middle East, our attacks will continue. We are not targeting Quebec; we are targeting you: Israelis and Zionists. Next time we will strike harder." It was signed, "The Brigades of Sheikh Ahmed Yassin." Yassin was the late leader of Hamas, killed in an Israeli missile strike. Sleiman El-Merhebi, a nineteen-year-old immigrant from Lebanon, was arrested and pleaded guilty.

Palestinian groups such as Islamic Jihad and Hamas have used Canada as a cyber-propaganda base. And members of Hamas, the PLFP and other radical Palestinian groups have been caught in Canada.

Among them was Qasem Ibrahim Qasem Hussein, a Hamas recruiter who had studied bomb-making techniques. "Mr. Hussein was complicit in crimes against humanity based on the widespread and systematic murder of Israeli citizens and Palestinian collaborators by Hamas between 1994 and 1998," when he was an active member, according to Citizenship and Immigration Canada's 2002 war crimes report. He was deported to Jordan on March 4, 2002. Issam Al Yamani, like his father, was a senior member of the PFLP, and was trustee of a million-dollar PFLP fund. He came to Canada in the early 1980s but by the time CSIS figured out who he really was, he had married a Canadian and had two Canadian-born children. "He has been the courier of information between different PFLP groups; he has been the contact between the PFLP offices in the USA and in Damascus. Mr. Yamani has played an important role within the ranks of the PFLP organization and has been the key instigator of the organization in Canada," the Federal Court of Canada said. "Mr. Yamani's behavior has shown a concern for the use of secrecy and hidden agendas. His use of counter-surveillance tactics and code words demonstrates a lack of transparency essential to convey a sense of truthfulness ... Mr. Yamani has been doing non-violent work for the PFLP organization in Canada on a daily basis since at least 1988. Nothing precludes the PFLP from having him perform other things in Canada. The mere presence of a Chapter Leader in name or in fact in Canada demonstrates the importance for the organization of remaining active in Canada."

In 1993, FBI agents heard senior leaders of Hamas discussing their lucrative fundraising efforts in Canada. At a clandestine meeting in Philadelphia, Hamas detailed its Canadian moneymaking success. "They also encouraged more fundraising activities in Canada," according to an FBI report, based on secret surveillance of the meeting. "They talked openly about opening an ... office in Canada. "It was mentioned that [a proposal for] such an office was submitted to the Canadian government three times and isn't approved yet." But donations flowed from Canada nonetheless. The evidence concerns the "Philadelphia meeting," a gathering of Islamic hard-liners who assembled at a hotel to discuss support for Islamic militancy, particularly against Israel. "All the participants without exception are Muslim fundamentalists," said the FBI report, an analysis of sixteen hours of recorded discussions. The twenty-five participants came from Washington, Virginia, New Jersey, Mississippi and Canada, the report says. Fundraising was the major topic of discussion. "A fundraising organization, an Islamic organization, in Canada collected $214,000 in six months, ending June, 1993. "It was also mentioned, they, in Canada collected $167,000 during the year of 1992. Another Islamic organization collected $189,000."

The international support network that feeds Middle East terrorist organizations has had a devastating effect on Israel, fueling the suicide death culture pervasive within what American columnist William Safire calls "the quadriad of terror": Hezbollah, Hamas, Islamic Jihad and the Al Aqsa Martyrs Brigade. The Israelis are not blameless for the mess in the Middle East, but they are faced with a foe that seeks Israel's destruction as a nation. "It's simple," explained Hamas official Mohamed Siam, during a December 1994 speech to the Muslim Arab Youth Association Conference in Los Angeles. "Finish off the Israelis. Kill them all! Exterminate them! No peace ever! Do not bother to talk politics."

One brilliant Saturday morning during a reporting assignment in Israel in the spring of 2002, I awoke hoping to have a day of rest after weeks of covering the fighting. Some American colleagues had rented a car for a jaunt to the Dead Sea, and I considered joining them. The skies were clear and the streets of Jerusalem were quiet, as they always are on the Shabbat. But there would be no rest. Word soon came in that there had been a massacre near Hebron, and I was off again into the hell of the Middle East war. Apache helicopters and Israeli ground forces were scouring the hilly terrain when I arrived at Adora, a cluster of coral look-alike houses, with red tile roofs, that were inhabited by fifty-two Jewish families, ten of them from the former Soviet Union. I saw a girl who looked no more than sixteen walking up the road with an Uzi slung on her shoulder. After some negotiation, police opened the gates and I went in to see what had happened. Two Palestinians armed with M-16s and Kalashnikovs had cut through the chain-link fence surrounding the mountaintop village that morning and gone house to house, gunning down residents. Four were dead, eight wounded.

"Be careful not to step on the blood," a soldier warned me, pointing to a vast stain on the kitchen floor of the Greenbergs' two-storey home, its carefully tended yard decorated with concrete garden gnomes. In the master bedroom, where Katya Greenberg had bled to death, the sheets and pillows were soaked a deep crimson. A Russian newspaper lay on the bed. Downstairs there were five bullet holes in the wall beside the bed of their teenaged son. A box of Hanukkah candles lay beside his blood-reddened bed.

Two doors away at the Shefi home, there were two bullet holes in the kitchen window and most other windows were shattered, the floor littered with glass shards. The hallway and bedrooms were peppered with bullet holes, suggesting the gunmen fired wildly. There were three bullet holes just above the bed of five-year-old Danielle, and a blood smear on the floor beside her school clothes and stuffed animals. Two more bullets had pierced the window of her brother's room. Her mother was shot when she ran to protect Danielle. "I think this raid was quite carefully planned," said Israeli General Amos Ben Avraham. Hamas later claimed responsibility. When I got back to the hotel that night, I took off my shoes and scrubbed them in the bathroom sink. But I just couldn't seem to get the bloodstains out.

The destruction that can be caused by one man and a briefcase full of explosives is astounding. On May 7, 2002, a Hamas suicide bomber walked into a crowded pool hall in Rishon Lezion and detonated his explosive vest. Hours later, Israeli police let me walk through the ruins to see for myself what a suicide bombing looks like. No tank shell, missile or other conventional weapon could accomplish such thorough devastation. Steel nuts and bolts had been packed around the explosive mix, and when the bomb detonated, they radiated out in all directions like hundreds of bullets, peppering the walls, ceiling, floor and everyone in range with chunks of hot metal. Some passed clean through bystanders before they became embedded in the walls.

The bomber himself was ripped apart. His legs were blown out of a hole blasted in the outer wall. Seventeen civilians died and more than fifty were wounded. "We saw bodies on top of bodies," said Ami Rene, a firefighter. The explosion lifted the roof off the three-storey building. The roof cracked when it settled again. The pool hall was at the corner of the building; both of its outer walls were blown off. The money trays of the crumpled slot machines were filled with token coins, knocked loose by the force.

I noticed a red splash on the ceiling. It looked as if someone had taken a can of red paint and tossed it upward. "That's where the bomber was standing," one of the police officers told me. I asked what had happened to the bomber's body, and he led me across the blood-soaked carpet to a green garbage bag. He opened it and pointed inside to a collection of bone fragments and unidentifiable body parts. What kind of coldness does it take to walk into a room filled with innocent people and obliterate them, I wondered. I put this question later to a Hamas leader in Gaza City, as I sat in his home. Ismail Abu Shanab responded by venting about how the world had become unjust and the United States was leading it into dark times of greed and immorality because it had become a puppet of "super-corporations that are in the hands of the Jewish lobby."

"And what is the solution," I asked "Islam?"

He nodded.

"Islam gives values," he said.

"And which Islamic values say you can blow up a bus full of Israeli women and children?"

"Islam is not against it, because it is self-defense. You are not initiating attacks, you are reacting."

A few weeks after I last visited his house in Gaza City, Ismail Abu Shanab was killed in an Israeli missile strike on his car.

Hamas and Hezbollah are a problem for Israel, but they are not just Israel's problem. Israel happens to be at the front line of a global phenomenon—the spread of radical Islam, which sees the non-Muslim world, and particularly the Western world, as a threat to be vanquished by force. The wrath of radical Islam is not confined to the Middle East, as Americans learned on September 11. In the absence of democracy in the Arab world, Islamism has moved in to fill the void, a potent blend of religion and politics all the more dangerous for its black and white world view. At its fringes, groups such as Hezbollah and Hamas employ terrorism, and suicide terrorism in particular, as a tool for realizing what radical Islam sees as its political destiny as expressed in its members' interpretation of the Koran.

While Israel bears the brunt of Islamist rage, that is only because it is conveniently located on the doorstep of some of the most fanatical Muslim homelands, such as Egypt and Lebanon. The unresolved status of Palestinians has fed Islamic terrorism in Israel, but those who believe that the creation of a Palestinian homeland will end terrorism are fooling themselves. If and when Yasser Arafat's dream is realized, Islamists will find another focus for their anger. Iraq, Chechnya and any of the assortment of Arab states with ties to the United States, such as Saudi Arabia, or even the exaggerated troubles of Muslims within North America, will then become the next big cause, just as Afghanistan was in the 1980s and Bosnia in the 1990s.

To think of Hezbollah and its look-alikes as an Israeli issue would be a big mistake. It ignores the security threat created by terrorist support operations within Canada. The United States realized this long ago, and has aggressively gone after not only Hezbollah but also Hamas and Palestinian Islamic Jihad, and particularly their U.S.-based fundraising networks. Canada has, for some reason, been reluctant to investigate Muslim charities with ties to Middle East terror. Canadian police and intelligence authorities have been watching Hezbollah for many years, but until December 2002, the federal government did not officially recognize that Hezbollah is at its core a terrorist organization.

Hezbollah's status began to surface as a Canadian political issue in December 2001, after the Liberal government passed its Anti-Terrorism Act. One section of the law allows the cabinet to draft a list of organizations that it deems to be involved in terrorism, and whose activities are outlawed. Based on Hezbollah's track record, there was an expectation that it would be quickly added to the list. The public debate exploded in the House of Commons in October 2002, after Prime Minister Jean Chrétien attended a francophone summit event in Beirut that was also attended by Hassan Nasrallah. When reporters told Chrétien he had been sitting only a few rows from the terrorist leader, the prime minister seemed to not know who Nasrallah was (so much for knowing your enemy) and said he was not responsible for the guest list.

A few days later Stockwell Day, the Canadian Alliance critic, accused Chrétien of "rubbing elbows with a world-renowned self-proclaimed terrorist whose stated goal is to disrupt any prospects for peace in the Middle East. Why did the prime minister at some point during this conference, while he was out on his weekend pass, not publicly condemn this terrorist and demand an apology from the Lebanese president who was already himself making one-sided comments about the Middle East situation?" Foreign Minister Bill Graham then spelled out his government's dual policy on Hezbollah. Canada would outlaw the activities of the "military wing" of Hezbollah while recognizing its "political wing" as if there were a genuine distinction. Graham said, "We condemn its military wing as terrorists and we engage in dialogue with those with whom we wish to gain peace," he said. "The policy of the government and the tradition of this country has always been one of seeking dialogue as a way of solving problems. It would not be consistent with that approach and in trying to defeat terrorism for us to name Lebanese members of parliament, teachers, doctors and farmers in southern Lebanon as terrorists."

The Canadian Arab Federation (CAF) stepped into the debate and sent letters to Solicitor General Wayne Easter and Bill Graham cautioning them not to succumb to political pressures to ban Middle Eastern terror groups. The letter criticized bans already in place on Hamas and Islamic Jihad, and called Hezbollah "a legitimate Lebanese political party." A Hezbollah ban would hurt Arabs, the federation argued. "The Arab and Muslim communities have suffered enough stigmatization following the events of Sept. 11 and we are fearful that the listing of Hezbollah will add to the marginalization of these communities," the letters said. Raja Khouri, the CAF president, said there was scant evidence Hezbollah had engaged in terrorism.

Lieutenant-Colonel Bob Chamberlain begged to differ, and as Canada's former military attaché to Lebanon and Syria, he had firsthand experience with Hezbollah. During the Lebanese Civil War he was driving through Lebanon's Bekaa Valley when his car was run off the road by Hezbollah members. He was forced to the ground, with an AK-47 pointed at his head, before being taken to an apartment and accused of being a spy. Using his fluent Arabic, the colonel convinced Hezbollah to release him after two hours. He said the notion that there is any difference between the so-called political and military wings of Hezbollah is a fiction. "The point that I'm making is that it wasn't the military wing. I know them. I know their quasi-uniforms and have seen them many times. This was slightly different; it was probably the political wing, including one cleric, and they're the leaders of the party." The foreign minister should listen to intelligence advisers, he said. "They put the military wing on the terrorist list. That's not good enough," he told me. "It's the whole organization and I'm sorry, Mr. Graham, you're wrong."

Why the government was recognizing two distinct Hezbollah wings and treating them differently was not adequately explained, nor was it even logical given that the terrorist branch is run by the Hezbollah political leadership. While there might be teachers and farmers within the organization, their aim is to turn Lebanon into an Islamic state and destroy Israel with terrorism—a goal that should be loudly condemned by the free world, the support of which should be deemed unlawful.

For the next six weeks, the topic of Hezbollah came up regularly in the House of Commons. The Opposition introduced a motion calling on cabinet to put Hezbollah on the terrorist list because it "has committed untold horror on the lives of innocent people" and "represents a security threat to Canada and its allies." The motion was predictably defeated. Canadian Jewish organizations also lobbied the Liberals, and B'nai Brith Canada launched a court action against the government.

The Liberal cabinet announced in December 2002 that, in its view, Hezbollah was indeed a terrorist organization. Foreign Minister Graham's policy of dealing with the "political" Hezbollah while shunning the "terrorist" Hezbollah lost out because it was not viable. Even Hezbollah's own agents admit there is no distinction between the various branches of the organization, and if Canada were to recognize such a separation for Hezbollah, it would be logically compelled to do the same for Hamas or, for that matter, Al Qaeda, which also has branches engaged in humanitarian activities. The decision was condemned by Hezbollah and the predictable pack of interest groups, as well as Lebanon's outspoken ambassador to Canada, who said it was the work of the Jewish lobby and the Zionist press. What the Lebanese ambassador failed to grasp was that advocating a ban on Hezbollah was not a Jewish conspiracy; it was a Canadian duty. Hezbollah's operations in Canada put the security of Canadians and their allies at risk, and that was why it deserved to be outlawed.

In late 2002, CSIS issued a "Secret Canadian Eyes Only" intelligence report titled Hezbollah and Its Activities in Canada, in which it described how "Hezbollah members collect money through the use of benevolent organizations," and use Canada for fundraising, propaganda and procurement. The report described a cross-Canada network, with operatives in Toronto, Montreal and Vancouver—a network identical to the one described a decade earlier by Al Husseini, whose offer to inform was declined. Canada learned the hard way that he was right.

The case of Fauzi Ayub shows that Hezbollah's Canadian branch is engaged in much more than raising money for the cause; it is also being used for high-level terrorist operations, directed by the most senior elements of the radical group's command. At about the same time that the Liberals were defending their policy on Hezbollah, Ayub was being interrogated by the Israelis, explaining how he had come to Jerusalem "as a volunteer to take part in one operation" to help those he considered to be oppressed Muslims. "My name is Fauzi Mohammed Ayub," he began. "I am originally Lebanese. I have Canadian citizenship." From Jerusalem, he drove forty kilometers south to the West Bank city of Hebron.

He could not have picked a more volatile city in which to operate. Like Jerusalem, Hebron is considered holy ground by Jews, Muslims and Christians, all of whom worship at the city's Tomb of the Patriarchs. Hebron is a tense and divided city. Most of it is controlled by the Palestinians, but Jewish settlers occupy the downtown, protected by Israeli troops. The first time I visited the city, I was stopped by a sullen-faced man standing in the doorway of his ceramics factory, Hebron Glass. The shop was closed, even though it was a Saturday morning. If not for the war, it would have been his busiest business day. We stopped to ask him for directions to downtown Hebron. He pointed the way, but reluctantly.

"You cannot go there at this moment," he added.

"But why?"

"They are hanging the collaborators."

During the night, at just before midnight, two Israeli Apache helicopter gunships had appeared over the city, just as Marvan Zalum, the forty-three-year-old leader of the Tanzim militia, was driving along Peace Street in his white Mitsubishi Lancer. With a chilling precision, a helicopter fired a missile directly through the roof of the car. When word of the assassination spread, Zalum's followers wrapped their checkered *kaffiyehs* around their heads, fetched their AK-47s from their hiding places, and took to the streets for revenge.

The Palestinian Authority security forces merely watched as Zalum's supporters hunted down three Palestinian men who were suspected of cooperating with the Israelis. There were no formal charges and there was no opportunity for defense. There was a mock trial, during which the three accused were lined up in front of

Zalum's demolished car while armed militants shouted accusations at them. The anger of the Tanzim militia was not directed so much at the three doomed men as it was at the very notion that anyone would deviate from the revolutionary path, for one of the unifying characteristics of a militant culture is its complete intolerance of dissent. Those who stray must be eliminated, and the sooner the better. Any pretext will do.

The verdict of the street trial was, of course, never in doubt. The men were guilty of crimes against the Palestinian people! The sentencing was swift. The men were executed with dozens of bullets, and their bloodied bodies were displayed for all to see. We left our car at the ceramics factory. It had Israeli license plates, and to drive into that crowd would have been suicidal. We hailed a local cab instead and made our way into the center of town. Hundreds of Palestinians were heading downtown, on foot, on horseback. Some carried weapons. They had awoken to the news that Zalum was dead, and that the collaborators responsible had been dealt with.

The first body was strung upside down from an electrical tower. It was hanging by a foot. The limbs were twisted at improbable angles and the bloodied head was about level with the onlookers who crowded around to hit the corpse and spit on the ashen face. "The people on this day are very happy," said one man. He said he hoped the public executions would let other people know they should not even think about helping the Israelis. "We should die before we do that. This is war." The second body was farther down the road, beside the Al-Ansaar Mosque. It was similarly dangling by a foot. The third lay in the road, encircled by a crowd of frenzied men who took turns kicking it.

The kicks were supposed to look like expressions of anger, as if the collaborators were the hated Israelis themselves. But watching the display, I had the sense that this was also theater, and that those laying their boots into the dead men were doing so not only out of hatred or anger, but to demonstrate that they, unlike these collaborators, were fully committed to the cause. The posthumous violence sent two messages simultaneously: First, "I hate Israelis," and second, "Don't do this to me because I am not a collaborator." Those who did not have the stomach to attack the dead were busy expressing these same two points in words, and in the joy with which they celebrated the murder of three fellow Palestinians under a perfect blue sky. "You want to know why everyone is so happy," an old man said. "They know these people are our people, and they are cheating us. These people are very dangerous; they give information to the Israelis!"

Those gathered around Zalum's car, which had been ripped open like a toy, echoed each other's thoughts. "You can see with your own eyes the terrorism of Israel," said a teenager who had brought a video camera to the scene to film the destroyed car. "But in the end we will have victory." An elderly man said he had come to see for himself the Palestinians accused of cooperating with the Israelis. "We like to know who are the kind of men who sell themselves for the enemy," he said, declining like the others to give his name. "That's it. To know how they look."

The other topic of discussion among those who jammed the streets for the carnival-like lynching was the virtue of the martyr Marvan Zalum, because in a culture as heavily radicalized as the Palestinian West Bank, to die for the cause is the highest of callings. No matter that Zalum was responsible for a string of terrorist attacks, including an April 12, 2002, suicide bombing at a bus stop in Jerusalem that killed six civilians and wounded eighty-five, as well as scores of other bombings and hundreds of shooting attacks, including one on March 26, 2001, that left an infant dead. "In security terms, Marvan Zalum was the equivalent of an entire armed militia," an Israeli official said. But to the Palestinians in Hebron, he was a *shaheed*, a martyr for Islam.

At some point, I lost my translator in the sea of people mobbing the street. I began to feel uneasy. I could feel their eyes watching me, questioning who I was. Was I an Israeli? Was I an American? A spy? I stood out because I was wearing my flak jacket, with the universal press symbol, "TV," written on the front and back in red electrical tape. There were more and more armed young men mixing in the crowd, so I decided to retreat. I made my way back to the glassworks and met up with my driver. Before we could leave, however, the man who owned the glass factory insisted that I come into his store and choose a gift. It was the last thing I felt like doing, but I did not want to offend, so I bought a ceramic plate and thanked him profusely. As I got back into the car for the drive to Jerusalem, I couldn't help noting how ridiculous this all was. Here I was, nauseous from the sight of fresh corpses, shopping for tourist trinkets.

Fauzi Ayub would have had no trouble getting into Hebron. Although Israeli soldiers had sealed off the roads with a series of checkpoints, the Palestinians had set up a backdoor pedestrian route that bypassed the troops. Once he reached the city, Ayub made contact with another operative who was to assist him with his mission. He began making plans to assemble a fragmentation bomb, but Palestinian Authority police became suspicious and brought him to their headquarters. He claims he was blindfolded, beaten and accused of being an Israeli spy. He told them he was Lebanese and they accused him of being a member of the pro-Israeli South Lebanon Army.

"I told them 'I'm from South Lebanon,'" Ayub testified in court. "They asked, 'What organization?' I told them I was with Amal and then I moved to Hezbollah. Only when I told them I was with Hezbollah were they satisfied. They said, 'You are in the resistance,' and I said, 'I am here in the resistance as well.'

"Right away they brought me coffee and they left me alone; they were satisfied with me. They said they would bring me cigarettes and chicken.

"I said that I was finished with being kicked and beaten up ... Later, one by one they came to me and asked me to tell them about my heroism."

He offered money to a sympathetic officer named Younis who had watched out for his welfare and brought him coffee, $5,000 now and another $5,000 once he reached Lebanon. But one day Younis stopped coming. Another officer brought Fauzi a copy of the Israeli indictment against Younis.

"He told me I made a big mistake.

"I asked why.

"He said Younis has told the Jews certain things about you."

On June 25, 2002, the Israeli military raided Hebron. An army convoy stopped outside the Palestinian police compound and, using a bullhorn, told everyone inside to get out. The guards fled and Ayub walked out alone, only to be arrested by the Shin Beit. The Israelis destroyed the building. When I visited it a year later it was little more than a pile of broken concrete and twisted rebar. Amid the wreckage of the security building I could see the white iron doors of a prison cell, perhaps the very one that had confined Fauzi Ayub.

Ayub was taken to a prison at Kiryat Arba and was held under Israel's Imprisonment of Enemy Combatants Law. The Israeli military claimed he had been sent to the West Bank to train members of Hamas and Islamic Jihad, and to help them build bombs and plan attacks "on a scale that hasn't yet been witnessed" in the country. But security officials have since concluded that Mugniyah, the Hezbollah terror mastermind, had bigger plans for Ayub. "He didn't take a guy from Beirut and send him to the West Bank just to do something that Hamas was already doing," an Israeli official said. Israeli investigators said Ayub was probably collecting operational intelligence about potential terrorist targets, as well as building an infrastructure within Israel and the West Bank for future attacks, but they also now suspect that he was part of an assassination plot.

Ayub's family in Toronto does not believe the Israeli claims. "We are worried about him," a brother told the *Toronto Star*. "We have no idea what he was doing but we don't believe what they say in the news. He is a religious man, he is devout. He went to Saudi Arabia once, to do the pilgrimage. Maybe he went to Israel to visit holy places." Of course, if he was simply a tourist in the Holy Land, he could have used his Canadian passport. The Canadian consular officials who visited Ayub after his arrest were immediately suspicious. Normally, when travelers are arrested in a foreign country, they want their embassy to move heaven and earth to get them home. All Ayub wanted was a prayer mat, cologne and a beard-trimming kit. He seemed resigned to his fate.

The Israeli Shin Beit made careful note of the parallels between the activities of Ayub, Jihad Shuman and another alleged Hezbollah operative, Hasin Makdad, who had accidentally detonated a bomb strapped to his body at a Jerusalem hotel in 1996. "It should be stated that there are many similarities between the way Ayub was sent to Israel and the way two other Hezbollah operatives infiltrated the country," according to an Israeli intelligence document. "In this framework, the three operatives sent by Hezbollah arrived in Israel just before an election campaign, apparently with the goal of influencing its outcome. Moreover, the three operatives were active in the area of Jerusalem containing many government buildings. The fact that Shuman was caught at a distance of 300 meters from the home of the prime minister is proof of this." The Israelis eventually concluded that their Canadian captive had probably been sent to assassinate the Israeli prime minister.

A few months later, on February 18, 2003, Ayub sat in a courtroom in Tel Aviv and explained that he was on a mission from God. He depicted himself as an Islamic soldier, dedicated to the downtrodden Muslims and willing to accept his punishment.

"My point of view on the world is that I protect the oppressed," he said. "I want to save the people from oppression. And always, whoever takes part in these operations goes to prison. I did not come for money or for dealing in drugs. I came to do something that is holy for me."

"Who are the oppressed you wanted to help here?" the judge asked. "Who are they?"

"The Muslims are oppressed," he replied. "The operation may be with the Palestinians or with others.

"You want to know the reason I came here? I came here by an order from God. This is my religion. To defend the oppressed."

The judge challenged Ayub's noble self-image, reminding him that he was part of a hijacking plot that had killed more than sixty people. Even if he had not intended to kill, he should have known that there could be fatal mistakes.

"A mistake is from God," Ayub shot back. "If innocents die, this is luck."

Fauzi Ayub compared himself to the Russian troops who had stormed a theater in Moscow to free hostages held by Chechen terrorists. Some of the hostages were killed during the rescue mission. "The officer that planned that operation to save the hostages did not intend to kill them," he said.

In Ayub's confused mind, he was the hero and the Russian police were the terrorists. "Your example is not good," the judge interjected. "You are not the person coming to save the hostages, as the Russians did. You are in the role of the Chechen, the hostage taker. Don't speak for the Russians, but the Chechens."

"Everybody" Ayub said, "has a different point of view."

On January 29, 2004, the same day a Palestinian suicide bomber blew up a bus in Jerusalem, Israeli guards removed Ayub from his cell and put him on a plane to Germany. There, Ayub and 27 others were handed over to Hezbollah in exchange for the release of Israeli businessman Elhanan Tannenbaum and the bodies of three Israeli servicemen. That night, Ayub landed at Beirut airport. Smiling broadly, he walked across the tarmac and embraced Hezbollah leader Sheikh Nasrallah. He was a free man again. Before he left his jail cell in Israel, he told a Canadian consular official he was thinking about returning to Canada.

The electronic detonator that the Montreal-based terrorist Ahmed Ressam built to blow up Los Angeles International Airport in 1999. US Customs agents found it hidden in the trunk of his car. (Photo by *Associated Press*) Ressam was a member of the Canadian wing of the Algerian Armed Islamic Group, whose leader Fateh Kamel (left) was captured in Jordan.

British Columbia Sikh extremist Talwinder Singh Parmar, an alleged leader of the Babbar Khalsa terrorist group, remains the prime suspect in the 1985 Air India bombings. He was killed during a "police encounter" in India on October 15, 1992. (Photo by Wayne Leidenfrost, *The Province*)

An airplane door bearing the Air India logo drifts off the coast of Ireland. The passenger plane exploded in mid-air on June 23, 1985, killing all 329 on board. Babbar Khalsa leader Talwinder Singh Parmar of British Columbia remains the prime suspect. (The Canadian Press)

In one of several surveillance photos shot by Canadian intelligence agents, Hezbollah member Said Harb crosses the Lynn Canyon Suspension Bridge, a popular tourist attraction in North Vancouver, B.C. A Hezbollah member told CSIS that the terrorist group collected videotapes of potential targets in Canada. "They film roads, life, everything."

Harb meets on a Vancouver street with Ali Amhaz, a Lebanese then living in Burnaby, B.C. The FBI alleges the two men, together with Vancouver resident Mohamad Hassan Dbouk, were members of a Hezbollah procurement ring that used the proceeds of cigarette smuggling to purchase military equipment for Islamic fighters in Lebanon.

Mohamad Hassan Dbouk, wanted by U.S. authorities for his role as a Canadian-based procurement officer for Hezbollah, meets in Vancouver with Harb. He has since returned to Lebanon.

Kassem Daher, an Alberta cinema owner accused of being the "prince" of an Islamic terrorist group, built this luxurious home in Lebanon's Bekaa Valley. (Photo by Stewart Bell)

A bomb planted by the Tamil Tigers gutted this office building in downtown Colombo, Sri Lanka (Photo by Stewart Bell)

Sri Lankan soldiers on patrol in the jungles of war-battered Jaffna. (Photo by Stewart Bell)

The World Tamil Movement office in east Toronto. The RCMP national security team executed a search warrant and removed documents in April 2006 as part of a terror-financing investigation called Project OSALUKI. (Photo by Stewart Bell)

Manickavasagam Suresh, an alleged Canadian fundraiser for the Tamil Tigers, arrives at the Supreme Court of Canada to argue he should not be deported back to Sri Lanka. (Photo by Tom Hanson, The Canadian Press)

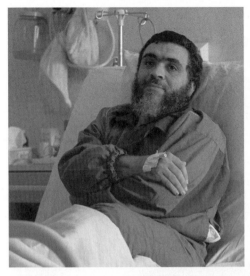

Ahmed Said Khadr, the Canadian aid worker whom Canadian intelligence says is close to Osama bin Laden, lies in a hospital bed in Islamabad in 1996 during a hunger strike to protest his arrest for allegedly bombing the Egyptian embassy. (Photo by Tom Hanson, The Canadian Press)

Palestinians in Hebron hanged a "collaborator" suspected of passing information to the Israelis about a local terrorist commander in May 2002.

Indonesian police examine the ruins of a nightclub bombed by members of the Al Qaeda-affiliated Jemmah Islamiyah on October 12, 2002. More than 200 were killed. Canadian Mansour Jabarah plotted several Jemmah Islamiyah bomb attacks in the region. (The Canadian Press)

Mohammed Mansour Jabarah, in the yearbook photo taken in St. Catharines, Ontario, before he went to Afghanistan to join Al Qaeda. After overseeing bombing plots in Singapore and Manila, he was captured and ended up in U.S. custody. (Photo by *National Post*.)

Jamal Akkal of Windsor, Ontario standing at Niagara Falls. He was later arrested in Gaza. Israeli officials claim he was trained by Hamas to carry out terrorist attacks in Canada and the United States. (Photo by Stewart Bell)

Jahmaal James, second from left, at his wedding in Lahore, Pakistan. James was one of 18 alleged members of an Al Qaeda-inspired terrorist group arrested in Toronto in 2006. (Photo courtesy of Stewart Bell)

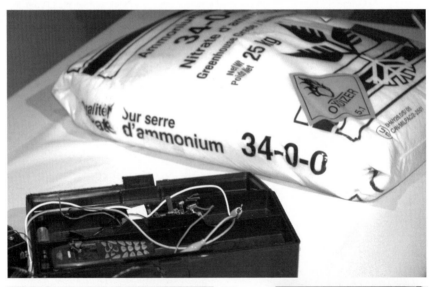

A sample of the evidence seized by the RCMP on June 2, 2006, during a series of counter-terrorism raids around Toronto. The explosives were allegedly to be used to create two or three truck bombs to be detonated in downtown Toronto. (Photos by Stewart Bell)

4

FATEH THE ALGERIAN

FATEH KAMEL is wearing a grey woolen sweater, drawstring pants and silver handcuffs as he is escorted by French *gendarmes* into the wood-paneled fourteenth chamber of the Palais de Justice. He shuffles to his seat in the prisoners' box and holds his arms up so the crew-cut guards can unshackle his wrists. Once seated, he buries his head in his folded arms. When he looks up to scratch his black beard, his face is the color of the drab green courtroom wallpaper, and there are coffee stains around his eyes. He looks like someone who hasn't slept well in a good long time.

The law-courts complex on Île de la Cité was once the home of kings and, later, a prison where Marie Antoinette and Robespierre were detained before being led to Place de la Concorde and guillotined along with thousands of others. But the trial on this chilly morning in February 2001 is about a different sort of revolution—the international jihad led by radical Muslims whose loyal foot soldiers believe it is their religious duty to do battle with infidels and the "enemies of Islam," notably America.

Outside the courtroom, a police officer uses a metal-detector wand to search the spectators and black-gowned lawyers who are lined up in the hallway. Another *gendarme*, wearing white gloves, digs through their purses and briefcases. Inside, police run their hands under the wooden benches, checking for bombs. An American television crew confronts Kamel's lawyer and peppers him with questions. Is it true Kamel was in Afghanistan, and that he met bin Laden? "He is Canadian," the lawyer responds, without answering the question directly. "He is free, he has done nothing, only travel."

Kamel is a forty-one-year-old Canadian with a wife and son back home in the suburbs of Montreal, where he once owned a small craft store. But for a simple shopkeeper, he is facing serious criminal charges. The indictment sheet on the judge's desk accuses Kamel of being a man known by the alias "Moustapha," wanted for "participating in a criminal association for the purposes of preparing acts of terrorism," as well as two counts of trafficking in fake passports for Islamic militants. French investigators say he is a "logistician" in the international jihad movement, a recruiter and organizer who has been instrumental in coordinating the movement of Islamic militants and in plotting terrorist attacks. Using the *noms de guerre* Moustapha and El-Fateh, he is said to have headed the Canadian cell of the Algerian extremist network, the so-called Groupe Fateh Kamel. Among the best-known members of his cell was a young Algerian bombmaker named Ahmed Ressam.

"Kamel was a key member of the international Islamist terrorist network of the mujahedin, or holy warriors ... determined to strike the Western world order that they considered corrupt and immoral," says an unclassified CSIS report. "As well, he played a central role in the wave of terrorist attacks that erupted in France toward the middle of the 1990s, notably the plot to commit bomb attacks in Paris metro stations and a series of attacks in the city of Roubaix, in northern France." One Paris magazine dubbed him "The Islamist Carlos."

Five days before his thirty-ninth birthday, in 1999, Kamel left his quiet neighborhood on Montreal's Île Perrot for a business trip. He flew to Athens, then Istanbul, and finally to the holy city of Mecca. The journey was a grave mistake for a man who, according to police, was an expert at arranging the clandestine passage of Islamic terrorists throughout Europe and North America. France had posted an international warrant for his arrest, and when Kamel made a stopover in Amman, he was arrested and quickly extradited to a cell at La Santé prison in Paris. He has been there ever since. To Western security agencies, Kamel is the new face of international terrorism, a force unlike anything the intelligence world has seen. Driven by religious zeal, radical Islamic terrorists have begun to work in loose cells placed strategically around the globe, sustaining themselves with criminal and business enterprises, communicating by cellphone and encrypted e-mail. They are mobile and highly motivated, and they come from any number of countries, which makes them nearly impossible to track. The only thing they have in common is their devotion to violent jihad.

The word "jihad" refers to the fight against evil, a duty that, according to Islam, must be fulfilled with the heart, tongue, hand and sword. Modern Islam focuses on the first three, emphasizing the inner, spiritual jihad. But radicals interpret Islamic law to mean that they should use violence to defend the faith and make non-Muslims surrender to Islamic rule. Those who die doing so will become martyrs awarded a special place in heaven.

Their generation emerged out of Afghanistan. In the 1980s, infuriated by the Soviet occupation of the country, idealistic young Muslim radicals from the world over made their way to the region to fight alongside the Afghan holy warriors known as the *mujahedeen*. The war turned into the Soviet version of Vietnam, resulting in fifteen thousand Russian deaths, and when the Red Army finally limped back to Moscow in 1989, the Islamists' sense of victory was intoxicating. The question for the Muslim volunteers was: what next? Most of them could not go home. The last thing their governments wanted was to see the return of battle-hardened Islamists. The holy warriors were soldiers without a war.

Osama bin Laden brought these veteran radicals together. He united the disparate band of Islamic extremists behind a declaration of worldwide holy war against Americans and Jews, and their allies. His Al Qaeda—literally, "The Base"—became an umbrella for the world's most extreme radical groups, such as the Egyptian Al Jihad and the Algerian Armed Islamic Group, of which Kamel was a member. They set out to combat the perceived enemies of their faith and, in doing so, to fulfill the destiny of Islam as the one true faith, under which all others would be subservient.

Some of the Afghan alumni (a term used commonly to describe veterans of fighting in Afghanistan) returned to Algiers and Riyadh to ignite Islamic unrest, while others fanned out across the globe to do the same in more clandestine fashion. They fought jihad in Bosnia, Chechnya, Kosovo, Kashmir and a long list of other countries, and they waged a low-level campaign of anti-Western terrorist attacks. The FBI put a US$5-million reward on bin Laden's head in 1998, but he evaded capture by aligning himself with the Taliban in Afghanistan and keeping on the move. Unable to bring bin Laden to justice, the United States and its allies instead set out to systematically dismantle the jihad network he had set up across Europe and North America through a series of criminal trials in New York, Los Angeles, London, Frankfurt, and now before an austere trio of judges from the Tribunal de Grande Instance de Paris.

In the early 1990s, however, if you had said the name Al Qaeda, few people within Canadian intelligence circles would have known what you were talking about. Sikh terrorism was still the priority of CSIS. In October 1992, several witnesses claimed to have seen Sheik Omar Abdel Rahman, an Egyptian cleric and Al Qaeda spiritual leader, preaching at mosques in eastern Canada. The sightings came just months before Rahman and his co-conspirators tried to blow up the World Trade Center with a truck bomb, an eerie foreshadowing of the infinitely more devastating strike that would come eight years later. The Security Intelligence Review Committee investigated the allegation but was never able to determine conclusively whether it was true. Following the 1993 bombing in Manhattan, the Americans approached CSIS for help chasing leads in Canada, drawing Canadian intelligence officials for the first time into the hunt for Sunni Islamic extremists.

One of Al Qaeda's member organizations, the Algerian Armed Islamic Group (known by the acronym GIA), was an increasing focus of Canadian investigators at the time. But nobody thought this was anything more than a spillover of the Algerian civil war. The notion that radical Islamists were gearing up for a worldwide jihad was only emerging in the West at the time of the 1993 publication of Samuel P. Huntington's "Clash of Civilizations" in *Foreign Affairs* magazine.

It wasn't until late 1995 that senior intelligence officials awoke to the threat posed by bin Laden and his band of Sunni Islamic extremists. Ironically, it was Canada's longtime Cold War foe, Russia, that first raised the alarm. Ward Elcock, the CSIS director, and Jim Warren, his deputy director of operations, visited Moscow in December 1995 to discuss the terms of post–Cold War security cooperation. But the Russians wanted to talk about something else: radical Islam. After their awful experience in Afghanistan, and brewing Islamic revolts in Chechnya and the southern republics, the Russians were well versed in the perils of Muslim militancy. The Russians also felt threatened by Islamic movements in Uzbekistan and Tajikistan, not to mention Bosnia, which they saw as a giant Islamic dagger pointed at the heart of Russia. Elcock and Warren listened and learned. They realized it was self-serving for the Russians to play up the threat of radical Islam at a time when the West was considering international intervention in Bosnia. Yet, even if there was some exaggeration by the Russians, the threat was undeniably real. "That's the first time that I had really sat back and thought about what they were saying and saw this as a war between Islam and Christianity," Warren recalled. "I am not sure I totally agreed with the Russians that this was a 'war' between Islam and Christianity. That was their language, but it is correct to say that this was the first time I ever really thought about a 'clash of civilizations' per se. Up to that point I think we were all conditioned to think of Mideast terrorism with its main focus on the Palestinians and, to a somewhat lesser extent, imperialism as personified by the French in Africa."

Almost hidden by the snowbanks on the sidewalks of St-Laurent boulevard in Montreal, next to the triple-X Cinéma l'Amour and a few doors up from an army-surplus store called Les Soldats de la Mode (Soldiers of Fashion), is a tiny boutique with a palm tree painted on the window. Imported tribal jewelry and heavy-knit sweaters fill the shelves. Bright mobiles in the shapes of tropical fish, parrots, and elephants dangle from the ceiling. Julie Lalonde and her husband, Mohamed Fenni, a native Algerian, had managed to keep the shop going for six years, but when a larger craft outlet named One World opened across the street, business suffered. "We couldn't compete. They were importing big quantities, whereas we were so small," Lalonde recalls. The couple worried about their worsening fortunes until a man appeared at the store saying he had heard about their troubles through the city's Algerian community. His name was Fateh Kamel and he offered to buy the business. "I turned to my husband and said, 'My God, he's been sent here from heaven!'" A problem emerged, however, when Kamel noticed that some of the merchandise depicted animals. He said it would be against his religion to trade in objects that represented life. Lalonde and her husband argued that if Kamel got rid of every craft in the shape of an animal, there would be nothing left. He eventually bought the entire stock, but it was clear to Lalonde and her husband that this was a man who was serious about his faith.

Fateh Kamel was born on March 14, 1960, in El-Harrach, Algeria, a part of the world where religion is deadly serious, a potent force in politics and war. He entered the world amid Algeria's bloody fight for independence from French colonial rule. His parents, Mohand Tahar and Fatima Mayouch, called him Fatah, which in Arabic means "Conquest," although he would later use Fateh, a variation. El-Harrach is a suburb of the country's ancient capital, Algiers, with a winning soccer club but little else. Two decades of socialism and misrule had wrecked the economy. Unemployment was at a 30 percent level, and 84 percent of the jobless were under the age of thirty. The optimism that followed the end of French rule vanished. Political unrest and a lack of opportunity prevailed. Many of the Algerians who were known as *hittistes* or "people who hold up walls" because they had nothing better to do than to stand on the streets leaning against buildings, decided to leave.

In 1987, Fateh Kamel and his brother Yazid joined the exodus. Yazid decided to make a new life in Paris; Fateh chose Canada, and arrived in Montreal just as the Algerian community there began to swell in size. In 1990, the Islamic Salvation Front (FIS) party began to show promise, winning local elections in Algeria and threatening to win power in Algiers as well. The military stepped in to prevent the Islamist victory. An extremist faction of the party responded by joining the Armed Islamic Group, which represented an emerging school of thought convinced that freedom from government tyranny would come only through Islamic rule, and that only war could bring about such a fundamental change.

The GIA emerged from the Mouvement Islamique Armée (MIA), which had been created by a veteran of the French colonial war who followed the preachings of Islamist philosopher Sayyed Qutb. During the war in Afghanistan, the MIA shipped thousands of Algerians through Saudi Arabia to fight the Soviets in the bleak Afghan mountains. When they returned to Algeria at the end of the war in 1989, they formed the backbone of the GIA. But not all the Afghan alumni returned home. Many of them went to Europe and North America, where they supported the war effort back home by raising money from expatriates and robbing banks. Toward the end of the Soviet war, Fateh Kamel journeyed to Pakistan and crossed into Afghanistan where, according to Canadian documents, he took part in combat. It was just the start of his great jihad. His lawyer argues Kamel just liked to travel, and that because he was a Muslim, it was simply easier to visit Muslim nations. But the region was hardly a tourist destination at the time. It was a war zone.

Kamel became something of a leader in the Montreal community in the early 1990s. He was charismatic and respected among the Algerian and North African émigrés. Sometimes they would come to him for help and advice. "All Montreal knows who is Fateh. Everybody calls him Fateh, that's all," says Abdellah Ouzghar, a Moroccan who met Kamel after moving to Canada and was later convicted in absentia by France on terrorism-related charges. Soon after he moved to the city, Kamel married Nathalie Boivin, a Québécoise special-education teacher from the Gaspé. But he didn't exactly settle down. Two years later Kamel traveled to the scene of the next Muslim jihad—Bosnia, where ethnic violence had erupted between Serbs, Croats and Muslims. Reports of Serbian ethnic cleansing in Bosnian Muslim villages had angered Muslims in Europe, Asia and North America, as well as in the Islamic world. They vowed to come to the aid of their brothers.

Groups of foreign volunteers made their way to Zenica, a Muslim enclave near Sarajevo, where they established the Mujahedeen Battalion, numbering several hundred.

The Bosnian jihad was modeled after Afghanistan. Training camps were established in Bosnia, and Islamic charities moved into the region to siphon money to the fighters, supply them with weapons and provide them with a cover story for their presence in the Balkans. "Access by Afghan Arabs to Bosnian or Croatian camps was largely facilitated by Islamic charity organizations, NGOs or governmental agencies, which, under the cover of humanitarian activities, stoked the Bosnian conflict and turned it into a jihad," says a 1996 confidential report by France's Central Antiterrorism Unit, UCLAT. A CIA report estimates that a third of the Muslim charities working in Bosnia were fronts for terrorism.

Kamel says he traveled to the Balkans on business. He had formed a company called Société Mandingo with a partner in Montreal, Pierre Aklil, and claims he was in Bosnia looking for contracts with a humanitarian focus, such as supplying pencils to schools. But it's now believed that he was there to fight, and that an early trip to the war zone sparked his involvement in the battalion's leadership. Kamel was riding a motorcycle on a Bosnian road when a shell struck nearby. He says a car swerved and struck the bike. Because of the extent of the damage to his foot, the French investigators claim, Kamel was taken to the mujahedeen base hospital in Zenica. The hospital medic was Christophe Caze, a young French medical-school dropout who professed a radical devotion to the jihad. What exactly happened in Zenica is not known, but according to the French authorities, from that point on, Kamel's principal activity became not commerce but organizing the shipment of mujahedeen recruits to Bosnia.

Over the next two years, Kamel traveled back and forth repeatedly between Canada and Bosnia and Croatia, making stops in France, Germany, Holland, Austria, Italy and Slovenia, searching for false papers and arranging convoys of recruits to Zenica. He eventually split up with his business partner at Société Mandingo. He says they parted because Aklil wanted to sell cigars, while he himself was opposed to smoking. Aklil told investigators they ended their partnership because Kamel was not reporting back from his travels with any contracts, and Aklil has denied any involvement with Kamel outside of their legitimate business dealings.

In 1994, one of Kamel's trips took him to Milan. The political chief of the Bosnian Mujahedeen Battalion, an Egyptian named Anwar Shaaban, was operating out of the Islamic Cultural Institute there. Italian police had launched Operation Sphinx to monitor his activities, and began eavesdropping on the institute. In their wiretaps, they started hearing about a man the others called Brother Fateh, or sometimes El-Fateh or just Fateh. It soon became clear to them that "Fateh the Algerian" controlled the movement of fighters to Bosnia. He worked closely with Shaaban, organizing Muslim recruits and getting them into Bosnia. His orders were passed on unchallenged, a sign of his authority within the mujahedeen. When international border controls were tightened, Brother Fateh would order a temporary halt to the flow of recruits. "Brother Fateh is responsible for the region," one caller says. French investigators say that the mysterious Brother Fateh was none other than Fateh Kamel.

By then, the Bosnian war had caught the attention of the Western allies, and the United States was trying to negotiate a peace settlement. The result was the Dayton Accord, which partitioned Bosnia into Serbian and Muslim ethnic enclaves. Any foreign soldiers involved in the conflict were required to leave or to lay down arms in order to stabilize the region and make way for North Atlantic Treaty Organization (NATO) peacekeepers. The Bosnian president thanked the holy warriors for their help, and even granted citizenship to those who had taken Bosnian wives, but they had served their purpose. The locals were relieved: they had tolerated the volunteer contingent for its role in combating the forces of Slobodan Milosevic, but they saw the volunteers as zealots and outsiders. The fighters would chastise them for saying "good morning" instead of "Praise Allah." "They didn't often smile," the journalist Ed Vulliamy writes in *Seasons in Hell*, his book on the Bosnian war. "They were feared by the Croats, disliked by most Bosnian Muslims, and totally estranged by the political project of Bosnia and

Herzegovina." Vulliamy quotes a source who describes them as "penguins in the desert."

The mujahedeen in Zenica were in disbelief. After spilling their blood fighting the Serbs, they were suddenly being told to pack up and go. Far from realizing their goal of turning Bosnia into an Islamic state, they had to hand the country over to soldiers from what they saw as the Christian West: the United States, Europe and Canada. Shaaban oversaw the suicide bombing of a Croatian police facility in Bijenkan, which was carried out by an "employee" of the Third World Relief Agency, and he began organizing terrorist attacks against the NATO forces. In December 1995, Shaaban was shot dead by Croatian security forces. The bulk of the foreign mujahedeen left reluctantly. Kamel, like the rest, returned home. But the jihad was far from over, and now the holy warriors had yet another grudge against the Western world.

In the color photograph, the wedding guests sit in their carefully appointed places inside a Montreal banquet hall. There are a half-dozen faces, all looking carefree. One of the guests, standing and caught in mid-motion, is a bearded man with a mane of black hair. A map hangs on the wall behind him. It could be Algeria, though it's hard to make out. The photo was the first frame on a roll of film seized by police (along with a cache of stolen passports and credit cards) from the Montreal home of Adel Boumezbeur. Also on the film were nine photos of Ahmed Ressam. American investigators interviewed a Vancouver man named Nabil Ikhlef about the photos, trying to confirm the identities of the subjects. In a videotaped interview, he identifies his own brother Mourad, as well as Boumezbeur's brother and Boumezbeur himself, who has since been convicted of aiding French terrorists.

"Anyone else you recognize in the photograph?" Ikhlef is asked.

"Fateh," he replies, pointing to the bearded man.

"Do you know the rest of his name?" the investigator asks.

"Kamel. He lived in the same neighborhood as me in Algeria."

It was at a get together like this, a Ramadan celebration, in fact, that Kamel first met an Algerian named Ahmed Ressam. Since arriving in Canada from France, Ressam had hooked up with other members of Montreal's Algerian community, including Kamel's sidekick Said Atmani. "It's somebody I hardly know at all," Kamel told me. Kamel was spending more time in Montreal now. The war over, he no longer had to spend long stretches on the road. He had returned to the apartment he shared with Nathalie. Their first child, a boy, was born in March 1996. Kamel spent the first six months of that year in Canada, but the jihad soon called again.

By then the GIA had become even more radical. It had evolved from a revolutionary movement into an apocalyptic group that sought to kill everyone who did not follow its fundamentalist ideology, including Algerians and Muslims. Its attacks became even more appalling. The GIA massacred entire villages and slaughtered foreign tourists. It began a campaign of attacks in the West, particularly France. The Notre-Dame metro was bombed; a Canadian was among those killed. The GIA hijacked a French plane over Paris. The organization got so extreme that even Osama bin Laden and Ayman Al Zawahiri, the top two in Al Qaeda, began to distance themselves from the group. Many members of the GIA abandoned the organization and drifted instead back to the ideals of the international jihad that had emerged from the Afghan war. They went to Al Qaeda.

Kamel started to hang out at a four-room apartment at 6301 Place de la Malicorne in Montreal's Anjou district. Also living there at the time were a Bosnian war veteran, Said "Karim" Atmani and two Algerians, Moustapha Labsi and Ahmed Ressam, who were small-time crooks. Other ex-mujahedeen guerrillas would often drop by for visits. The apartment served as the Canadian headquarters of the Algerian jihad network. Telephone records linked it to other cells in France, Italy, and Turkey, where mujahedeen fighters had settled after leaving Zenica.

But European investigators were closing in on Kamel. Christophe Caze, the medic from the Zenica battalion, had formed a gang in northern France called the Groupe Roubaix to raise money for the GIA. They robbed stores and banks, killed at least one man, and planted a bomb in a car outside a police station near a gathering of G7 leaders. Police finally cornered them in March 1996, in a Muslim ghetto, but they did not surrender quietly. They set fire to their hideout and started a shootout. Four members of the gang were killed, including Caze. Inside the burned-out house, police found Kalashnikov assault rifles, automatic pistols, grenades, ammunition and documents from a radical Algerian extremist group. In Caze's electronic organizer was a Montreal phone number with the name "Fateh-Can."

Members of the Montreal cell raised money through theft and fraud for Islamic militants abroad. While Kamel's task during the war had been to get recruits into Bosnia, he was now charged with what the French call "exfiltration," which is obtaining bogus documents for the former fighters so they could travel to carry out terrorist operations such as assassinations. It marked the next phase in Kamel's career as a jihadist. He had crossed the line from guerrilla warfare into full-blown terrorism.

Phone records show a flurry of calls in the months that followed between the Montreal jihad apartment on Place de la Malicorne, Kamel's home, and the Foundation for Human Rights and Humanitarian Relief, a Muslim charity in Turkey also known as IHH that was involved in passport and weapons trafficking. Then, in June 1996, a man named Laifa Khabou flew to Montreal on a mission to get black-market passports for four Islamic militants hiding in a ghetto in Istanbul. He was picked up at Mirabel airport and taken to the apartment, where he stayed with members of the Groupe Fateh Kamel. Atmani, whom the French call Kamel's "right-hand man," came up with three Moroccan passports, one short of the target, and Khabou left two weeks later. He took the passports to Belgium, where the photos were switched and delivered to Turkey.

In Milan, meanwhile, police were continuing to monitor the Islamic Cultural Institute, eavesdropping on two of its associates, Youcef Tanout and Rachid Fettar, coordinator of the European GIA network, in a new police probe code-named Operation Shabka. "Where is Moustapha the terrorist?" Tanout says in an intercepted phone call. "We don't see him anymore." On the evening of

August 6, 1996, a man whom Tanout and his associates identify as a Canadian arrives at Tanout's Milan apartment. At times they call him Moustapha, at other times Fateh. During the next four days, the men talk frequently and openly about terrorist activity related to the GIA and the global jihad. "I am not afraid of death, and killing does not scare me," Moustapha tells his hosts. "Long live the jihad!"

In conversations recorded that summer, the men discuss a terrorist attack in France. Moustapha asks Tanout if he has obtained "the powder." When Tanout says no, Moustapha replies, "What are you afraid of? That everything will explode on you? Tell me at least whether Mahmoud has taken the bottle of gas?" The three men describe how best to ship the explosives, which they refer to in code as shoes, to France. Moustapha proposes sending half by courier, but the others are uneasy with this. Tanout fears the "shoes" will be discovered. Moustapha appeases them, saying, "You send lots of things and you slip them inside."

"Have you hidden everything?" Moustapha asks. "Yes, in the truck," says Fettar. A few days after that conversation was recorded, Italian police raided the apartment and found two canisters of gas, a timer, five transmitters and thirty-eight metal cylinders that investigators said could have served as bomb containers. But Moustapha slipped away. Using video cameras hidden outside the apartment, Italian police would later identify Moustapha as Fateh Kamel.

Kamel traveled that fall to Bosnia, Germany and Turkey. In late 1996, he left home again for Bosnia, then flew to Istanbul, Belgium, Istanbul, back to Bosnia, then to Istanbul for a third time, and, finally, to Amsterdam, where he helped secure a fake passport for a former mujahedeen fighter before heading home. In 1997, he went back to Bosnia in March and April, then to Istanbul and Holland, returning to Montreal on April 24. And then his travels came to an abrupt stop. The end of his adventures coincided with the publication of a brief item in a Paris weekly magazine, *L'Évènement du Jeudi*, that linked Kamel to terrorism investigations in Italy and France. The article named Kamel as a veteran of combat in Afghanistan and Bosnia and a "big fish" ("*le gros poisson*") in the GIA, suspected of plotting terrorist attacks against France. It also noted possible links to a terrorist bombing at the

Port-Royal metro station in Paris that killed four and injured 122 (he was never charged for this), and linked him to the Groupe Roubaix through Caze.

Over the next few months, as French investigators delved into the workings of the Groupe Roubaix, they cracked the mujahedeen secret code. They discovered that phone numbers were recorded by replacing the digits 0 to 9 with the letters of the word m-o-h-s-a-l-e-d-i-n. (Saledin was the Muslim leader in the war against the Christian Crusaders in the twelfth century.) Once again, Kamel's name and telephone number turned up in several address books seized in raids on jihad cells in Belgium, Italy and Canada.

Canadian intelligence was by now closely monitoring Kamel, whom they considered a major player in the international Islamic extremist movement. Intelligence officers tailed Kamel and his hangers-on as they hung around mosques and coffee shops, and carried out their petty crimes. CSIS was fairly certain the proceeds of this theft and passport fraud were being funneled to the cause, but it was difficult to pin down. The main challenge were those on the periphery, like Ressam, who had no known past in jihad and whose link to the core of the cell seemed to be mostly criminal. The investigators' strategy was to focus on the figures at the centre of the group and hope that the rest would flow from there. Kamel seemed unaware he was being watched. CSIS agents thought he behaved as if he felt secure. Only once did one of Kamel's men confront an intelligence agent, accusing him of being a police officer. The agents even caught Kamel brazenly shoplifting. They passed the information to the RCMP, but the Mounties were not interested in petty crimes. That was the frustrating thing about counterterrorism investigations. CSIS could identify people with connections to terrorism, but they lacked the tools to really do anything about it. They knew about his travels, about his petty crime and his connections.

Telephone records, for example, showed calls between Kamel and Islamic terrorists. But strictly speaking, a terrorist is not a terrorist until it's too late. On what basis do you arrest somebody like Kamel, a Canadian citizen who had not killed anyone but who was clearly working to support the terrorist jihad? All they could do was keep watching him and his network, which required an incredible amount of manpower. As they watched, the CSIS agents made note of a man they considered a minor figure in the cell, more of a groupie than a hard-core jihadist. His name was Ahmed Ressam.

Ahmed Ressam, the firstborn son of a veteran of Algeria's independence war, grew up in Bou Ismael, fifty kilometers west of Algiers, in a poor neighborhood where the only hope was to emigrate. The graffiti scratched on the building walls betrays the preferred escape hatch: "Canada," it reads.

His father, Belkacem, was an observant Muslim who prayed five times a day. His mother and two sisters wore *hijab*. He had four brothers. They played soccer in the streets and went to school. His parents hoped Ahmed would qualify for a free university education, but he developed an ulcer as a child and the pain kept him out of school for so long that he failed the tests and had to settle for waiting on customers at his father's café. When the Algerian Islamist movement began recruiting in Bou Ismael, seeking volunteers for jihad, Ressam showed absolutely no interest, preferring the nightclub scene to the austerity of radical Islam. He made a decision to follow the advice of the graffiti. He went by boat to Corsica, where he made a living picking grapes and oranges and as a painter at a tourist resort, but he was soon identified as an illegal and was to be deported. Instead of leaving, he adopted a new identity, acquiring a doctored French passport in the name Tahar Medjadi. It worked. He boarded an Air Canada flight to Montreal, landing at Mirabel airport on February 20, 1994.

Upon his arrival, he was stopped by an immigration officer, who was suspicious of his passport. He admitted his real name and made a refugee claim in which he gave a concocted story about having been imprisoned in Algeria for arms trafficking and association with terrorists. Although this should have set off alarm bells in the immigration department, it didn't, and he was soon released. It would be just the first of the government's many mistakes in handling his case.

Ressam roomed at the Montreal YMCA at first, but then moved in with fellow Algerians, including Moustapha Labsi; Adel

Boumezbeur; and Karim Atmani, Fateh Kamel's deputy. He supplemented his welfare income with the proceeds from pickpocketing and passport theft. "I used to steal tourists, rob tourists," he said during court testimony in New York. "I used to go to hotels and find their suitcases and steal them when they're not paying attention ... I used to take the money, keep the money and if there are passports, I would sell them, and if there are Visa cards, I would use them up, and if there were any travelers' checks I would use them or sell them."

When he came across identity documents, such as Social Insurance cards, he would sell them to his friend Mokhtar Haouari. Ressam was arrested four times and convicted once. He paid a fine. During more than four years in Canada, Ressam held only one legitimate job, distributing advertising leaflets. He quit after a week.

On Fridays, Ressam attended a mosque where recruiting videos that called for martyrdom were distributed. "Come to Afghanistan," said one of the videos. "Come for jihad. If you are real believers, Allah is expecting you to do an extra job." CSIS agents were well acquainted with Ressam. "He was on our radar screen but he clearly wasn't the key," a former intelligence official said. But the time that Ressam spent at the knee of Fateh Kamel and Kamel's cell of veteran holy warriors got him to thinking about Afghanistan. "My friends came back and talked to me about the training that they had received, the learning that they have gotten, and about jihad, and I got, they encouraged me so I got interested." Abderaouf Hannachi, an Afghan-trained mujahedeen in Montreal, contacted Abu Zubayda, a recruiter in Peshawar who kept bin Laden's training camps supplied with eager young men, and told him Ressam was coming. In March 1998, Ressam bought a round-trip ticket to Karachi via Frankfurt. Before he left, he made sure he could return. Using a blank baptismal certificate stolen from the Notre-Dame-des-Sept-Douleurs parish, he forged a new identity as Benni Norris. Then he applied for a passport. The Canadian Passport Office was happy to comply.

That same month, a letter typed on a sheet of white paper was delivered to the Montreal police. It said biological and chemical weapons would be detonated at the Montreal subway and there was nothing anybody could do to stop it. The letter casually promised 1,000 people would die. It was signed World Islamic Front. Canadian authorities were not quite sure how to handle the threat. Some thought it a hoax. And then another letter arrived. And another. They were filled with radical Islamic rhetoric and references to the CIA. "There were multiple letters sent, each one of a threatening nature," said Staff Sergeant John Bureaux, the RCMP's top bomb expert, who was involved in the three-month operation. "The important thing was we felt they were doing surveillance on the Canadian authorities, the way we were responding. They said, 'We know how you're operating. You won't be able to defeat our means.'" Several people were eventually arrested and deported and, although no explosives were ever found, some of those involved were linked to Ressam.

Ressam's refugee case fell apart when he failed to appear for a hearing. He said he had just forgotten to show up. His claim was rejected, but it didn't matter. At the time the immigration department had placed a moratorium on deportations to Algeria because of the violence there. He didn't have to leave, but he did have to comply with conditions set out by immigration authorities, and even those he neglected. He failed to turn up for a meeting with an immigration officer and a warrant was issued for his arrest on June 2, 1998. By then, however, Ressam had already gone off to jihad.

During the Soviet war in Afghanistan, Peshawar became the gateway used by young Muslim volunteers who came from all over to fight holy war and, in the name of Allah, to die as martyrs. Later, the border town gave birth to the Taliban, and then it was the hub for Al Qaeda, the place where recruits were screened, indoctrinated and sent off into Afghanistan for terrorist training. The man in charge of this revolving door to jihad was Abu Zubayda, a Palestinian and one of bin Laden's most trusted aides.

"He receives young men from all countries," Ressam said of Zubayda. "He accepts you or rejects you. And he takes care of the expenses of the camps. He makes arrangements for you when you travel coming in or leaving." Nobody in the camps used their real names, so when Ressam arrived in Peshawar he became "Nabil." Zubayda accepted Ressam for training and wrote him a letter of introduction in the local Pashtun language. He told Ressam to grow a beard and gave him Afghani clothes. A car took him to the border and then, early in the morning, he and a guide set off by foot into the mountains. There were about a hundred people at Khaldun Camp—Saudis, Jordanians, Chechens, Algerians, Turks, a few French, Germans, Swedes and even a fellow Canadian. They were grouped by nationality, so Ressam went with the Algerians, who numbered about thirty. One of those he encountered during training was a man he knew as Zubeir Al-Maghrebi, a Moroccan. CSIS says Al-Maghrebi is actually Adil Charkaoui, a pizza shop owner from Montreal.

For the first month, the instructors showed Ressam how to use handguns, machine guns and RPGs. Then they moved on to explosives training. Ressam learned how to make bombs using TNT and C4, and how to use them in sabotage operations "to blow up the infrastructure of a country." The ideal targets were military bases, electrical plants, gas plants, railroads, corporations, hotels and airports. There were lessons on urban warfare, assassination techniques and surveillance. "When you go to a place you would wear clothing that would not bring suspicion to yourself, you would wear clothing that tourists wear. You would observe or you would also take pictures." And there was the required instruction about security, which impressed upon the recruits the requirement for absolute secrecy, that everyone should know only what they needed to know.

One day a sheet of paper was distributed showing a picture of Sheik Omar Abdel Rahman, and claiming he had issued a *fatwa* to "fight Americans and hit their interests everywhere." It is unlikely it came from the blind cleric, however. He was imprisoned in the United States for his role in the 1993 World Trade Center bombing. But such religious incitement was part of the training ritual, and one of the most important parts. Ressam's team crafted its attack plan. "We were all to meet in Canada and we were all to carry out operations of bank robberies and then get the money to carry out an operation in America; the discussion was about an airport, a consulate," he said.

Ressam moved to the Dharunta Camp near Jalalabad for another six weeks, learning bomb-making techniques: how to mix chemicals into a volatile cocktail; how to put together a circuit board into a detonator. They also experimented with chemical weapons. While Ressam watched wearing a face mask, his chief led a small dog into a box and placed a small quantity of cyanide inside. Then he added sulfuric acid. The dog was dead within five minutes. Imagine, the instructor told Ressam, what would happen if you placed this gas at the air intake of a building in America.

With six months of training under his belt, Ressam returned to Peshawar and went again to Abu Zubayda. They said their goodbyes and Zubayda asked him to send some Canadian passports. Ressam did not go home empty-handed. He carried with him US$12,000 in cash, a notebook with instructions on how to make a bomb, and a small amount of hexamine tablets and liquid glycol—bomb-making chemicals.

He flew to Los Angeles, where agents checked his Canadian passport and waved him through. While he waited for his connecting flight to Vancouver, it no doubt occurred to him that this was an opportunity to try out the surveillance techniques he was taught. At Vancouver International Airport, Ressam was admitted without difficulty by Customs and Immigration. When Ressam had left Canada, CSIS had notified virtually every intelligence service in the world. CSIS agents were watching for him in Canada, suspecting that he would eventually return. "We had our sources looking for him," an official said. But the intelligence service was not looking for a Canadian named Benni Norris. It was looking for an Algerian named Ahmed Ressam.

By the time Ressam returned to Canada, the Groupe Fateh Kamel was in serious trouble. Atmani had been arrested in Niagara Falls on charges of credit card fraud, and deported. Arrested with him was Ahcene Zemiri, one of Mokhtar Haouari's friends. (Zemiri later fled Canada for Afghanistan, where he was captured at Tora Bora and taken to Guantanamo Bay. During his detainee hearings, he told the U.S. military he had taken weapons training in Afghanistan "for fun.")

Kamel stayed put, at first. His Montreal lawyer, Joseph Elfassy, said Kamel was angered to discover that he was being called a terrorist by French investigators. Kamel also suspected that Canadian intelligence was watching him. "He is married, he had a kid, he was doing his thing and to me he looked like a gentleman. He was upset about what was happening to him, he was contesting, fighting; he wanted to sue everybody."

Kamel had moved his family out of Montreal, renting a brown duplex in Pincourt, a suburb of ten thousand that is close enough for daily commuting but far enough into the country to have signs marking the snowmobile crossings. The house had a big backyard that overlooked nothing but trees, and the place had a friendly, small-town feel. "He looked like a nice guy," his landlord, Pamphile Thibodeau, recalls. "He told me that his business was import-export. I had no trouble with him. I didn't see him very often."

Then, in March 1999, Kamel sold his St-Laurent boulevard craft store to an Algerian named Mokhtar Haouari, and bought a ticket to the Middle East. He was halfway through his journey when he was apprehended in Jordan and turned over to French authorities. Nathalie, his wife, told the *Toronto Star* at the time, "It's absurd what is happening. It's inconceivable what they are saying ... All I know is that when people go abroad to bring aid as Catholics, no one is suspicious. But if you go there as a Muslim, then people are suspicious."

Ressam stayed in Vancouver with an Algerian friend named Abdelmajid Dahoumane. His circle of friends also included Haouari, who was involved in a Visa-card scam with another Algerian, Samir Ait Mohamed. Samir had not trained in Afghanistan, but was eager to do so. His fervent wish was to go to Afghanistan to impart his knowledge of explosives to trainees at bin Laden's camps. He was passionate about the Islamic fundamentalists' uprising in Chechnya and spoke about joining the Chechen jihad. He told Dahoumane he could make explosives, and offered to do so if Dahoumane would plant them.

Ressam asked Samir to get him a gun so he could start making money with a robbery spree. Ressam specifically asked for a Scorpion pistol with a silencer, as well as hand grenades. Samir got him a 9mm Heckler & Koch instead, stolen of course. The plans initially hatched in Afghanistan began to go awry, however. The other cell members from Khaldun Camp could not get to Canada. Moustapha Labsi was stopped in Britain and arrested. Ressam called Abu Doha, an alleged Algerian terrorist cell ringleader in the United Kingdom who had also trained in Afghanistan, who told him the plans had changed. The others were going to stay in Europe. Ressam was on his own.

In August 1999, Ressam told Samir about his plans, and they discussed possible targets. Their first thought was to strike a Jewish neighborhood in Montreal. Samir suggested a suburb such as Outremont, and mentioned the area of rues Laurier and Parc because of all the Jews he had seen "walking about with long, curly sideburns." The bomb should be placed inside a gasoline truck to magnify its force, Samir said. But Ressam recalled his training in Afghanistan. Strike at the enemy's infrastructure, its companies, its military bases—its airports. He decided to bomb a U.S. airport—in fact, Los Angeles airport. The plan was almost naive in its simplicity. He would get a baggage cart, load a suitcase on it and leave it unattended, then observe how long it would take security to find it. Once he had the timing figured out, he would do it again, only this time the suitcase would not be empty. He bought a map of California and a tourist guide. Then, working from his apartment on rue du Fort in Montreal, he started building the electronic detonator, shopping at Radio Shack and Active Électronique for the circuit boards and wiring he needed to make the timer that would set off the explosive charge. He made four such timers, using Casio watches.

Jean-Louis Bruguiere, a French anti-terrorist judge, had been probing the Canadian link to the Groupe Roubaix since it emerged. He realized that Montreal had become a base for Algerian extremists and he turned for help to Canada. He had heard about Ressam in

1996, but back then Ressam was not a major player. Following Ressam's trip to Afghanistan, however, "there was a change in attitude and also [in] status. After the arrest of Fateh Kamel, Ressam moved in to fill the void, assuming a higher rank in the cell and a more direct operational role."

Bruguiere sent a letter to Canadian authorities in April 1999 concerning his investigation, but the RCMP took its time responding, and it was not until October that the paperwork was done and police finally searched Ressam's apartment. By that time the safe house on Place de la Malicorne had shut down. So police searched Adel Boumezbeur's new residence, on Sherbrooke. In addition to an array of stolen passports and credit cards, officers found photographs of Fateh Kamel, Nabil Ikhlef and others, as well as a Swiss bank book. Written inside the bank book was the number of a post-office box connected to Abu Zubayda; some phone numbers; and the addresses of an electronics store in Montreal and a chemical supplier, Evergro Products in Delta, British Columbia. The RCMP did not connect the dots, and simply passed the evidence to the French.

CSIS agents tried to find Ressam but he skillfully evaded them. "It's pretty hard to monitor somebody who is proceeding under a name that is different from the name you know," a high-ranking Canadian intelligence official told me. "Even if we knew he was here and heard rumors that he was here, you've still got to find him and you've got to find him under a name you don't know he has. This is a big country. You're trying to find a needle in a haystack."

A week after the search, Canadian authorities interviewed Abdellah Ouzghar at France's request. The interview was introduced at Ressam's trial. "If you do not want to convert to Islam, you will have to pay the *gisia*, meaning a certain amount of money," Ouzghar explained. "And we are going to take care of you, protect you. And if you do not want to convert or pay for the protection, it's war between the prophet and the country that refuses to convert to Islam." Ouzghar demanded that the court recess so he could pray. Judge Bruguiere's suspicions of a Canadian cell seemed to be right.

But where was Ressam?

On November 19, Ressam and Dahoumane checked in at the 2400 Motel in Vancouver. They took room 118. Using chemicals he had bought and stolen, Ressam began mixing up explosives on the kitchen table. Dahoumane was there to guide Ressam. He had done this before. He had been involved in a 1992 bombing in Algiers, at an airport. At one point, Ressam spilled one of the compounds, burning his thigh. The hotel maids noticed that although it was winter, he left the windows wide open. He would not let the maid into the back bedroom. Following the formula in the notebook he had brought from Afghanistan, he made a batch of hexamthylene triperoxide diamine (HMTD), a primary explosive. He poured it into a Tylenol bottle. He mixed up some cyclotrimethylene trinitramine (RDX) and poured it into a zinc lozenge bottle. And finally he blended a small quantity of secondary explosives, ethylene glycol dinitrate, which he put into an olive jar. To amplify the blast, he filled green garbage bags with urea and aluminum sulfate.

Ressam rented a car a Lo Cost Rent-A-Car, but returned it because the spare wheel well was too small. Instead he rented a green Chrysler 300M from Thrifty Car Rental. At the hotel parking lot, Ressam and Dahoumane removed the spare tire and packed the bomb into the cavity. On December 14, they boarded a BC Ferries vessel to Vancouver Island, and then parted. Dahoumane returned to Vancouver, while Ressam continued with the mission. He took a second ferry to Port Angeles, Washington. His car was the last off the ferry.

A U.S. Customs agent grew suspicious about the nervous-looking Canadian. When asked for proof of citizenship, Ressam handed over a Costco membership card. The agent ordered him to step out; he ran. He was tackled at a nearby intersection, where he was trying to car-jack a motorist stopped at a stoplight. He was soon identified as Ahmed Ressam. The bomb was found in the trunk. The agents also found, scrawled on paper, the phone number, in Pakistan, of one of bin Laden's closest aides. For years, Canadian intelligence agents had been investigating the Algerian network in Canada, but not until then did they realize that the GIA had become part of Al Qaeda and that it was using Canada to attack the United States. "That was in a sense the wake-up call of Ressam," a senior Canadian intelligence official told me.

The Ressam affair was an early indication of the coming war being planned by radical Islamists. Just as the Cold War began in Canada, when Soviet cipher clerk Igor Gouzenko defected in 1945 with a pile of documents that revealed the existence of a massive KGB spy network, so too did Ressam's capture begin to wake the West to the infiltration of Al Qaeda operatives trained for terror. Like Gouzenko, Ressam soon began to tell all, naming the members of his network, resulting in more arrests. The difference was that Canada did not have custody of Ressam. He was in U.S. hands, and Canadian agents would have access to him only through their American contacts. And his boss was in the hands of the French.

The man who represents Fateh Kamel's only shot at persuading the French court it's got the wrong guy is an elderly, stooped lawyer with a musty office above the crowded sidewalk cafés on boulevard St-Germain, in Paris's Latin Quarter. On a clear, sunny afternoon a few days before the conclusion of Kamel's trial, Mourad Oussedik shuffles slowly to his simple wooden desk and lights a cigarette. A native Algerian, Oussedik is a self-avowed left-wing lawyer who has represented accused Islamic militants for years. In the course of his human rights work, he has succeeded in freeing scores of war prisoners held in Morocco under deplorable conditions. His firm also represented Carlos the Jackal. (Unsuccessfully, it turns out. Carlos was jailed for life in 1997 for the 1975 murder of two French intelligence operatives.)

With its two old chairs and ghetto blaster atop a bookcase, Oussedik's office is the workplace of a man who lacks either the taste or the money for the material trappings of the legal profession. There is not even a sign outside identifying the law firm. Those who need him know where to go. He recalls how a letter arrived at his office. Kamel had written it from his cell at La Santé prison, seeking the veteran lawyer's help. As he dug into the case, Oussedik became convinced Kamel was innocent, or at least that he had broken no laws in France. "Mr. Kamel has done nothing wrong," he says. Kamel may have innocently met Islamists during his travels, the lawyer says, but there is no evidence he was complicit in acts of terrorism.

Oussedik suspects the United States is to blame for Kamel's troubles. FBI agents came to Paris to try to convince Kamel to appear as a government witness against Ressam in Los Angeles, the lawyer says. Kamel would not talk. Oussedik says the CIA was obviously behind them. He does not elaborate, but the implication is that he sees the trial as Fateh Kamel's punishment. Oussedik's legal strategy is not entirely clear. He rarely shows up for court and, when he does, he does not look actively engaged in the proceedings. By the final week of the trial, a younger lawyer is speaking on his behalf. Not that it matters. In France's legal system, the judge leads the trial, asking questions, arguing with the witnesses. The defence lawyers seem more like spectators than advocates.

On the final afternoon of Kamel's testimony, national police in blue kepi hats pace the sidewalks outside the Palais de Justice, a sand-colored fortress that occupies the western half of Île de la Cité, the narrow island that separates Paris's chic Right Bank from its bohemian Left Bank. A black, wrought-iron fence encircles its perimeter. Gargoyles grimace from the steeple of the chapel in the courtyard. Across the plaza, the spires of Notre-Dame Cathedral reach for the high winter clouds. Kamel wears a light-brown jacket over a black turtleneck. He appears to have trimmed his beard and hair. As Kamel waits for the proceedings to begin, a young lawyer sitting near him takes a clear plastic bag out of her leather purse and places a wad of chewing tobacco under her lower lip. At 2:13 p.m., the presiding judge rings the door buzzer announcing her arrival and those in the courtroom rise as she takes her place behind the mountain of folders strewn across her desk. She reads aloud the charges against Kamel, and asks if he has ever gone by the name El-Fateh. "No," he says. Moustapha? Again, "No."

The judge turns quickly to events in Milan in August 1996. The prosecution reads from transcripts that it says describe the buildup to a terrorist attack in France. "We need lots of money," Moustapha says in one transcribed conversation, recorded with a secret microphone by Italian police. Then, dispensing with the practicalities of the mission at hand, Moustapha begins to vent. "You know, people imagine a Muslim on the back of a camel, four women behind him, and bombs that explode ... terrorists, terrorists, terrorists. But all these problems are the result of the publicity of the Christian world on the GIA, but why don't they say jihad? There's a big difference." To his mind, terrorism and violent jihad are not synonymous.

There are more mundane discussions about the movement of light weapons, referred to in code as tomatoes, and black-market passports that can be purchased for $3,000 from Algerians in Montreal. In the candid conversations, captured on tape, Moustapha casts himself as a fearless jihadist, willing to do anything for the cause.

"I am GIA," he says. "Killing is easy for me."

But just before leaving Milan, his bravado slips and he laments his difficult life as a militant. "I almost lost my wife. I am thirty-six years old, with a son four-and-a-half months old. My wife is playing with him and I am here. I am almost a soldier. I don't know if I am going left or right."

It's as if the Canadian holy warrior wants out.

In court, standing in the prisoner's box, Kamel maintains with convincing indignation that he is not Moustapha. He says he hardly knows Ressam and Atmani, and visited them only a handful of times. He has never heard of the Islamic Cultural Institute and has never met anyone named Fettar or Tanout—although when shown the secret police photos of "Moustapha," he concedes that "it's possible" it is he. He says his phone card was stolen, which may explain why suspicious calls were on his phone bill.

"What have I done?" he pleads. "For two years I have been here. Tell me, what have I done, Madam Judge ... I was not arrested with weapons. Not once! Not once did I have false papers, not once had a weapon."

The judge looks at Kamel like a teacher addressing an errant pupil. She says that, in effect, what he is saying is that there is someone who looks like Kamel, who uses his name and phone, and travels to the same destinations at the same time, but that it is not really Kamel. Kamel rubs his eyes, folds his arms, and hangs his head. At the end of the trial, the prosecutor demands a ten-year sentence, saying Kamel "is an important member of the GIA, in league with the international jihad" and that he "sought out false documents for terrorist actions targeting France."

On April 6, 2001, Kamel was convicted on all counts and sentenced to eight years. Sixteen others were convicted, including Ressam and Adel Boumezbeur, who both received five-year sentences. Since then, almost every suspected member of the so-called Groupe Fateh Kamel has been arrested. They were just "people at the wrong place at the wrong time," maintains Joseph Elfassy, who has acted as a lawyer for both Kamel and Haouari. "Guilt by association," he calls it. "I know the other one who bought [the store] from Haouari is twenty-four hours under surveillance. He doesn't know what to do." Elfassy continues, "The more guys like you publish and do things, the better it is for newspapers and the better it is for police officers." Why would police arrest innocent men? He replies, "The system is based on frenzy."

Trying to make sense of the terrorist underworld is like peering into a murky version of Plato's cave, where the closest you get to truth is to observe the faint shadows cast on the wall by firelight. State counterterrorism work is shrouded in official secrecy, and international terrorists are equally hard to pin down. They wander invisibly through Western cities, meeting at mosques and safe houses, planning their activities unnoticed. Sometimes they don't do anything suspicious at all. They simply wait—try to melt into Ottawa or Montreal as best as they can, and keep off the radar screen until the time is right to strike. If luck prevails, or if investigators have good informants, ask the right questions and chase the right leads, the attack might be stopped. In the case of the Groupe Fateh Kamel, if Ahmed Ressam had not been so nervous when he was crossing the Canada–U.S. border, he might have slipped through and realized his devastating millennial bombing plan. And that is perhaps the most frightening aspect of the jihad: that a collection of shopkeepers and low-level crooks have proved such an even match for the world's most advanced counterterrorist forces.

Still, it is not easy to reconcile the terrorist described in the evidence with the dejected Canadian being cuffed by gendarmes and led out of the prisoners' cage back to his cell at La Santé jail. This is, after all, a man who refused on principle to sell cigars or parrot mobiles. When Kamel was arrested, police found a photo of a young girl inside his address book. Written on the back was: "For Uncle Fatah and Nathalie and of course Karim," an innocent inscription from an adoring niece. During his initial interrogation, Oussedik says, Kamel wept. It's not clear for whom, or for what, he was crying.

Perhaps the answer can be found in the gap between the way the Western world views terrorists, as dangerous lunatics, and their noble self-image. The jihadists see themselves as freedom fighters, holy warriors willing to make the ultimate sacrifice for the cause. They know they are expendable, and when one falls, there are others to take his place. In a conversation with a police informant, Abdel Ghani Meskini, the man who had been assigned to help Ahmed Ressam in the United States, made a bold statement. "Allah will shake up this world," he said. "A new generation will punish America." Some thought it was no more than bravado. They could not have imagined, back then, that Al Qaeda meant exactly what it said.

Four years after Kamel was convicted and sent away, I walked up the front steps of a Montreal townhouse and rang the bell. A bearded man wearing jeans and a white sweater answered the door. He looked older and wearier than the last time I saw him, but it was Kamel. Since returning to Canada on January 29, 2005, after completing his prison sentence in France, he has kept a low profile, although he has taken the Canadian Passport Office to court.

When he returned to Montreal, Kamel applied for a new Canadian passport. The Passport Office refused to grant him one due to his involvement in the use of fraudulent documents for terrorist purposes. At the time of this writing, the case was still working its way through the courts. But I was the first journalist to track him down to the street where he lives with his wife and son. He told me his trial in Paris was "cinema" and that he did nothing more than help Bosnians during the civil war. "I went to help in Bosnia because the media was showing a lot of atrocities against the Bosnians," he said. "We helped them and now we are war criminals." He denied knowledge of Ressam. "I don't know him. I've seen him here like anybody. He's in the hands of American justice. They do their work."

"It's not my problem."

5

A BRIEF ENCOUNTER WITH A
(SUSPECTED) CANADIAN TERRORIST

THE ROAD that winds high into the cypress hills above Beirut cuts
through mountain villages where Lebanese escape the heat of summer, then comes to a dead end at the Roumieh prison, a massive
complex that looks fashioned after the castles of forgotten empires
scattered in the stark deserts to the east. Soldiers clad in desert camouflage and blood-red berets guard the prison gates. Visiting women
and children wait in lines at the guard posts, trying to balance the
plastic shopping bags filled with bananas and cigarettes that they
are carrying for their jailed husbands and fathers. Inside, a fountain
gurgles in a sunny courtyard encircled by dark cell windows, from
which the prison laundry hangs like white flags of surrender.

It is visiting hour. The inmates flood into a long, narrow room
where they are separated from their loved ones by whitewashed iron
bars and mesh. There are so many people in the visiting room that
everyone has to shout to be heard, and the result is a deafening chorus of Arabic and French, as husbands and wives, boyfriends and
girlfriends, fathers and sons and daughters exchange yells of affec-
tion until their voices go hoarse.

The metal door opens and Kassem Daher pushes through the
crowd, stopping when he stands opposite me. He is wearing glasses with large frames and a golf shirt with a red maple leaf crest.
Not long ago, Daher was a successful businessman, the owner of

cinemas; he was a family man and a respected member of the community. But his life has become a hopeless routine of bad meals, bad sleep and sporadic prison visits. Lebanon claims he is an Islamic holy warrior, the leader of a terrorist cell loyal to Osama bin Laden. Intelligence agents have long suspected his involvement in the jihad, and have linked him to Al Qaeda extremists.

"I used to have the best life in Canada," he says, screaming to be heard above the chatter. "I had movie theaters, everything. I have four Canadian kids. My wife is Canadian too.

"I am Canadian."

The civil war that ripped apart Lebanon and made it synonymous with terrorism and kidnapping left its indelible mark on Beirut. The reminders are everywhere, from the gutted high-rises pock-marked with bullet holes to the scarred memories of bitter survivors. The country is in the midst of a massive reconstruction, but it is far from complete. Modern buildings sprout along the Mediterranean waterfront and the city known for its car bombings now has a Virgin Records Megastore and a McDonald's, Burger King and Starbucks. The war, however, just doesn't seem to go away.

Traveling through Beirut, my car is overtaken by a Mercedes covered with radio antennae and filled with bearded men. "Hezbollah," my translator, a local journalist, says. Hezbollah still controls parts of Beirut and South Lebanon, and in the Bekaa Valley I see truckloads of Syrian troops in simple green fatigues. The newspapers this morning are reporting on the assassination of a Christian warlord. A Lebanese group opposed to Syria's military presence has claimed responsibility, but everyone blames the Israelis.

Adnan Adoum has six telephones in his office in the justice building. One of them, presumably for emergency calls, is fire-engine red. He is Lebanon's prosecutor-general and has a big wooden desk cluttered with law texts, a bowlful of gold-wrapped candy, a bottle of water, a vase of roses and a silver statue of an eagle. A Lebanese flag sits on a stand and a portrait of the Lebanese president, Emile Lahoud, hangs on the wood-paneled wall. Adoum gestures for me to sit on his black leather couch.

He knows why I have come calling.

The Canadian at Roumieh prison is accused of the worst sort of crimes. Kassem Daher, Adoum says, was an "emir" of an Islamic terrorist group that tried to overthrow the government by force. "You know what is an emir?" he says, making sure I am following him. "It means a prince."

This prince was part of a group of hard-core Islamists that wanted to turn Lebanon into an Islamic state. They were led by a veteran of the war in Afghanistan named Abou Aycha. Daher, the businessman, collected money for the group in Canada, although Adoum could not say how much. Daher came to Lebanon and met Bassem Kenj, another of the leaders of the insurgency. Then he traveled to South Lebanon and met a weapons dealer at a Palestinian refugee camp to arrange the purchase of firearms, Adoum says.

Late in 1999, the insurgents established a paramilitary training camp in the Bekaa Valley at the start of Ramadan, the Muslim holy month, and called on Muslims to join the jihad. The Lebanese security services got word and moved in to dismantle the operation. Fighting broke out at Tripoli. The Muslim warriors fought hard, and most were either killed or injured. The last thing Lebanon wanted was another civil war; it did not take kindly to yet another insurrection, particularly one led by Sunni fundamentalists such as Daher.

By February 2000, the Lebanese were moving aggressively to crush the Islamists. Fifty Lebanese troops descended on Karaoun, in the Bekaa Valley. A gunfight ensued—local press accounts called it "spectacular"—and nine suspected Muslim extremists were caught. The soldiers came to Kassem Daher's home at 4 a.m., his mother Umm Kassem told me. "And that was it. He was wearing his pajamas."

A search of the village turned up four caches of weapons— rocket-propelled grenades, mortars, mines, explosives, detonators. "We found a lot of arms," Adoum says. "These people had light and heavy weapons." During their search, the army came to the home of another Canadian, Ahmed Aboughousch, a young computer expert from Edmonton who ran an Internet café in the Bekaa Valley and was married to one of Daher's cousins.

"They were asking, 'Where's Ahmed, where's Ahmed?' and I said 'Why do you want him? He hasn't done anything',", his mother, Fatima Aboughousch, told me. When Ahmed got home, the soldiers had left, but his mother told him they were looking for him. "I said, 'Are you sure, my son, you haven't done anything?' and he said, 'No, I'm going to go see what they want.' And he went and he never came back."

The Canadians faced charges of participating in an organization seeking to overthrow the Lebanese government by force. "They collected money and they prepared arms and they were readying to fight, when it was time." Daher was also looking at more severe charges because of his leadership role in the movement.

Adoum says while he has no solid proof that Osama bin Laden was ultimately responsible for the violence, such a conclusion was a logical deduction. Indeed, deduction is one of the only ways to get at the truth behind the rebellion, because most of the fighters were killed. "All of them were determined to fight to the end," Adoum says. The insurgents, he notes, were members of a group called Takfir wal Hijra, a radical Sunni group with ties to bin Laden, although CSIS says Daher is actually a member of Asbat al-Ansar.

Adoum seems remarkably talkative for a prosecutor-general, and when he speaks about Daher there is no doubt in his voice: "I know that this man collected money for this organization. He had good contacts outside Lebanon."

"How can you be sure?" I ask.

He looks at me as if I am the only one who does not know. "This man has confessed."

The name Kassem Daher first surfaced publicly in connection with terrorism in a report by CSIS, which described him as a "contact" of Mahmoud Jaballah, a Toronto refugee claimant and member of the Egyptian Al Jihad who had links to the Canadian Al Qaeda terrorist Essam Marzouk. "On February 3, 2000, Kassem Daher was arrested along with eight other individuals in the Bekaa Valley, Lebanon following clashes with Lebanese authorities," the report said. "Those arrested were tied to an Islamic extremist group."

A Brief Encounter with a (Suspected) Canadian Terrorist

Later, I went to Jaballah's trial at the Federal Court of Canada in Toronto and watched as a CSIS officer identified only as "Mike" testified about Daher. "My Lord, Kassem Daher is a Canadian citizen," Mike said. "He is believed to be a member of a particular Islamic extremist organization that was operating in Lebanon. Prior to February 2000 there was an effort on behalf of the Lebanese to try to contain the level of terrorist operations or terrorist organizations that were operating out of Lebanon. At one point there was a gunfight between this particular religious extremist group that Mr. Daher was attached to and Lebanese forces.

"It is our assessment, my Lord," he continued, "that anybody who had significant contact with Mr. Kassem Daher would likely be part of that particular Islamic extremist organization."

Intrigued by these vague mentions of a Canadian doing such things in Lebanon, I set off to find out more about Kassem Daher. In Ponoka, Alberta, I found his sister, Samira, who told me how the family had originated in the Bekaa Valley, but like many Lebanese, a sizable people in a tiny country, they had headed overseas in search of opportunities. Daher's father opened a general store in Colombia that sold "everything and anything," she said. "From clothes to shoes to perfume, just name it."

Kassem Daher was fourteen when he moved to South America, but he did not stay. At some point he traveled north to Alberta, at first to visit his sisters and his brother, Yaya. Impressed, Kassem went home to Lebanon, applied to immigrate, and returned in the late 1980s as a business-class immigrant. He settled in Leduc, a town of fifteen thousand just south of Edmonton, and in 1990 bought the Leduc Twin Theatres through his company, Afendy Theatres Ltd. He was a 33 percent owner and a director. His wife, Badar, was also a director. They remained active in the company until May 1998.

"He worked at the theater, he was the manager of the theater," the current manager responded when I asked about Daher. "He worked here four years ago, he used to manage the theater." But, like everyone else I spoke to about Daher, the cinema manager clearly did not want to talk about the man. "I'm sorry, sir, you're asking too many questions and I will not help you any more."

Daher bought a second Alberta cinema in 1994, the Capitol Theatre in Ponoka, a town of six thousand between Red Deer and Edmonton. He signed the sale papers to purchase the tiny cinema, a heritage building across the street from the railway tracks, but the owner is listed as Daher Bros. Daher used to go to mosque in Edmonton, which is where he met Ahmed Aboughousch, also a native Lebanese, who had moved to Canada as an infant, grown up in Edmonton and studied at the Northern Alberta Institute of Technology. Daher and Aboughousch would sometimes talk after Friday prayers.

By 1993, Daher was being investigated for his role in a network that financed and recruited for jihadist conflicts in Afghanistan, Bosnia, Chechnya, Somalia and even Eritrea. Using a group called the Canadian Islamic Association as a cover, U.S. authorities allege, he worked with several U.S. contacts, notably Kifah Jayyousi, to send money and recruits overseas—or in the words of U.S. prosecutors, to "murder, maim and kidnap."

A follower of the "blind sheikh," Omar Abdel Rahman, Daher published a booklet titled *Terrorism is a Duty and Force is an Obligation*. Intelligence agencies infiltrated his group and monitored his telephone calls as he "communicated and coordinated with mujahedin field commanders and violent jihad leaders overseas," prosecutors allege. He often spoke in code, but sometimes he was open. "As long as there is slaughtering, we're with them," he said in one 1995 conversation. "If there's no slaughtering, there's none ... that's it, buzz off."

After the death of his father in Lebanon, Daher returned to his home village, ostensibly to care for his mother. He took his wife and children too, all of them Canadians. At about the same time, Aboughousch, then twenty-four, went to a village eight kilometers away called Lala, also to care for his elderly parents, who had decided to return to Lebanon. "They liked the old country better and he went along with them, just to take care of them," said his brother Mohammed. Aboughousch married Daher's cousin, Sarab, and they had a son.

The two Canadians spent less than a year in Lebanon before being arrested. "He spent one year there and boom!" Samira said in January 2002. "They just pick up whoever they want. There is no law there. We don't know anything yet. They told us this year we will know, but we are hoping because there is nothing so far against them. I'm here and they are there so it's hard to know, all I know is there is no case against them. They haven't been charged with anything."

Despite his circumstances, Kassem Daher plays the role of the charming host, as if welcoming me to his home in the prison.

"I'm fine," he says. "Very good. They treat us very well."

"What about the allegations against you, that you tried to overthrow the government?" I ask.

"That's not true at all," he says. "My main reason to come here was to care for my mother."

He says he wants nothing more than to move back to Alberta and resume the life he had before returning to Lebanon. "This is my intention. My family want to move back." Canadians often remark that traveling abroad makes them appreciate the life they have in Canada, and I sense that Daher feels this way too. "We are very proud to be Canadians. I used to have the best life there, movie theaters, everything."

The allegations are "all politics," he says. He denies ever fundraising in Canada for terrorism. Sure he collected money, he says, but it was for charity. CSIS agents came to his mosque at one point asking questions, he says. "I told them I'm a Muslim, that's true, but I'm a Canadian. That's very important to me." Besides, he adds, he has an argument that proves the accusations could not possibly be true. "They said we are radicals," he says. "Radicals never watch movies."

The Canadians were taken at first to Beirut and held in the basement of a defense ministry building that was so filthy the inmates contracted a skin disease. Daher and Aboughousch claim they were tortured and forced to sign confessions they had not read. Aboughousch says he was kept standing for three days and denied access to a lawyer until he signed the confession. He claims he signed the paper even though he did not know what it said. "I basically had no choice," he says. The prisoners went on hunger strike to protest their conditions and, after six months, were transferred to a regular prison to await trial.

The court hearings opened in the fall of 2000 but have moved slowly, in part because the cases involving two dozen alleged members of the terror group are being heard simultaneously. "The judgment is going to take some time," says Bassam El Halabi, Aboughousch's Beirut lawyer. "I came here for a humanitarian cause and this is where I end up," Aboughousch says, sounding disgusted but resigned. "This is a made-up story. They say I belong to this group? I've never seen them in my life."

"It's a political issue, 100 percent," says Mohamed Khaled, a British doctor who is also among those arrested on identical allegations. He too says he returned to Lebanon from London at the request of his parents. He claims he was arrested because his phone number was found on a militant. He says he signed a confession only after soldiers threatened to rape his wife and make him watch. "Actually, I was thinking of going back to the U.K. three days before they arrested me."

Working against these men, however, are a few untimely and unfortunate incidents. First, a car belonging to the judge hearing their case was blown up, raising obvious suspicions. Then seven cabinet ministers received written death threats from militants claiming to represent the imprisoned men. "The situation does not look good," Aboughousch admits. On May 14, 2003, Lebanese authorities arrested nine Islamists they said were planning to attack the U.S. embassy and kidnap officials in order to free those arrested in the 2000 uprising.

It is difficult to tell whether these are just remarkably unlucky men, or whether they are doing what most criminals do—deny all and hope for the best. Many Islamic terrorists confess when confronted because they don't believe they have done anything wrong; they were simply fulfilling God's will. Then again, if you need to lie to carry out the holy commands of God, why not? For a terrorist who is willing to kill, lying is a small thing.

I put each of the allegations to Daher and he denies them all. He doesn't know Mahmoud Jaballah. He never bought arms from the Palestinians in South Lebanon. In fact, he says he has never even been to South Lebanon. And he was not part of any Islamic uprising.

"I have nothing to do with this," he says. "This is the truth."

Karoun is just off the main north-south highway that runs through the Bekaa Valley, bookended by the Mount Lebanon range to the west and the Anti-Lebanon mountains, beyond which Syria lies. The Daher home is tucked behind an auto shop, and you have to pass a graveyard of car wrecks to reach the driveway. It is a palatial home, worthy of any upscale California neighborhood, overlooking an olive grove, lake and mountains. The house was built for eight, and has a four-car garage. I knock on the door but nobody answers, although I can hear activity inside. Finally, the kids come out onto the balcony above me and ask what I want. There are three girls and one boy, aged ten, twelve, fourteen and fifteen. "I want to go home," one of the girls says, "I don't like it here."

"It's very difficult for me to raise the children on my own," Mrs. Daher says. But she will not say any more. I wait, hoping to wear her down. Eventually the children emerge and I join them in a game of basketball. Still, the mother will not talk to me. I take out my camera to photograph the home, and the grandmother emerges. She yells angrily, berating me in Arabic.

"He's a good boy," she says of her son. "His father died and he came so he could look after me. At least give him a trial so we know where he stands.

"This is malicious. This is all lies. They came to the sons of Karoun, they take money from them and then they stick this accusation to them.

"This is a religious family and we don't play around with militias."

Down the road in Lala, Sarab Aboughousch invites me in for coffee. We sit in a living room with a wood stove and a Sony television set as her two-year-old with flaming-red hair plays. Sarab pulls out her wedding album and turns the page to a photograph of herself in her white bridal gown. The photo had been ripped in half, so that there was no groom. "The army came and tore this off so they could have a picture of Ahmed," she says. Her life has likewise been torn apart—whether by terrorism or the overzealous fight against it, it is difficult to tell.

Six months later, on August 20, 2002, Aboughousch was released. The Lebanese had completed their investigation and decided not to lay charges. He phoned the diplomats at the Canadian embassy in Beirut three days later to thank them for their help. Daher was later released from the Roumieh prison, but remains a wanted man.

U.S. Attorney General Alberto Gonzales announced on November 22, 2005, that Daher had been indicted for terrorism, murder conspiracy and conspiracy to kidnap, but he is unlikely to ever stand trial, because Lebanon and the United States do not have an extradition treaty. His friends in Canada say he is now living in his village in the Bekaa.

He is apparently wanted by Canada as well. After the September 11 attacks, the RCMP sent out a request through Interpol for information on eight people, including Daher. The notice described Daher as an associate of Hassan Farhat, the former imam at the Salaheddin mosque in Toronto who had gone off to northern Iraq to join the Ansar Al Islam. It added that Daher was "a partner" of a man named Ahmed Said Khadr.

6

THE AL KANADI FAMILY JIHAD

THE INTERSECTION of Kennedy Road and Eglinton Avenue East is all parking lots, strip malls and dull apartment blocks. In the eighteenth century, this was called Glasgow Township until Elizabeth Simcoe, the wife of Upper Canada's first lieutenant-governor, remarked that it reminded her of Scarborough in North Yorkshire, and the name stuck.

Today, northwest Scarborough is a mixed bag of cultures, a home for the world's displaced where businesses with names such as Good Luck Chinese Restaurant, Yoga's Supermarket and Filipino Cuisine compete for customers on the same strip. More than half of Scarborough's 550,000 residents are visible minorities and immigrants, mostly from China and South Asia, but also the Caribbean, the Philippines, Latin America, the Arab world, Japan and Korea. The result is a disorienting community where store signs are as likely to be in Tamil or Arabic as in English, and it would be easy to forget what country this is, if not for the Canada Post building and the Tim Hortons.

Beneath two hulking transformer towers, on a corner lot surrounded by chain-link fencing, a mosque dome rises from a pale blue building that looks like a hockey arena. Atop the dome sits a crescent moon, the universal symbol of Islam. The sign at the gate reads, Salaheddin Islamic Centre. It is one of Toronto's largest mosques, the place of worship for thousands of devotees, among them several suspected of involvement in the Al Qaeda network, including the former Imam Hassan Farhat (now believed to be dead); Amer El-Maati, wanted by the FBI for a plot to hijack a plane in Canada and crash it into an American building; Mahmoud Jaballah, a member of the Egyptian Al Jihad who served as principal of the mosque school; Fahim Ahmad and several other young men arrested on terror charges on June 2, 2006; as well as Ahmed Said Khadr.

Khadr lived a few blocks away, on Khartoum Avenue, in his mother-in-law's small brick house. The street is wide and open, with a few short maples and firs, surrounded by tall apartments. The untended yard is full of dandelions with a patch of tulips—red like the Canadian flag—hanging from the front porch. "Western blood is very expensive and our blood is very cheap," the woman of the house, Fatimah Elsamnah, tells me. She is talking about the war in Afghanistan, which she clearly does not support. Instead of bombing the Taliban and Al Qaeda, the Americans should be asking themselves why they were attacked, she says. "If something wrong happen to me, I will ask myself first before I go and punish somebody because I must have done something wrong."

She is worried because her daughter, Maha, and six grandchildren were in Afghanistan with Khadr, who calls himself an aid worker, when the Americans went to war. She has not heard from them since. "Nothing, nothing for some time now," she says.

She is fully aware of the accusations that have dogged her family, that Khadr, also known as Abu Abdurahman Al Kanadi, is close to Osama bin Laden, that his charity is just a cover for his activities in support of Islamic fundamentalism, that he is the hub of the Canadian Al Qaeda network. According to one CSIS report, "Khadr is a close associate of bin Laden and is reported to have had contact with bin Laden in Afghanistan."

"Why you treat us like that?" she responds. "When they do that they push people to be bad. If you are good and do something good and you try to be a good person and they always accuse you for something else, maybe you're going to go and be this person or do something bad.

"Like if you always see someone and you said, 'You are a killer, you are a killer,' he's going to be a killer one day."

If there is one world event that can be said to have shaped the current state of international terrorism more than any other, it is the 1979 Soviet invasion of Afghanistan. That one conflict radicalized scores of young Muslims all over the world, who saw in Kabul an assault on their religion, and by communists no less.

Moved by the plight of the Afghans, both those who fled and those who fought, Muslims formed a series of Islamic aid organizations to assist. But many of these were used, mainly by wealthy Saudis, to channel money to the mujahedeen holy warriors in Afghanistan and Pakistan. The charities were also frequently used as fronts for moving fighters into the Afghan war zone. If a Muslim youth wanted to fight jihad in Afghanistan, he was accredited as a representative of a Saudi aid group so he could get the required travel visas.

Ahmed Khadr was living in Ottawa when the war broke out. He had moved to Canada from Egypt in 1975, studied computers at the University of Ottawa and worked at Bell Northern Research. He married Maha Elsamnah, the daughter of Palestinian immigrants who ran a bakery in Scarborough. They started a family, but when war broke out in Afghanistan, he could think of nothing else. The stories of communist invasion and the suffering of refugees had a powerful effect on him. He joined a Muslim aid organization called Human Concern International (HCI), which had formed a year after the war started, and became regional manager of its Pakistan office, which was supposed to provide relief to refugees displaced by the fighting. Its money came from Muslim donors in Canada as well as the Canadian International Development Agency (CIDA), the humanitarian aid arm of the government of Canada.

Once he had traveled to Pakistan, Khadr was hooked. For a devout Muslim, the war was the perfect mission. It brought to life everything preached in the more radical mosques of the Arab world—the oppression of Muslims by a non-Muslim force and the duty of jihad to aid the afflicted and defend the faith. Afghanistan was the land of jihad.

Khadr would arrive early at his office and stay until nightfall, talking on the radio to the mujahedeen on the war front, assessing the needs of the refugees and soliciting donations. An acquaintance described him as a "burning flame, full of enthusiasm," who "wanted to give whatever [he] could to [his] brothers who were raising the flag of jihad." Khadr was so impassioned by the Afghan war that he moved his family to a compound in Peshawar, where he had established an HCI office. Soon after arriving, Khadr met a tall Saudi from a wealthy family who, like himself, had come to participate in the great jihad. His name: Osama bin Laden. "He knew Osama bin Laden," Khadr's daughter Zaynab told me during one of our interviews in Pakistan. "If you want to say they were friends, well, they were friends twenty years ago."

In 1986, Khadr wrote an angry letter to the *Ottawa Citizen* lamenting the lack of aid for the Afghan refugees, who by then numbered in the millions. "Will we as Canadians encourage our government, ourselves and other relief agencies to support the Afghan refugees today in their distress?" Human Concern International was building a compound called Hope Village, which would accommodate women and children displaced by the war, feed them and educate them, he wrote. There was to be accommodation for widows and orphans; health care; social services. He ended by asking for donations. "We issue tax-deductible receipts."

Tim Deagle was a young freelance journalist when he heard about Hope Village. It was the winter of 1988 and he was killing time in Pakistan, waiting for the Soviets to withdraw so he could go into Afghanistan with the mujahedeen. He was stringing for Canadian publications, so he decided to pay a visit to Khadr and write a story about the work of his charity. He tried again and again to reach HCI by telephone but was never able to get an appointment, which he found odd because the other nonprofit groups working with Afghan refugees were desperate for media attention. One day he arrived unannounced at the charity's office in Peshawar. It was just a room with a broken computer. A group of young men armed with AK-47s sat on the floor drinking chai.

He told them he wanted to visit Hope Village but he did not get the sense they were eager to assist. Three weeks passed before he got the okay to visit the refugee camp.

Two hours outside Peshawar, near the border of Afghanistan, he came to the entrance. It was marked by a shabby sign with the words Hope Village written in English. Deagle had seen many refugee camps but none quite like this. "There was absolutely fuck all there," he told me. It was run-down, with little in the way of humanitarian activity; Deagle saw a group of about two dozen kids weaving carpets and a lot of heavily armed young men. "All they did in Hope Village was weave carpets," he said. "It was politicized, militaristic and it smacked of Hezb-i-Islami," the armed faction of Gulbuddin Hekmatyar, a strongly anti-Western Afghan warlord.

Deagle shot one roll of film and left. But he still wanted an interview with Khadr, so he kept calling. Three weeks later, he was told to go to the Islamabad Marriott and wait. A van filled with armed men picked up Deagle and a colleague at 11 p.m. They weaved through the empty streets before turning into an alley in Rawalpindi that was guarded by two fighters. He found it bizarre that all this was necessary just to speak to the head of a Canadian charity. "The whole thing was so cloak-and-dagger," he said. "I mean, he was getting millions from the Canadian government! This was like a covert operation."

The journalists were taken into an upstairs room and offered tea. Khadr showed up forty-five minutes later. He looked nervous. Deagle began asking questions about Hope Village, what it was doing and the number of children living there. "He knew nothing whatsoever. It was absolutely ridiculous," Deagle said. But Khadr was sure about one thing: he needed more money. It became clear to Deagle that Khadr was using him to solicit money from donors in Canada for a camp that did not appear to be doing much of anything. "He was not a very nice man; he wasn't polite," he added. When Deagle ended the interview, Khadr did not shake his hand.

A Canadian government official who met Khadr and toured his aid project had a similar experience. "Visiting HCI was an eye-opener. Massive facilities with almost no one around, as if he had cleared everybody out before our visit. All of his colleagues were dual passport holders, Canada and Egypt." The official recalled "sitting in a briefing room in Islamabad one day and a Chinese diplomat, Yu, asked me whether I knew anything about 'The Canadian' who had been involved in a border incident in Baluchistan. Chinese diplomats at that time were by far the best informed and the least talkative, so I found it curious Yu would ask me this. This incident involved Khadr, the HCI aid worker, who had been carrying large amounts of cash from Saudi Arabia into Afghanistan. Yu informed me that this was not the first time that Khadr had been involved in money running and actually seemed proud to announce it to me as if we were on exactly the same side. For months the Afghan scene in Islamabad buzzed with this and other information on 'The Canadian'." The most the official could find out was that Khadr was rumored to be carrying Saudi money to one of the radical mujahedeen leaders. "No one really knew, though, and my sources were unsure of the destination of the funds. There was no doubt, however, as to the unsavory character and shadowy reputation of Khadr. On this all my Pakistani and Afghan sources were agreed." Khadr's daughter Zaynab confirmed the story to me. "During the war in Afghanistan, Osama bin Laden and my father were taking money into Afghanistan."

Intelligence documents show that CSIS believed Khadr's camps were actually mujahedeen bases, used by Islamic fighters entering and exiting Afghanistan. "Afghanistan has benefited from substantial HCI assistance since the 1980s, including aid to the same Afghan refugee camps along the Pakistan/Afghanistan border that have served as transit points and safe havens for many Arab mujahedeen volunteers," CSIS noted in a "Secret, Canadian Eyes Only" report. Another CSIS report says that HCI "was one of many organizations that were helping refugees fleeing to Pakistan from Afghanistan and supporting the mujahedeen freedom fighters, who waged war against the Soviet occupying forces throughout the 1980s."

At least some of Khadr's money was coming through the Saudi Benevolence Committee, run by Adel Baterji, according to a U.S. indictment. Baterji was a Muslim who financed the mujahedeen resistance during the Soviet war. He later founded Benevolence International Canada whose president, Enaam Arnaout, was convicted of diverting money from charitable fundraising and shipping the funds to Islamic militant groups. Canada took no action against Baterji until December 24, 2004, when it ordered banks to freeze his assets. In November 1988, Khadr was accused by one of his financiers, the Saudi Red Crescent Society, of having "contacts with suspicious non-Islamic agencies." In a measure of the level of organization involved in the Afghan financial pipeline, the dispute was sent to a secret "arbitration committee." The judges were "Dr. Fadhl," an Islamic scholar for the Egyptian terrorist group Al Jihad, and Abu Hajer al Iraqi. Both were members of the Al Qaeda fatwa committee. They ruled in support of Khadr.

Khadr's activities may have gone beyond financing the anti-Soviet Islamic resistance. Reports that he was actively fighting alongside the mujahedeen also surfaced. Khalid Khawaja, a friend of the family, told me he believed that Khadr took up arms against the Soviets. In a photograph seized by the Pakistanis, he is shown posing with an anti-aircraft gun. Then, in 1992, Khadr was seriously injured. He claimed that he had been hit by shrapnel from a mine while visiting an aid project near Kabul. His leg was badly shattered and he had severe wounds to his abdomen. Newspapers reported that his kidneys failed and he was hospitalized in Peshawar until he stabilized, and then he and his family returned to Toronto. He was treated at Toronto's Sunnybrook Hospital, and later underwent rehabilitation at Riverdale Hospital. A nurse who treated him said he was a demanding patient. "You wouldn't believe the stuff he asked for," she said. "We gave him everything. The doctor said we gave him everything but the potato peeler."

The Khadrs lived initially with the Elsamnahs on Khartoum Avenue, but the house was small for such a big family, and they moved into an apartment in Toronto's west end. The children attended an Islamic school. This was a decisive time for Khadr. His friends and family wanted him to stay in Canada, to get a stable job and settle down. "When he [was] injured, we thought he was going to stop doing the refugee work, but you know you get injured you feel more about the other people," his mother-in-law told me. "So we thought he's going to stay here, he will not go back, because he got injured there and he would feel bad to go back, but he feel more like to be with these people, people who need help ... He found he cannot run away from this. It's hard. Not everyone can do that.

"For me, they ask me many times, 'We need your help, come, there are so many girls and women who need help, they need somebody.' But I am afraid. I said I can't come. But for them, because they are used to these people and they know the language, you can't run away and just leave the people like that. But nobody appreciate that. They say he's bad. He's disabled [he walked with a limp since his injury] and he has six children and he still work there to help these poor people because they need help because too many organizations left the country after they fight with each other. They would just run away. But if everybody run away, who is going to take care of these poor people?"

And so Khadr, his wife and their children returned to Peshawar.

By the mid-1990s, Al Qaeda was fast developing into a formidable terrorist force. The international network that had coalesced to support the Afghan resistance during the Soviet war had turned against the United States, which was now considered an infidel country and a foe. The financial network that had been set up to support the fight against the Soviets was now being harnessed by Al Qaeda. Khaled al-Sayed Ali Mohamed Abul-Dahab, Al Qaeda's financial officer in California, was moving tens of thousands of dollars around the world to finance jihadi violence.

Some of the cash was raised at his Santa Clara, California mosque. Ayman Al Zawahiri, the Egyptian Al Jihad leader and bin Laden's deputy, even visited the mosque to raise funds. Abul-Dahab would receive bundles of cash from a wealthy California gynecologist who worshiped at the mosque, or a relation who was a New York pharmaceutical company executive, and deposit the money in his account at the Wells Fargo Bank in California. Then he would transfer it to account numbers supplied by Al Jihad members. In 1993, he received a money transfer from bin Laden with specific instructions: go to Canada and post bail for a man named Essam Hafez Marzouk.

Marzouk may well have been the first bin Laden operative to enter Canada. Six-foot-two, with a short beard and thinning black hair, he was the son of a well-off Cairo businessman who lived in the upscale El Mohandeseen neighborhood, in a fifth floor apartment at 2 Doctor El-Mahroky Street. One day at the gym, Marzouk, just out of the Egyptian military, met a man who told him about the jihad against the Soviets in Afghanistan. Almost immediately, Marzouk traveled to Pakistan as a volunteer for the Red Crescent Society and later the Muslim World League. He claims he was no more than an ambulance driver, but investigators say he was a training camp instructor and that he learned how to make improvised explosive devices.

When the war in Afghanistan was over, Marzouk bought a couple of fake passports and flew to Khartoum, then to Damascus and Frankfurt, where he boarded Lufthansa Flight 492 for Canada. On June 16, 1993, a man calling himself "Fawzi Alharbi" disembarked at Vancouver International Airport at 3:30 p.m. dressed as an Arab sheikh and handed a Saudi passport to the Canada Customs inspector. At the baggage carousel, a roving Customs officer named Gordon Peterson pulled "Alharbi" aside for a chat. Mr. Peterson soon grew suspicious. He noted inconsistencies in the Saudi's story and ordered a search of his luggage. In his suitcase, the inspectors found a brown paper bag filled with ID with "Alharbi's" photo but different names—an Egyptian passport, a New York identity card, an Egyptian military service record and a Pakistani student card.

An RCMP constable looked at the documents and noted the obvious giveaway: the passport described "Alharbi" as five-foot-three, while this man stood almost a foot taller. "Alharbi" responded that he must have grown. Police noticed a man was waiting at the airport for "Alharbi." His name was Ali Mohamed and he had come from California to meet his friend. Mohamed was questioned and let go, but "Alharbi" was arrested and charged with three counts related to his fake identification. By then, however, police had established that "Alharbi" was in fact a twenty-four-year-old Egyptian named Essam Marzouk.

Canadian investigators did not know it then, but Marzouk's friend Ali Mohamed was actually a member of the terrorist group

Egyptian Al Jihad. The year before, he had been in Afghanistan, teaching basic military and explosives training at an Al Qaeda camp. Six months after Marzouk landed in Vancouver, Mohamed returned to Khartoum, where bin Laden was planning the next phase of his expanding jihad.

Bin Laden sent Mohamed to Nairobi to look for worthy targets. Mohamed scouted the U.S. embassy, U.S. Aid headquarters, the U.S. Agricultural Office, the French embassy and cultural center, as well as British and Israeli buildings. "I took pictures, drew diagrams and wrote a report," he told a New York judge later, adding the targets were chosen as revenge for U.S. military intervention in Somalia. "I later went to Khartoum, where my surveillance files and photographs were reviewed by Osama bin Laden, Abu Hafs [al-Qaeda's late military chief], Abu Ubaidah [also dead] and others. Bin Laden looked at the picture of the American embassy and pointed to where a truck could go as a suicide bomber."

His reconnaissance mission complete, Ali Mohamed returned to Vancouver to help Marzouk, who was still imprisoned. Abul-Dahab, who went with him, described the trip to Vancouver as a "jihad mission." He had been instructed to withdraw $3,000 money from a California bank account and give it to Ali Mohamed. He was told that "this money was from Osama bin Laden to help Essam Mohamed Hafez [a reference to Marzouk] who was imprisoned in Canada."

The money was transferred into his bank account from an Al Qaeda account in Sudan. He said bin Laden's money was delivered to Marzouk's Vancouver lawyer. But the lawyer, Phil Rankin, says he does not recall getting any money from Marzouk's colleagues. "I have no recollection of ever receiving money from anybody but Marzouk. Maybe his wife brought me some money at some point; I can't recall that even."

Marzouk was facing charges of using a forged document, fraud and illegally entering Canada, but from behind bars he applied for refugee status, claiming he feared religious and political persecution in Egypt. "He was very polite and respectful and easy to get along with," recalls Mr. Rankin. "The general impression I had of him was very favorable in the sense that he obviously came from a well-to-do family and had very good manners. He was very poised."

During his refugee hearings, Marzouk maintained he had only driven an ambulance in Pakistan and that he had never set foot in Afghanistan. He even brought forward a witness to support his claim—Ali Mohamed—who told the refugee judges that Marzouk was nothing more than a humanitarian aid worker. Following two days of hearings, his refugee claim was approved on December 12, 1994. The passport fraud charges were dropped.

Marzouk married an attractive Canadian of Egyptian heritage, got himself off welfare and found a job at a seafood company. He worked out at the gym and prayed at mosque. He behaved like a model citizen. But on paper, he was exactly what counter-terrorism investigators were watching for in the months after the botched 1993 World Trade Center bombing. He had arrived in Canada with a suitcase full of fake ID. A check of his travel patterns was also worrisome; he had recently visited Syria and bin Laden's new base, Sudan. He had military training, having served in the Egyptian armed forces. And most important, he had spent five years as an "Arab volunteer" in the war-ravaged Pakistan–Afghanistan frontier, a bastion of rising Islamic militancy.

CSIS put Marzouk under surveillance. Intelligence officers followed, listened and watched. But he did nothing untoward. CSIS interviewed Marzouk at a federal office building in downtown Vancouver. They showed him a *Time* magazine article about the World Trade Center bombing and pointed to the photographs of the suspects. "Do you know that person?" the intelligence officers asked. "Have you ever met that person?" "Have you heard of that person?" Marzouk denied knowing any of them and maintained he had only been an ambulance driver.

The surveillance turned up little worth forwarding to headquarters in Ottawa, nor did some 300 interviews. But investigators believe they know his secret: between 1988 and 1993, he was a training camp instructor and a member of an Arab fighting faction led by Ayman Al Zawahiri.

By 1998, Marzouk had started his own business in suburban Surrey, B.C. Together with his friend, Amer Hamed, he launched 4-U Enterprises. They had business cards printed. Hamed was also an Egyptian and, like Marzouk, an athlete. He had played on the Egyptian national basketball team before crossing into Canada at Lacolle, Quebec, and making his way from Montreal to the West. Sometimes the two friends would disappear into the bush for days to recite the *Koran* in the awesome solitude of the Coast Mountains. In retrospect, Marzouk's behavior was textbook Al Jihad. Operatives hiding in the West behaved perfectly because they had been told to. Following the war in Afghanistan, they were instructed to go somewhere safe and lay low—for now.

Marzouk's efforts to gain Canadian citizenship, however, were bogged down over unresolved concerns about his past. His wife, Yasmien, grew impatient over the delay. Their marriage soon foundered. Yasmien and Marzouk had a child but she found him too secretive, among other things, and they divorced. The same month that bin Laden issued a proclamation calling for the death of Jews and Crusaders, Marzouk sold off his company assets and left B.C. with his friend Hamed. But first he stopped in Scarborough, at a small brick house on Khartoum Avenue—the house of Ahmed Khadr's in-laws. Marzouk flew to Turkey, where authorities believe he met an alleged Egyptian extremist named Ahmad Agiza. Then he flew back to eastern Afghanistan, the hub of bin Laden's training camp network. Investigators believe Marzouk was assigned to train two men, a Saudi and an Egyptian, who were being prepared for a suicide bombing mission. One of the trainees was being sent to blow up the U.S. embassy in Kenya; the other was to hit the U.S. embassy in Tanzania.

But Al Jihad, the Egyptian wing of Al Qaeda, would hit another embassy first. In 1995, a California doctor gave Abul-Dahab US$4,000 to deliver to Al Jihad. Abul-Dahab gave the cash to Ali Mohamed (also known as Abul-So'ud), who transferred it to Pakistan. "I later learned from Abul-So'ud that this money was used to bomb the Egyptian embassy in Islamabad," Abul-Dahab told Egyptian police later. The man suspected of overseeing the financing of the bomb plot was a Canadian aid worker living in Peshawar—Ahmed Said Khadr.

Seventeen people were killed and sixty injured when a truck packed with explosives rammed into the Egyptian embassy in

Islamabad on November 19, 1995. The attack came amid a surge of violence by Egyptian Islamists trying to topple the government of Hosni Mubarak. Two weeks later, twenty Pakistani troops came to Khadr's door. They knocked at 11 p.m., but his wife would not let them in. She said that, as a Canadian, she did not believe she had to. "I felt so proud that I'm Canadian," she told the *Ottawa Citizen* later. "I told the officer I'm a Canadian citizen, and he said, 'To hell with you and your Canada.'"

Khadr was not at home; he was away in Afghanistan. The family was taken to the police station and released after two hours. When Khadr returned five days later, he found out he was wanted and, before he had even sat down to greet his children, he set off to a government office to complain. He was arrested. Police returned to the house and seized Khadr's papers and roughly US$40,000 in cash. He said the money was partly his, partly HCI's, and that he kept it at home because there were no banks in the area. But Pakistani authorities accused him of involvement in the bombing and said that Al Jihad members caught fleeing the country after the attack had identified him as the financier of the plot.

"I am not Egyptian. I'm Canadian," Khadr told the police.

"No, you're Egyptian," they replied.

"No, I'm Canadian. My residence, my applications, everything is as a Canadian citizen."

"No, you are Egyptian," the police said.

"See," Khadr insisted, "this is my Canadian passport.'"

The arrest came as no surprise to CSIS, which was already aware of Khadr and knew his "refugee" camps were being used to support the war effort. It was also not the first time HCI had been associated with terrorism. According to a 1996 CSIS report, just before Khadr's arrest, newspapers in France had tied a bombing by Algerian extremists in Paris to Human Concern operations in Croatia. "Press reports indicated that HCI's Zagreb office has sheltered militants of the GIA [Armed Islamic Group] and that this HCI office may have served as a staging ground for the Paris bomber." The report does not indicate that the allegation was ever proven, and HCI denies any association with terrorists. CIDA, however, was caught off guard by Khadr's arrest. The government aid agency had given hundreds of thousands of dollars to HCI. CSIS prepared a report for CIDA but it has been too heavily censored to see what was said about Khadr, although it did mention that Muslim charities were often used to support fighters in Afghanistan.

Secret internal memos sent to Don Boudria, then the minister for international cooperation, show that the federal government believed it would be too politically risky to continue funding HCI. The government feared that while there was no solid evidence of the charity's involvement in extremist activity, if proof surfaced, it would prove highly embarrassing. The government pulled its funding. Marc Duguay, the charity's lawyer, traveled to Pakistan to investigate but told me he found no evidence the group had been involved in terrorism. The agency began lobbying Ottawa to restore its funding, but CIDA refused. HCI then sued the Canadian development agency, but was not successful. Although CIDA suspended funding to HCI in 1996, the organization still has charity status and remains active in providing humanitarian aid.

Shortly after Khadr's arrest, two Al Jihad members arrived in Canada. The first was Mohamed Mahjoub, a member of a faction called Vanguards of Conquest, who flew to Toronto in December 1995 and stayed at Khadr's in-laws' house in Scarborough. He got a job at Food World, a twenty-four-hour corner store in downtown Toronto, and married a Canadian. Mahjoub was eventually arrested, and admitted that he had met bin Laden and worked for one of his companies in Sudan. Telephone records also showed that Mahjoub had been in regular contact with Essam Marzouk, the bin Laden loyalist from Vancouver. Mahjoub admitted that he knew Khadr. When I visited his shop shortly after the September 11 attacks, when Mahjoub was in custody, the manager was standing at the cash register, transfixed by the newspaper spread across the counter. "It's unbelievable," he said, staring at photographs of the rubble of the World Trade Center. A Federal Court judge later ruled that Mahjoub was indeed a terrorist.

Then another Al Jihad member named Mahmoud Jaballah arrived in Toronto and became the principal of the Islamic school at the Salaheddin mosque. CSIS also tied him to Khadr and top Al Qaeda members, including bin Laden's senior lieutenant Ayman

Al Zawahiri. Jaballah likewise denied the allegations, but once again a judge ruled that the government had presented a convincing case. CSIS regarded the timing of Mahjoub's and Jaballah's arrival in Canada as suspicious. Asked about it by a Federal Court judge, CSIS agent "Mike" said: "Interestingly, my Lord, this was shortly after the Egyptian embassy in Islamabad was bombed by Al Jihad members … A number of Al Jihad operatives, shortly after that bombing, my Lord, fled that part of the world looking for sanctuary. One of the other individuals is a Canadian citizen by the name of Ahmed Said Khadr who, according to open reporting, was involved in this particular operation. He has apparently used the facilities of an aid organization for logistics for that particular operation."

Khadr protested his innocence by refusing to eat, and consequently was hospitalized in Islamabad. "I feel very saddened," he said from his hospital bed, "I never did anything." The Pakistanis, however, considered him a radical and said they had information that he had given "extremist speeches" and was active in religious extremism. Maha Elsamnah moved the children to a hotel in Islamabad near the hospital and gave updates on Khadr's condition to the press in Canada, complaining that her husband had been arrested only because he was an Egyptian. "We are being treated like rats," she said.

Muslim lobby groups in Canada took up Khadr's cause, and urged Jean Chrétien to intervene, suggesting that Canada should threaten to withhold aid money from Pakistan. Khadr grew weak and developed a fever. The Islamic Schools Federation of Ontario offered to raise money for a lawyer to defend him. The timing was most fortunate for Khadr. As it turned out, Chrétien was already planning a state visit to Pakistan. A spokeswoman for the prime minister assured Canadians that Chrétien would "definitely" raise the issue with Prime Minister Benazir Bhutto.

Chrétien's visit was billed as Khadr's "last hope." Days before Chrétien was to meet Bhutto, Khadr spoke to reporters from his hospital bed. He had lost twelve kilograms during his month-long hunger strike. He accused police of blindfolding him, pulling his hair and beard, and threatening to rape Maha. Pakistani officials said Khadr had financed the bombing by funneling money through HCI, and that three of his businesses, including his carpet-weaving operation, were covers for his aid to extremist groups. "I had nothing to do with that," Khadr countered. "I have never aided, I have never financed anything like that. I do not believe in violence."

Chrétien and Bhutto met on January 15, 1996. "I wanted to make very clear that due process is followed in this case and they gave me all the guarantees that I could have expected under the circumstances," Chrétien told reporters. Three months later, Khadr was released without charges after a judge ruled there was not enough evidence to hold him. He parted company with Human Concern International and returned to Toronto with his family. According to friends, when Khadr arrived back in Canada, he kissed the ground. In the words of Khadr's son, Abdurahman, "Jean Chrétien used his influence on Benazir Bhutto."

In Toronto, Khadr was again encouraged to stay and settle down. Aly Hindy, the imam at the Salaheddin mosque, spoke with Khadr about what he should do next. He was thinking of staying in Canada to work as an engineer. "He thought about it and then he said, 'No, I already committed myself to those children and I already have camps of children and orphans,'" Hindy said. "He had the feeling like he would be betraying all these people, so he said, 'No, I'm going back.'"

In 1996, the Khadrs returned to the region, this time to Jalalabad, Afghanistan. They had a house in the city and another farther north, in an Al Qaeda compound called Nagim Ulgihad, where bin Laden lived with his senior leadership. The Khadr and bin Laden children were schoolmates. "We studied poetry," Zaynab recalled in an interview with the Arabic-language newspaper *Al-Sharq Al-Awsat*. "Bin Laden was very fond of poetry. He used to reward the children who recited poetry well." Bin Laden even attended Zaynab's wedding.

"I believe that this man was an ordinary person who had a noble humanitarian sensitivity," she continued, describing bin Laden. "Sometimes he was moody. I do not, however, know what used to happen inside his house. Those who surrounded him were different from him but they all agreed on one thing, namely, that they were prepared to sacrifice their lives for his sake. I used to notice that Dr. Ayman al-Zawahiri and Abu Hafs al-Masri had a special place in his heart.

"When my family went to live in Jalalabad in the same compound as bin Laden I was already 19. We visited them sometimes but he did not have daughters of my own age. At this time he had three wives and around 20 children. He had seven or eight with his first wife. Not all the children lived with him. I saw him several times. He did not deprive his children of anything but prohibited them from buying any U.S.-made products, even if it were only soft drinks or ice cream. We still follow his example. We do not buy U.S. products."

The Khadrs followed bin Laden's example in another way as well. They began sending their sons to bin Laden's training camps. Abdurahman was just eleven when he was sent off to take weapons training during the summer. Although those who knew the family regarded Abdurahman as a reluctant recruit, more interested in having fun than dying a martyr, he trained at Al Qaeda's notorious Khaldun Camp. "I became famous in the camp for being the youngest trainee ever to come to Khaldun," Abdurahman testified later. "It's a normal thing in Afghanistan," he said. His mother said, "We wanted to get him into something just to be disciplined." According to a Canadian intelligence report, Abdullah, the eldest, "is believed to be an Al Qaeda member, possibly having commanded an extremist training camp in Logar Province of Afghanistan."

After leaving HCI, Khadr launched his own organization, Health & Education Project International (HEP-I), which had an office adjacent to the Scarborough mosque, where he raised money, and made use of former HCI facilities in Pakistan. According to Khadr's Internet site, his charity was running orphanages and working in cooperation with the Taliban "Department of Martyrs' Families." Photos posted on the site show schoolboys, sheep being slaughtered and a building with a sign that reads "Canada." In Jalalabad, Khadr was considered a fierce Islamist close to bin Laden. "We had great problems with this man, great problems," French aid worker Alain de Bures told *The Globe and Mail.* "I never met such hostility, someone so against the West. He was pro-Islamic to the core ... he refused to even talk to Westerners."

In Canada, however, Khadr had no trouble raising money. "The family used to come every year for fund collection," Imam Hindy said. Khadr would speak at the Salaheddin mosque, and then pass the collection bucket. He did the same in mosques around Toronto, as well as in Winnipeg and Vancouver. "He was proud of [being a] Canadian citizen," Hindy said. "That's why he was coming here all the time, because of the generosity of the people. This is our duty to help other nations. We are really fortunate people to have all these things, so he was actually talking to people to open their heart, to open their wallets."

By 1997, Al Qaeda was determined to take on the Americans in a big way. The organization recalled a number of operatives to prepare for a massive assault. Essam Marzouk left Vancouver for Baku, Azerbaijan, where high-level Al Jihad and Al Qaeda members such as Ahmed Salama Mabrouk were gathering to plan a major terror attack. A plan was devised to crash truck bombs into the U.S. embassies in Kenya and Tanzania. Marzouk flew to Nairobi in July 1998 to help with the final preparations, then went to Baku.

A day before the bombings were to take place, the Baku cell sent a fax to an Al Jihad–affiliated center in London, advising that the embassies were about to be attacked. On August 7, 1998, trucks laden with explosives blasted into the U.S. embassies in Nairobi and Dar es Salaam. More than two hundred were killed. It was Al Qaeda's biggest attack yet. Bin Laden's involvement was quickly determined, and two weeks later U.S. President Bill Clinton ordered missile strikes against terrorist camps in Afghanistan. When one of the Tomahawk missiles landed near Khost, Marzouk's friend Amer Hamed was standing in the kill zone. "He was cut into pieces," said Ahmed Khadr's son, Abdurahman, who was there with Hamed that day. "So I had to collect his pieces off the ground and that is what built rage in my heart. So that day I hated America as ever."

Marzouk was undone by a telephone call. Mossad intercepted a phone call indicating that a suspected Egyptian terrorist named Ihab Saqr was planning to meet an unidentified member of the Iranian intelligence service MOIS. The meeting was to take place the following week at a hotel in Baku. The "signals intelligence" was handed to a veteran Mossad officer, ironically a Canadian, who was the Israeli agency's counterterrorism liaison to the U.S. intelligence community. The Mossad liaison officer called his contact at the CIA station in Tel Aviv, and they decided to make a fast trip to Baku. "Let's pick them up," they agreed.

The CIA operation was run out of Frankfurt. The agency quickly assembled a team of eight or nine. Mossad was going along for the ride, but it was to be a U.S. operation. Officially, the Israeli officer was not even there. The raid was swift and brutal. The police waited until Saqr was in his hotel room having coffee, and then burst in like a ton of bricks. There were, it turned out, three men in the room. All were dragged away. It happened so fast their shoes were left behind. It soon became clear the Iranian intelligence official the Israelis were hoping to catch had not arrived. The two men with Saqr were not Iranians. They were fellow Al Jihad members, Ahmed Salama Mabrouk and Marzouk. All three were sent to Cairo. "He was not the main focus," the Mossad officer said of Marzouk. "He was an incidental catch."

The six Khadr children were raised with one foot in the East and one in the West. Their childhoods were spent shuttling back and forth between Canada and the fringes of the war. Asked where she was from, Zaynab gave a telling response: "Canada, Pakistan, Afghanistan, or you can say I'm from all over." But they were also proudly Canadian and had a fondness for Western culture. Abdurahman, in particular, seemed more interested in North American life than the strict religious codes of his father. Khadr tried to put him in boarding school, but he kept running away. Likewise, Omar, the youngest, was a fan of Hollywood action films. A family friend who visited the compound in Peshawar was struck by the Khadrs' collection of videos, which they would watch for hours at a time. Omar's favorite was the Bruce Willis adventure *Die Hard*, in which terrorists seize a Los Angeles corporate building, take hostages and are ultimately outwitted by a resourceful American cop.

Omar was a "very sweet, simple and easygoing person," Zaynab said. "Very loved by all his family and friends. He finished Grade 8 before the school he was in closed. He speaks Arabic and a little English. He is known to be trustworthy. He mainly sticks with my mom and dad." Said Abdurahman: "He can't kill a fly." But he would also fall into the grip of Al Qaeda, training in weapons and explosives near Khost, in eastern Afghanistan.

For the Khadrs, it seems, holy war was a family affair.

The Khadr family moved to Kabul in 1999, and lived in the Wazirkhan neighborhood, where the Western embassies were located. The houses were big. There were "broad tree-lined avenues," Zaynab said. "It was as if you were living in a Western capital." When Canadians came to Afghanistan for jihad they would sometimes stay with the Khadrs. "Otherwise, if they didn't stay in our house, then we would know that there is a Canadian coming, you know, to go to Afghanistan and he is going to Khaldun [training camp] or he is going to the guesthouses," Abdurahman said.

"I know a lot of people that are living in the West and are living in Canada and that live their everyday life now and are not under arrest or anything, that have been to Khaldun," he added. "I had a lot of friends that were Canadians that came to Afghanistan and went to training. Some of them are back in Canada and some of them are under arrest." Among those Abdurahman said he saw in Afghanistan was Amer El-Maati, a Kuwaiti-born Canadian from Toronto who would in May 2004 be named by U.S. Attorney General John Ashcroft as a "clear and present danger to America" because of his membership in Al Qaeda and his desire to attack the United States homeland.

El-Maati was born in Kuwait, where his Egyptian father worked for the Kuwait State Audit Bureau, but the family immigrated to Canada in 1981. Later, El-Maati traveled to Pakistan and in 1998, appeared at the Canadian High Commission in Islamabad claiming his passport had been stolen. A new passport, Number BC077265, was issued on December 2. That was the last anyone heard of Amer until the war in Afghanistan, when some of his identity cards were found in the rubble of an Al Qaeda safe house that had been bombed by the Americans.

El-Maati's brother Ahmad has also surfaced in connection with terrorism probes. Arrested in Syria, in 2001, he "admitted to having planned a suicide attack on the Parliament Buildings in Ottawa," according to a Canadian intelligence report.

A Buffalo cruise boat employee thought he saw Amer photographing a passenger vessel in May 2004 and called the FBI, but Imam Hindy said he has heard that Amer was killed in 1999 in Chechnya. When I told him that Amer might have been spotted in Buffalo, his father Badr replied, "That's nice. I would like to see him."

Perhaps not surprisingly, given the assistance he had received from Canada to date, Khadr did not hesitate to seek the help of Canadian authorities. When the Pakistanis seized his passport at the border in November, 2000, Khadr sent a fax to the Canadian High Commission in Islamabad, complaining about the incident. "Mr. Khadr has informed us that he was planning to return to Canada in the beginning of the holy month of Ramadan, as he arranges [a] fundraising campaign there for his organization, and if he is unable to leave, it will be a great loss for his organization," an embassy official wrote in a memo to Ottawa. Canadian officials contacted the Pakistani's foreign ministry and asked for an investigation into Khadr's allegations.

Khadr eventually stopped making his fundraising tours of Canada sometime in the late 1990s, but his wife would come with the children to collect money. Hindy recalled seeing one son, Omar, on her last visit in the spring of 2001. But he did not make much of an impression on the imam, who saw only a quiet boy of twelve or thirteen, in the tow of his mother. Abdurahman came back to Scarborough that spring as well and lived with his grandmother; he got a job and was planning to go to school. CSIS agents soon approached him and started asking questions, he said. Spooked, he returned to Afghanistan.

In the last letter posted on their Internet site, Khadr and Maha spoke of the harsh Afghan winter and pleaded for donations. "It is the second year with no rain. While many Muslims were enjoying various types of delicious food, the poor Afghan children and women were roaming the streets searching for any food to survive on ... If you are willing to share the bounties, the price of one sheep is 100 Canadian Dollars, and the price for a share of Cow is 45 Canadian Dollars."

In the summer of 2001, Egyptian police went to Pakistan to hunt for Khadr and, after weeks of searching along the Afghan border, they found him in Peshawar. The Egyptians were there as guests of the Pakistanis, so before moving in to arrest Khadr, they notified the head of Pakistan's intelligence service. That night, a car bearing diplomatic plates raced up to the building. A group of Taliban members jumped out, grabbed Khadr and fled over the Khyber Pass to Afghanistan, according to one press account.

Fatimah Elsamnah recalled a similar story. She said her son-in-law was sitting in a taxi in Islamabad with her daughter and some of the children when eight men tried to pull him out of the car. The family hung on to the father and the attackers fled. Khadr returned to Afghanistan at once. "I think my grandchildren had to learn to fight back," she said. "Omar and the other kids, everyone, they trained to learn how to fight back."

At one point, Khadr tried to convince his son Abdurahman to become a suicide bomber. "He sat me down with this scholar and the trainer and they talked about it," Abdurahman testified. "We even discussed which clothes I would be wearing, that I would shave my beard, that I would wear a Walkman, anything. And I was like, 'No, no, no.' ... Because for me to become a suicide bomber is a pride for my dad. It is a pride for the family. He said even a pride for Islam." Khadr condoned bin Laden's ideology and violent methods, and was a member of Al Qaeda, Abdurahman said. "To him it was not terrorism. To him it was a freedom fight. To him this was a group of the last Muslims surviving to defend Islam. That is what it was to him."

Well before the 9/11 attacks, CSIS already had "intercepts" that placed Khadr close to bin Laden. The intercepted communications, together with what intelligence agencies already knew about Khadr, showed that his role in the bin Laden network was primarily financial, Canadian officials told me. He knew how to raise money in the West, and he knew how to use his charitable work as a cover. During a single trip to Canada, Abdurahman picked up more than $50,000 and brought it back to Afghanistan. Khadr also sent supplies to the Khaldun training camp, including a shipment of clothes and medicine from Canada. The United Nations was the first to take action against The Canadian. It ordered governments to freeze his assets as part of an effort to isolate Afghanistan, the Taliban and Al Qaeda.

After the September 11 attacks, as the United States led the war against terrorism, Ahmed Khadr's name quickly surfaced again, appearing, along with seven of his aliases, on a list of suspects sought in connection with the 9/11 investigation. The White House placed his name on its own list of individuals whose assets were frozen for terrorism. Canada added Khadr to its list of terrorist "entities," forcing banks to freeze his accounts.

The Khadr family was living in Afghanistan when the Americans went to war to bring down the Taliban. On November 11, 2001, as the forces of the Northern Alliance were poised to liberate the capital Kabul, Khadr sent Abdurahman and Omar out of the city. They went to Logar province, where Khadr had a school. They spent the night, but Abdurahman returned to Kabul in the morning. He said he needed money to pay their driver. "On my way back I saw that there was a flee [Sic] from Kabul. Everybody was running away from Kabul." By the time he got to his house, his mother and father had already left for the Pakistani border.

In a posting on the HEP-I Internet site, Zaynab described being in Afghanistan during the war and advised that "Maha and Ahmed are good and safe and send you all their salaam [peace]." Zaynab angrily recounted that "while the world was happy and celebrating, we and many others were being bombed day and night. Is this what Muslims are for? Watching? I don't think so.

"So Muslims, try to help first by making lots of dua'a and then by standing in the face of kufer and evil, try to stop world destruction and put your hands together to save Islam and the Muslims. Follow the news. Watch what they do to our brothers in Guantanamo.

COLD TERROR

"What would you do if he was your blood brother?"

The U.S. warplanes swept in great arcs, drawing chalk-white lines in the sky with their vapor trails as they placed laser-guided bombs along the ridgeline of the Kalakata Hills. On the plain below, debris rained down—bullets, tank shells, rockets and artillery shells. The U.S.-backed Northern Alliance rebels and the Taliban forces were pounding each other with everything they had.

At an abandoned farm on the outskirts of Khojaghar, I climbed onto the roof of a mud outbuilding to watch the battle, along with a dozen rebels dressed in shalwar kameez (tunic over loose pants) and rolled-brim pakul hats. Kalashnikov rifles lay across their laps. They were laughing and joking, happy their commanders had at last given the order to begin the land assault to reclaim Afghanistan from the Taliban.

The commander handed me his binoculars and pointed across the plain to the foot of the mountains, where his tanks were rolling across the Taliban lines. The ancient field glasses were shaped like a periscope, for peering over trenches—a useful feature in northern Afghanistan.

When I stood and looked through the scratched lenses, I could see the Russian-made T-55 tanks of the Northern Alliance rebels rolling up hills the Taliban had occupied for months. Puffs of smoke erupted from the gun turrets as they blasted the Taliban strongholds, softening them up for the advancing troops.

The old commander said something in Tajik and waved his hand downward, as if wanting me to lower the field glasses.

I did so but could see nothing. Again he said something, this time with more urgency, and again he waved his hand. But I could not understand. My translator had stayed behind at the Kotchka River and nobody here spoke English, so hand gestures and facial expression were the only way we could communicate.

And then I understood: the commander and his troops were sitting while I was standing. He wanted me to get down.

It was too late. A faint whistle arose from the West. It grew louder—then louder still, its pitch falling as it approached. It was a mortar round fired by the Taliban soldiers, who were sitting in a trench not two hundred meters away. They had spotted me and were trying to hit our rooftop.

The smiles fell from the rebels' dirty faces as they realized they were about to get hit with chunks of burning shrapnel. They scrambled off the roof, down a makeshift ladder made of lashed sticks.

The shell thudded into a pasture.

A moment of dead silence followed, then another faint whistle. Rebel soldiers scattered in all directions, not sure where to run, but needing to run somewhere just to feel as if they were getting away. The next round came in, this time closer. The Taliban fighters were adjusting their mortar launchers; they were homing in on us.

There was nowhere to hide. The plain was flat and empty. Anyone who tried to run from the farm would be mowed down by snipers in a few seconds. There was nothing to do but sit it out, so I hid behind a mud wall and waited.

Crossing into Afghanistan early in the U.S.-led war was like going back in time. It was nearly midnight when we reached the Amu Darya, the broad river that divides Afghanistan from Tajikistan. The only way across was by raft. An old tractor was strapped atop the raft, with a cable wrapped around one of its wheels. We loaded our gear on board the raft and a soldier fired up the tractor, which pulled us across as the wheel turned. The crossing, we were told, was within shelling range of the Taliban positions, hence the need for a night crossing. As we neared the far shore, I began to make out the shapes of the Afghans who awaited our arrival. I could see the dark outline of their turbans, their flowing cotton clothing and Kalashnikovs. They moved like shadows on the riverbank, like ghosts from another century.

The Soviets pulled out of Afghanistan in 1989 but left behind a puppet communist regime that was finally toppled by Ahmad Shah Massoud's commandos in 1992. Then the Taliban religious movement, which had developed in the Afghan refugee camps in Pakistan, launched its own military campaign, pushing from town to town in Toyota pickup trucks to impose their austere version of Islam on a people too war-weary to resist. The Taliban seized power in Kabul and pushed Massoud's men north into the Panjshir Valley and the plains along the Tajikistan border. With the capture of Taloqan, the rebel capital became Khoja Bahauddin, a collection of mud compounds and dusty roads crammed with vendors, camels, donkeys, old Russian jeeps and the occasional tank.

Khoja Bahauddin is a militaristic town, where men of all ages walk the streets in camouflage jackets and brown pakul hats. The women are all but invisible. At the Saturday market, where imported Iranian soaps, cookies and cans of Pepsi are laid out in the dirt for sale, the men carry their rifles slung over their shoulders. Camouflage clothing, some of it left behind by the Soviets, is heaped in great piles. Even children wear camouflage. The stall where an old man repairs Kalashnikov rifles is always crowded. Metal workers forge pots and pans out of old tank and artillery shell casings picked up from the battlefields. Those held in highest esteem are the bearded old men who tell tales of defeating the mighty Soviets in the great jihad.

There are no hotels here. Television networks with considerable budgets have rented out the only available houses. Journalists can stay at the ministry of foreign affairs; it's a one-level, L-shaped building featuring a few rooms packed with reporters, many of them ill with stomach infections. I end up at the compound of a French aid organization that is trying to build roads through the north. At first I sleep on the floor of a screened porch, and then I move to a tent outside. On my first morning, a distraught French journalist comes limping into the compound. "I need a doctor," he yells. "I've been bitten by a scorpion."

The refugees have it worse. Thousands of Afghans have fled the Taliban advance for camps dotted around the north. The camps that encircle Khoja Bahauddin are the worst I have ever seen. Usually refugee camps are distinguishable because of all the blue and white United Nations tarps. Here there are none: the UN pulled its workers out of the region because of the war, and only a handful of humanitarian groups have stepped in to help. The refugees live in improvised tents made of sticks, canvas, tarpaulin and basketweave, and they tell horrific tales of Taliban abuses that seem totally at odds with the stated ideals of radical Islam. Stories of rape, abduction and murder are common here.

At night on the front, when the shelling subsides and the temperature drops, the Northern Alliance soldiers leave their trenches to eat rice and beans and lay their sleeping bags in caves dug out of the hillsides. They switch on their walkie-talkie radios and listen to the Taliban across the valley talking among themselves. But often the radio chatter is in languages the rebels recognize as Arabic, Urdu or Russian. "I talk with them, but suddenly they start using their own language and I cannot understand," says a teenage rebel at the hilltop command post at Puza Pulkhumry, a heavy machine gun slung over his shoulder and a walkie-talkie in his hand.

The troops opposite are the Taliban Foreign Legion—Muslim fighters waging what they believe is a holy war in defense of their radical religious beliefs. About one-quarter of the soldiers protecting the ruling Taliban regime are non-Afghans. Most are Pakistani. But there are also brigades of Saudis, Chechens, Algerians and Islamic guerrillas from western China and the neighboring former Soviet republics of Uzbekistan, Tajikistan and Kyrgyzstan. Filipinos and Indonesians are said to have joined the Taliban ranks, and a British citizen of Pakistani origin has been captured by the Northern Alliance rebels.

"They are the people of Osama bin Laden," complains Mullah Nazamudeen, a Muslim priest from the village of Imamsahib, which was overrun by the Taliban. I had come to Afghanistan to watch the Americans uproot the terrorism that was hitting at the West. But as I soon learned, there was another dimension to the war on terror. The Afghan people were enduring great suffering at the hands of the foreign terrorists who had seized their country and turned it into a base for Islamic radicalism and holy war. I knew that Afghanistan was exporting its terror to the outside world. What I had not realized was how devastatingly we were also exporting terror to the Afghans.

Arabs account for up to three thousand members of the Taliban armed forces. Most are loyal to, and financed by, bin Laden. "Generally, Arab units are deployed in an infantry role armed with nothing heavier than rocket-propelled grenades, PK machine guns and mortars," according to *Jane's World Armies*. "They are, however, widely recognized as currently the most aggressive and committed fighters in Taliban ranks."

And some of them are Canadian citizens, the sons of Ahmed Khadr.

By the end of October, Afghanistan is consumed with just one question: when is the Northern Alliance going to attack? U.S. warplanes have been pulverizing the Taliban positions for two weeks. The U.S. Special Forces are all over the place. The Alliance has new uniforms, guns and backpacks. Dozens of Russian-made tanks and armored personnel carriers are lined up at a military base near the front. I visit Barylai Khan, the rebel deputy defense minister, at his fortress near Ay Khannom. He is unshaven and looks tired and stressed.

"When does the offensive begin?" I ask.

Instead of answering, he reaches into his camouflage jacket, pulls out a Palm Pilot and asks me to define "offensive." He listens to my explanation of the word's multiple meanings and makes a note on his electronic device.

"And when will this offensive begin?" I ask again.

"Soon," he mutters. "Inshala!"

At the Kotchka River, I hire a horse and join a group of French journalists heading to the front to look for signs of the impending assault. We ride for an hour across the plain, traveling through empty villages on our way to the foothills, and then we climb on foot up narrow goat trails to the trenches. On the barren hilltop near Chagatay, bored Northern Alliance soldiers wait in a trench. One of them spots a group of Taliban fighters moving along the opposite hill. They have left their bunker and are walking in the open.

A young rebel soldier loads an ammunition belt into a heavy machine gun mounted on a stand. He takes careful aim, grimaces and pulls the trigger. Nothing. The gun jams. He fiddles with it, gives it a kick, but it still does not work.

Another rebel takes over and manages to load the gun properly. He takes his time aiming. There is a deafening crack. A few seconds later, a puff of dust erupts across the valley as the 150-mm shell rips into the sand. He's missed.

The Taliban realize they are under fire and clamber into their pickup trucks. The soldier aims and crack! This time he fires too high. The bullet sails over their heads. The Taliban are by now circling erratically in their trucks, hoping to make themselves difficult targets.

The rebel soldier squints and aims his massive gun once more. The dust explodes below the trucks. Another miss. He tries again and again, but no luck. He gives up. Six bullets gone, no damage done.

As we leave the front behind us, the Frenchmen get their old horses up to a gallop and are laughing and joking as if this were a day in the Normandy countryside. When will this war ever begin, they complain. We will be here for months and still the Alliance will be waiting for the Americans to drop a bomb from three thousand meters to kill the last Taliban! This war will never start. We cross the river on our horses and drive back to camp for another meal of beans, rice and flatbread, not realizing that as we sleep the war is already getting underway.

"The troops crossed the river at midnight," one of the journalists proclaims as I emerge from my tent. We race to Dasht-e Qala and take the road to the riverbank, where we can hear the boom of the advancing tanks. We are almost at the river when a rebel soldier with a Kalashnikov stops us. Nobody is allowed across the river. The front is closed. We try hitchhiking on a military truck, but again the soldiers stop us. Desperate to get to the fighting, we turn back for the compound of the local warlord, Momar Hassan. He cannot give us permission to cross the river, but he agrees to give us one of his men, who will show us where we can cross. The soldier leads us through town to a spot upriver where two boys keep a raft made out of old inner tubes and sticks.

In a field that lies between the Northern Alliance tanks that are blasting volleys of shells overhead and the Taliban troops who are firing back with every weapon they can find, a white mongrel barks wildly and runs in circles, driven mad by the noise of war. The rebel offensive has veiled the Kalakata Hills in smoke, but it is the deafening sound of the fighting that is most unnerving—the boom of the tanks, the swoosh of rockets and the sickening scream of incoming artillery shells. The villagers trapped in the middle of the war seem unmoved by it all. In one frontline hamlet they watch the battle from graveyard mounds, as if this were nothing more than a fireworks display. As machine guns rattle nearby, an old man paces through his pile of drying rice, mixing it with his bare feet. Two children work a cattle-drawn plow in a field littered with shell casings, while their camels stand gnawing the greenery from the trees. A girl walks a donkey laden with water jugs past a row of rebel tanks that are warming up their engines in preparation for an attack. War is such an everyday occurrence in Afghanistan that even the thunderous start of the battle to reclaim the country from the Taliban cannot nudge the people from their daily routines.

At Khojaghar, I make the deadliest of mistakes. Watching the tank battle to the west from the roof of a farmhouse, I am completely oblivious to the fact that there is a second Taliban trench just two hundred meters to the south. It takes the Taliban just a few minutes to spot me and begin their artillery assault. For more than two weeks, I had waited for the offensive to begin, cursing the rebels for not attacking, and now, pinned down behind a flimsy mud wall while the Taliban lob mortars at me, more than anything in the world I just want it to stop. As the mortar bombs rain down, each one closer than the last, I wait at first but then decide that the only sensible thing to do is to get out of there. I fasten my backpack on tight and run back along the road. I cannot risk cutting across the fields because they are mined. As I run, the Taliban mortars follow me until I am out of range.

By mid-afternoon, it is clear this coordinated attack will combine the world's mightiest military force with one of the planet's most backward guerrilla armies. Two U.S. fighter-bombers, flying side by side, arrive at 3:30 p.m. to join the B-52 bomber already pulverizing the Taliban front. At about the same time, the rebels begin firing into the hills from a row of tanks lined up on the outskirts of Dasht-e Qala. The rebels shell over the heads of the villagers. The chorus of shelling gets so loud that it almost winds anyone below, and it starts coming without pause. Every so often, an incoming tank or artillery shell whistles past as the Taliban respond with unexpected resolve. A Taliban cluster bomb of some sort soars overhead and breaks apart into a dozen smaller bombs. One missile strikes deep inside Dasht-e Qala, hitting a market filled with watermelons and imported Iranian biscuits. Two of Commander Hassan's men are killed and a third loses his leg.

The fighter-bombers swirl in tandem in the deep blue above, leaving a maze of scribble in the sky. Beneath them, the mountain ridges that had been held by the Taliban for months are vanishing behind clouds of black smoke. The Alliance unleashes its big guns late in the afternoon—rocket launchers, missiles and tanks positioned on a mountain overlooking the Taliban line. The mud houses shake as the heavy weapons are fired. The battle is still going strong as the sun starts to sink in a haze of smoke and dust. By 6 p.m. there is quiet. Darkness descends. The stars come out. Occasionally, a trail of tracer fire and the white flash of an exploding shell flashes in the blackness, but the battle has subsided for the night. The first day of the land war to capture the lair of Al Qaeda has come to an end.

The next night, after another day at the front, I am at Commander Hassan's house when Australian correspondent Paul McGeough calls on his satellite phone to say there has been a terrible accident at Chagatay. A group of journalists was riding atop an Alliance armored personnel carrier when it was ambushed. Three of them are dead—a German magazine writer and two French reporters who had been staying with me at the aid compound in Khoja Bahauddin.

I switch on my shortwave radio two days later and hear the BBC news announcer proclaim that Kabul has fallen to the Alliance, setting off scenes of celebration, as Afghans are freed from the grip of the Taliban. People dance in the streets to music that was previously banned, and they shave their beards; children fly paper kites, also banned by Mullah Omar. But while the festivities are underway on the streets, the rebel forces are still combing neighborhoods for Taliban and Al Qaeda members, and their search soon leads them to a Canadian, Abdurahman Khadr, who is taken into custody and sent to a prison in Kabul. He is eventually handed to the Americans and agrees to become an informant. The CIA interrogates him about his father, about bin Laden, the training camps and those who had trained there. Then they send him to spy on the detainees at a makeshift detention facility for captured terrorists called Camp X-Ray, at Guantanamo Bay.

The scorching tropical sun is high over Cuba when a fat-bellied C-141 Starlifter appears over the Caribbean and aligns itself with the airstrip. Dozens of heavily armed U.S. Marines stand guard on the tarmac; a helicopter circles above them. A riot squad crouches as the heavy transport plane hits the ground and slows to a dead stop. Humvees with mounted machine guns quickly encircle the plane. The rear cargo door lowers like a drawbridge and thirty-four prisoners wearing orange jumpsuits stumble out, one at a time. They wear gloves, orange hats, goggles with blackened lenses and surgical masks over their mouths to protect the marines from tuberculosis and whatever other diseases the prisoners might have picked up in Afghanistan. The marines frisk them and check their shoes before leading them to two yellow school buses.

It has been a long flight from Kandahar and the latest shipment of enemy combatants shuffle across the tarmac like stickmen, their legs stiffened by hours of immobility. A third of them have gunshot wounds. One man has to be carried off the plane. There are Saudis, Pakistanis, Egyptians, Algerians, Ethiopians and Tanzanians, and even a few Brits and an Australian. "There's many countries represented," says Colonel Terry Carrico, a U.S. Army commander. The broad assortment of nationalities at the camp shows how the Taliban has been propped up by radical Muslims from around the world. But their nationalities are not apparent as they are escorted from the aircraft on a clear Sunday morning in January 2002. For now they are all citizens of Guantanamo Bay.

Camp X-Ray lies in a valley between the harbor and the mountainous frontier of communist Cuba. Ten guard towers surround the camp, and each one of them is occupied by a sniper armed with an M-16 assault rifle. There are three layers of fence, topped with coils of barbed wire. Spotlights propped on poles keep the camp lit like a baseball field at night. When the prisoners look out through the rows of fence, they see at least a half-dozen U.S. flags strung from guard posts and a lush tropical forest that is the exact opposite of the Afghan moonscape they left behind. The only thing they might find familiar is a small sign nailed to the eastern guard post bearing the symbol of Mecca. It informs the prisoners of the direction to which they should pray.

Only a few of the prisoners were from Canada. They included Ahcene Zemiri, who had been part of the Algerian network in Montreal. Zemiri had been captured at Tora Bora. Mohamedou Ould Slahi was also there. Slahi had preached at the Montreal mosque attended by Ressam and the other Algerian extremists. Transcripts of U.S. military detainee hearings de-classified in 2006 allege he "actively recruited" for jihad. "An al-Qaeda operative identified the detainee as an Al Qaeda facilitator who played a part in recruiting jihadists to fight in Afghanistan and Chechnya and to become suicide hijackers in the West," a military officer said during the hearings. "The detainee convinced the Al Qaeda operative and three future World Trade Center suicide hijackers to undergo Al Qaeda basic training in Afghanistan. ... An Al Qaeda operative stated that the detainee facilitated the operative's initial travel to Afghanistan and his initial introduction to Osama bin Laden."

He was also accused of being "a suspected facilitator" of Ressam's 1999 plot to bomb Los Angeles airport. He said he "hated Canada" when he left in 2000 because he was being pressured by CSIS, but he said at his detainee hearing that he wanted to return. "Man, just give me a couple of million dollars and just let me go on my own and I will be just fine." Slahi admitted he had sworn loyalty to bin Laden in 1991, that he underwent weapons training in Afghanistan and that his goal was "to become a martyr by dying for Islam." He also conceded that he had signed a confession admitting that "while I was in Canada, I was planning for a terrorist attack," but he said he only did that because he was being tortured.

Also at Guantanamo were the sons of Ahmed Khadr, Omar and Abdurahman. Omar's journey to Guantanamo began in June 2002.

His father had arranged for Omar to receive a month of "one-on-one" training from a man named Abu Haddi. The course "consisted of training in the use of rocket-propelled grenades, rifles, pistols, hand grenades and explosives," a U.S. indictment says. He did further training in the use of land mines in July, and then joined a group of Al Qaeda operatives who were planning attacks against U.S. forces in Afghanistan, the indictment says.

Sergeant 1st Class Layne Morris was at the U.S. Army base near Khost, Afghanistan, when a local man walked in and offered to sell information about two Arabs. In those days, the Americans were offering money for tips about the remnants of the Al Qaeda and Taliban forces.

"My neighbor is Al Qaeda and he's hiding all these antitank mines in the backyard," the man said.

"How do you know this?" Morris asked him.

"Well, I helped him bury them."

"When?"

"Last night," the man replied.

A team of special operations troops were assembled and they drove out to storm the home. The search turned up more than two dozen antitank mines and a how-to guide on planting them to inflict maximum damage. The Americans took one prisoner, but the second Arab could not be found. They asked around and were told he had fled to another village called Ab Khail.

So early on July 27, thirty members of the Special Forces and the 82nd Airborne set off for Ab Khail, along with twenty members of the Afghan Militia Forces. Sergeant Morris drove in a tan Toyota Tacoma pickup truck with five other soldiers, among them Sergeant 1st Class Christopher J. Speer, a twenty-eight-year-old medic assigned to the unit just a week before.

Sergeant Speer had joined the army in 1992 and had already served in Rwanda, Kenya and Uganda. The youngest of three brothers, he loved to draw and was always sketching. He had decided to marry his wife, Tabitha, on their first date six years earlier. "Chris treated me like a princess, always very loving, putting me before everything," Tabitha says. "I had never met such a genuine, honest and giving man ... He called my dad for his blessing after asking me to marry him." The Speers have two children, Taryn and Tanner. "He was able to phone once from Afghanistan. He spoke to Taryn and told us both that he loved and missed us. I was to give both the kids a hug and kiss and tell them he loved them. I asked him to be careful and he said not to worry."

It was shortly before noon when the Americans reached Ab Khail. "It didn't seem to be that big; it was mainly a lot of farms, a lot of isolated buildings," said Specialist Christopher Vedvick, part of the 82nd Airborne contingent. One of those buildings was quickly identified as their target, the compound where a group of Al Qaeda fighters were said to have been training with firearms and explosives. Inside they found women and children, but there was also a man with a severe leg injury. He said it was from a car accident but an army medic said the injured man had obviously been hit by a mine. "We knew we had the right guy," Morris said.

Then the team commander noticed something as he was checking the readings on his Global Positioning System. Communications specialists had been tracking a suspicious signal for several days, a signal they thought might be a satellite phone, which indicated Al Qaeda might be present. They had traced the beacon to a spot that they now realized was just a few hundred meters away. They decided to check it out. A small team of Special Ops and Airborne approached the compound, and Morris peeked inside. He saw five men holding AK-47 assault rifles, and they looked as if they were preparing to use them. He backed out and had troops surround the perimeter.

As Morris waited for reinforcements, a group of Afghan children wandered over. Morris pulled out his camera and took a few pictures. The kids smiled but never let on about what they must have known—that all hell was about to break loose. More troops arrived after five minutes, and two Afghan soldiers were sent in to try to talk to the armed men inside the compound. The two soldiers were crouching beside a wall when two gunmen jumped up and shot them in the head. "They just slaughtered them,"

Morris recalled. Then a hail of grenades and bullets came flying out at the Americans.

"It was mayhem."

The first grenade exploded less than two meters from Vedvick. Shrapnel hit his left side. The metal fragments also tore into Private 1st Class Brian S. Worth. Moments later, a second grenade hit Vedvick. Rifleman Michael Rewakowski ran to help, but another grenade knocked him to the ground and fragments embedded in his right calf, left forearm and left temple. Vedvick was hit by three grenades altogether and had wounds to his shoulder, arm, elbow, thigh and calf. "There were bullets all around," he said.

Morris pulled one of the injured soldiers to safety and took cover. He tried to triangulate the source of the fire and pointed his rocket-propelled grenade launcher at what he decided was the most likely target. Just as he fired, something slammed into him "like a sledgehammer." Shrapnel had struck the right side of his nose, ricocheted in behind his eye, and blown out the side of his face. "The lights went out," he said. He recovered sufficiently to retreat to where, just a few minutes before, he had taken photos of the Afghan kids, and someone got on the radio and called in air support.

Two A-10 Thunderbolts, maneuverable planes designed for providing close-range support to ground troops, were accompanied by two AH-64 Apache attack helicopters and a pair of F/A-18 Hornets. The air strikes were intense. Rockets, canons and 250-kilogram bombs struck the compound. "They laid waste to that place," Vedvick said. Yet even as the bombing destroyed the compound, the armed men inside continued to fight. A Black Hawk helicopter swooped in to evacuate the wounded to the Bagram Air Base, almost two hundred kilometers to the north. The last thing Vedvick remembers seeing was a dark mushroom cloud rising high above the compound.

The bombing lasted three hours, until the Americans decided it was safe to send troops inside. One of the first to go was the medic, Speer. Six days earlier, Speer had walked into a minefield to rescue two wounded Afghan children. He applied a tourniquet to one and bandaged the other, then waved down a passing truck to take them to the U.S. Army hospital. It was risky, but Speer may have been thinking about his own children. Before leaving for Afghanistan, he had hidden letters for them at home: "It's no secret how much I love you. Take care of each other. Love, Daddy."

Inside the obliterated compound, the Americans found four bodies. They continued searching for more. Watching them from behind a pile of rubble was fifteen-year-old Omar Khadr, who had been injured in the air strikes but was the only fighter left alive. He held a pistol in one hand and a grenade in the other, according to a U.S. military report. When Speer was within range, Khadr threw his grenade, the military report said. The shrapnel struck Sergeant Speer in the head. As the soldier fell, U.S. troops opened fire on Omar, shooting him in the chest. The American soldiers approached Omar and saw he was still alive. He begged them to finish him off, but the troops refused. Instead, they loaded him onto a helicopter to Bagram.

The injured U.S. soldiers spent only a day at Bagram before being airlifted to a hospital in Landstuhl, Germany. Speer had the worst injuries. His wife flew in to sit at his bedside. "She held his hand, whispered to him and gave him a kiss on the cheek," said Morris's wife, Leisl, who had flown to Germany. "And he turned and puckered to kiss her." Sergeant Speer died on August 6.

Omar was treated at the Bagram Air Base, north of Kabul. Then one day he surprised the Americans by claiming he was a Canadian. U.S. officials notified Ottawa, which confirmed he was indeed a Canadian citizen, the son of Ahmed Khadr. Despite everything Omar had done, the Department of Foreign Affairs decided to treat him as it would any Canadian detained overseas. "This should be treated like a standard consular case," the department wrote in a memo three days after Omar had killed a U.S. soldier while fighting with the enemy. Foreign Affairs began pressing the Americans to allow Canadian diplomats to visit the wounded teen and argued that because he was a juvenile, Omar should be treated differently from other prisoners. Their pleas were ignored. Omar arrived at Guantanamo Bay on October 28, on a flight with thirty other enemy combatants.

I never heard any Canadian politicians express their regrets for the death of Sergeant Speer and the wounding of his colleagues, who had gone to Afghanistan to fight a global menace that threatens Canada as much as any other Western nation. Secret documents show that concerns were raised at that time with the prime minister, who was warned that the Khadr family's exploits could come back to haunt him, given that he had taken the highly unusual step of intervening in the case of Ahmed Khadr. The only official I ever heard express anger about Speer's death was an aide to Foreign Minister Bill Graham, who castigated me for reporting on Omar and the way he had killed a U.S. soldier. My stories, she said, had put the youth at risk. A U.S. military investigation later determined that Omar had attended an Al Qaeda training camp in Kabul, had worked as a translator for Al Qaeda and conducted surveillance missions at an airport near Khost to collect information about U.S. convoy movements. He also planted ten landmines in the mountains between Khost and Ghardez, according to U.S. military documents, at a choke point where U.S. forces patrol in vehicles.

"There are many ways of explaining it," Omar's sister Zaynab told me in one of several e-mails we exchanged. "You can get a [firearms] license very easily so he might have had [the gun] for protection; he is Arab after all. It is very dangerous there now. Or he could have been given it by someone.

"Would Omar do such a thing as kill someone? If what the Americans say is true it could have been self-defense or an accident or he could have been forced to do it. I was not with him and I don't know the situation he was in, but I know that I can trust Omar to do the right thing, so if he did it then he must have had his reasons," Zaynab wrote.

Khadr's wife and daughters stayed for a while at Logar but eventually crossed the border into Pakistan and made their way to Islamabad, where they were assisted by one of bin Laden's close friends. When I interviewed them later, they did not conceal their admiration for bin Laden and his ideals. "Osama bin Laden did not say that Americans should evacuate America or else we'd kill them. He just said this is our country and we would like you to leave, and I think he has a right," Zaynab told me when we met at an Islamabad hotel. She glanced at her toddler, who was playing with my Nikon. "If I was to choose for my daughter to live a life of no meaning or die a martyr," she added, "I would choose for her to die a martyr. I'd love to die a martyr. It's a desire that I believe that any Muslim would have, or should have."

In 2003, Ahmed Khadr was given "operational responsibility" for mounting attacks against U.S. and other foreign troops along the Pakistan–Afghanistan border, according to the police documents based on interviews with his eldest son Abdullah that were conducted in Pakistan and Toronto. "Khadr's father asked [Abdullah] to assist in this effort by procuring munitions to use against the U.S. and coalition forces," says an affidavit written by RCMP Corporal Richard Jenkins. "During a six-month period in 2003, Khadr purchased approximately $20,000 worth of AK-47 rounds, rocket-propelled grenades and mortar rounds."

Ahmed Khadr crossed from Afghanistan into Pakistan but remained in South Waziristan, a remote, mountainous region of Pakistan under the control of tribal warlords sympathetic to the Taliban and Al Qaeda. Because Khadr was partially crippled, his youngest son, Abdul Karim, then fourteen, went to live with him late in the summer of 2003. The youth wrote to his mother and sister in September, asking them to send warm clothes and food. But the border region was not a perfect sanctuary. Pakistani and U.S. forces were operating intensely in the area, searching for bin Laden and his followers.

Late in September, the Pakistanis received an intelligence report indicating that a group of Al Qaeda fighters had taken over six abandoned mud huts in the village of Baghar, about five kilometers from the Afghanistan border. Intelligence agents tracked their movements for several days and on October 2, a Pakistani army unit moved in after nightfall to surround the village.

At dawn, the troops called out toward the houses, urging the occupants to surrender. Ten women and children walked out and were searched and taken into custody. Then the Al Qaeda fighters opened fire. The gun battle lasted all day, as the soldiers cleared one compound after the next. Abdul Karim was shot and captured but Khadr continued to fight. The ground troops could not flush him out, so they called in a Cobra attack helicopter, which sent a small rocket screaming into the compound.

By the time it was all over, two Pakistani soldiers were dead, along with eight Al Qaeda fighters. The troops seized what was described as "a massive cache" of rifles, anti-tank mines, grenades, foreign currency and videotapes. Six of the dead were soon identified, but two of the bodies were so badly mutilated that forensic tests were required to determine who they were.

One turned out to be the leader of a Chinese Muslim extremist group. A bone fragment from the other body was compared to a DNA sample taken from Omar Khadr at Guantanamo Bay. On January 15, the Pakistani foreign ministry sent a "Secret" memo to Ottawa advising that there was a match.

"Thus, Ahmad Sa'id Khadr is confirmed dead by DNA analysis," the note said.

A Pakistani official would not tell me where the body was buried but said Khadr was "a very high ranking member of Al Qaeda. He was on our watch list. He has been a close associate of bin Laden. He was suspected of the Egyptian embassy bombing in Islamabad in 1995. He was also a fundraiser for Al Qaeda. So, he was wanted by us." Another Pakistani official told me Khadr was a member of Al Qaeda's Egyptian wing, the Al Jihad. "And he was also a member of bin Laden's inner circle, and he had close relations with his deputy Al-Zawahiri." The official also told me Khadr collected money in Canada for charity but that the funds were redirected. "Instead, Khadr misused the money to fund a terrorist camp and assist Al Qaeda operatives."

Early in 2004, Khadr's wife was allowed to return to Toronto with Abdul Karim, who needed hospital treatment for his gunshot wounds. Many Canadians protested their arrival, but the government took no action, aside from withholding their passports. Former prime minister Brian Mulroney, who had enjoyed good relations with the U.S. during his term, criticized "the limp and pathetic manner the Liberal government handled the case of the Khadr family, intimates of Osama bin Laden ... some of whose members have taken up arms in support of terrorism, and yet are welcomed back to Canada with open arms. Imagine the signal that these images send to the White House and the civilized world."

But to radical Islamists, Khadr was a hero. The Islamic Observation Centre in London issued a statement praising "the Knight Ahmed Said Khadr" as a founding member of Al Qaeda who had been "martyred for his goodness and correctness." The eulogy spoke of a life of trials and then stated: "You kept your calm to assist your brothers instead of returning to Canada with its clear water and greenery and beauty ... They could not remove you from the land of heroes and sacrifice."

Zaynab Khadr returned to Toronto from Pakistan in 2005 for the first time since the 9/11 attacks. She was greeted at the airport by RCMP officers armed with a search warrant. The warrant alleged that "Zaynab Khadr and her family are Al Qaeda" and that she had "participated in the activities of a terrorist group" by collecting money in Canada and delivering it to her father, who used it to "fund and supply Al Qaeda camps in Afghanistan." She has not been charged.

That fall, on November 7, the U.S. military announced it had filed criminal charges against Omar Khadr, who was by then 19. In addition, the widow of the soldier killed by Omar won a lawsuit in a Utah court that could force the Khadr family to pay damages. Later in November, Omar's older brother Abdullah, then 24, flew back to Toronto from Pakistan to join his family. Police questioned him upon his arrival.

"Khadr told me that he never killed anyone personally," wrote FBI Special Agent Gregory T. Hughes, who interviewed Abdullah. "However, at another point in the interview he said that he sometimes regretted not 'doing something.' Khadr believed, like his father, that Canada should not be attacked unless the country did something against Muslims to warrant it. However, Khadr said that the United States was a different matter as it had oppressed Muslims in many places around the world. When asked if the United States was a target, Khadr smiled and looked away."

A few days after his return, police obtained an arrest warrant. The U.S. is seeking his extradition to stand trial on charges that he sold weapons and explosives to Al Qaeda and the Taliban for attacks against coalition forces. According to investigators, when Abdullah was arrested in Pakistan, he was in the process of buying missiles from a former member of a Pakistani terrorist group for $1,000 each. He intended to re-sell them to an Al Qaeda weapons broker. Two days before Christmas, Abdullah appeared in a courtroom in downtown Toronto for a bail hearing, wearing a T-shirt with a Muslim logo. His lawyer asked the judge to release Abdullah into the custody of his grandparents, the Elsamnahs, so he could live at the house on Khartoum Avenue with what the lawyer called "a simple, typical immigrant family."

7

WHITE MEAT

SOPHIE SUREAU keeps the photos she took during her trip to Bali in a small hardcover album, just big enough for one picture per page. She opens the book of memories to a photo of five friends smiling and relaxing on a beach under a backdrop of blue sky and waves. The next frame shows Sureau with her best friend, wearing the bikinis they packed for their holiday in paradise.

She turns the page to the next photo.

It shows Sureau lying in a hospital bed in Singapore. Her body is a patchwork of scars. Her neck, left arm and hand, and the whole left side of her back are swollen and red. There are open sores. It is painful just to look at. A quarter of her body was scorched in the hellish minutes after the bomb went off.

"They wanted to kill me," she says.

Sureau is a talkative, friendly French Canadian. She has blue eyes and a brilliant smile. She has lived abroad and has friends all over the world. At university in Montreal she was active in a student organization called AIESEC, which works to increase cultural understanding. She is a model global citizen.

It was not because of anything she did that Osama bin Laden's radical Islamists wanted to kill her. It was because of what she represented. "Whites deserved to die," one of the bombers said during his trial. The group behind the bombing, Jemaah Islamiyah, is a regional affiliate of Al Qaeda that wants to establish a Muslim state in Southeast Asia. To Al Qaeda, Westerners are nonbelievers who must be killed and subjugated for the glory of God. And so Sureau was coldly attacked along with the hundreds of others who were killed or maimed at a bar in a tourist resort that night on October 12, 2002. That is the hardest part to take. "I don't dream about fire," she says. "It's about people wanting to kill me."

Sureau was working at the Brazilian office of the Montreal marketing research company Ipsos when she started planning a Bali vacation. Her boyfriend, Jeff Syslo, is an American who also worked in Brazil. Her best friend, Christèle Berthelot, a dual Canadian and French citizen, lives in Hong Kong. Together with Andres, an Uruguayan working in Denmark, and Morgana, a Brazilian living in Hong Kong, they decided to have a holiday together. "We decided to meet in Asia for two or three weeks," she says. Sureau and Syslo went to Malaysia first, and they were to rendezvous with the rest of the group in Bali.

It had been barely a year since 9/11, and they were well aware of the risks. Syslo thought it unwise to travel at all. Wherever they went they contacted the U.S. and Canadian embassies. They ruled out visiting areas close to the Philippines because of terror warnings. Sureau flew to Bali with Syslo on October 11. They rented bikes and looked into renting a car. The others arrived late Saturday afternoon and they had a little reunion. It was the first time they had been together in months. They went to a Mexican restaurant, Sureau wearing a red silk dress with pink flowers and Syslo in his yellow sneakers.

They were planning to go snorkeling in the morning, and then get a car and spend the week scuba diving. "After dinner we were kind of like, 'Well, do we want to go out or not?' And we said, 'We can go walk around for a little bit,'" Syslo says. On the main tourist strip in Kuta, they passed Paddy's Irish Bar, but Morgana said her sister had been to a place called the Sari Club and that it was the place to go. There was a small lineup outside, but it moved quickly. The time was 11 p.m. "We got in and it was packed," Sureau says. "It was full of Westerners and we thought, 'What are we doing here, so far from home? It's all full of blond hair and blue eyes.'"

They squeezed into a spot near the entrance and stood in a circle. "There was no place to sit down. It was totally crowded. I don't think any of us really felt like being there." The drinks arrived—a local concoction made of fruit juice and alcohol.

"I took one sip. Then everything exploded."

Syslo was facing Paddy's and saw right away that a bomb had gone off across the street. He and Sureau looked at each other, as if to say, 'Thank God it didn't happen here.'

Then the second bomb went off.

This one was far more powerful. There was a flash and a deafening boom, and then all went dark. "I just remember something hitting me," Syslo says. He compares it to the time he got walloped playing football. Whether it was debris or just the force of the blast, he does not know. He was thrown toward the street. He got up and looked around. It was like a dream. Everything was dark and there was smoke, almost like fog. Nobody was moving. "This can't be happening," he thought. "I'm the only one who survived." He walked out to the street and saw nothing but mangled cars. Then he heard screaming in Paddy's and saw people moving. He looked back at the Sari Club. "There was really nothing left." It was all rubble and smoke. Flames started to rise.

Sureau had blacked out. When she came to, she was lying face down on the floor near the entrance. People were walking right over her as they flooded out of the bar. Every time she tried to get up, somebody would step on her back or shoulders and she would go down again. Syslo thought he heard her screaming and went back in to find her. He came across a semiconscious woman and pulled her out to the street. Then he went back and helped carry a heavy man; he believes it was one of the rugby players who died. He went back in but he could not hear Sureau anymore. He saw some local people screaming and pointing at a woman who was pinned down with a beam across her waist. He tried to get her out but couldn't. (It wasn't Sureau.) She was on fire, and the flames around her were getting bigger. He was getting burned. He had to get out. He had to leave her behind.

Sureau was sure she saw Syslo, or at least his yellow sneakers—who else in Bali would be wearing yellow sneakers? But he never heard her call. Syslo took a scooter to the hospital. Maybe Sureau was fine. Maybe she was already back at the hotel. Or maybe she was dead. In fact, she was still on the floor. She could feel the flames against her skin. Her dress was on fire. She put her face in her hands. "I said to myself, 'Sophie, you're going to burn here and you're going to die.'" It was so hot, and it started to really hurt. "That's it," she told herself. "I have to let myself die." But then she started thinking about her family, her nephews and nieces, especially the newborn, Valerie, whom she hadn't even met. She gave one last push and managed to lift herself and throw off the debris piled on top of her. She ran outside into the chaos. "I didn't even look behind me."

Her only thought was survival. Her feet hurt terribly, as if she were walking on broken glass. It was the third-degree burns. She remembered there was a little store on the corner that sold beachwear, and she went over and took a pair of plastic flip-flops. She didn't bother assessing her injuries. She didn't have to. She knew they were bad. She could see the bone poking through her melted skin. She started asking around for a hospital. She saw an Australian. He offered her some bottled water and pointed the way to the hospital. It was a long walk, though. She saw some locals with motorcycles and asked one to take her to the hospital. He agreed and she climbed on the bike.

The hospital was packed. There were ambulances and trucks lined up outside, each with dozens of wounded, some unconscious. Some looked dead. The lobby was full of beds and people. "It was awful." She decided she had to go somewhere else. She got back on the bike and they headed for the airport, thinking there might be a first-aid station there. On the way they passed a small clinic, but it did not look well equipped so they kept going until they came to a foreign medical clinic run by a humanitarian aid group.

There were fifteen or twenty beds, all full. Those with injuries deemed less serious were lying on the floors and standing. The staff showered Sureau in cold water and put her in an ambulance to take her to a maternity hospital. There was no surgeon. All they could do was bandage her up and give her morphine. She needed to get to a hospital.

At about 7 a.m., Syslo walked in and saw her. "Jeff, you're alive!" she yelled. He had gone back to the hotel and met a German anesthesiologist who told him that his burns were serious and that he needed to see to a doctor. The first hospital was full. He was turned away from a second hospital too, and at the third he walked in and saw Sureau. "That's my wife!" he shouted. (From that day on, he has called Sureau his wife, and she has called him her husband.)

Sureau's parents were just finishing dinner with their daughter Christine and her husband and three kids when the phone rang at 8:45 on Saturday night. The caller identified himself as an official at the Department of Foreign Affairs. He asked Real Sureau if he was Sophie's father. He said yes. The official asked if he knew Sophie was in Bali. He said yes. He asked Real if he was aware that something had happened in Bali and that Sophie had been hurt. Real switched on the television set. The phone rang again at 2 a.m. This time it was Syslo and Berthelot. They said they were with Sureau and that while she was badly injured, her life was not in danger and she was awaiting an emergency room examination. "Of course we were very shocked by what was looking like a terrorist act," Real said, "but we were happy that she was alive and with friends."

Syslo called again at 3:30 a.m. This time Sureau got on the phone and reassured her parents that she was all right. But Syslo knew she was in bad shape. She needed to get out of there, to a proper hospital. That meant an air-ambulance evacuation, but the operators wanted $20,000 up front. One of Sophie's friends at HSBC Bank in Sao Paulo got the money and transferred it to South Asia to cover the airlift to Singapore. Sophie boarded an ancient South African military plane on Monday morning. There was another stretcher beside her, but the body was so badly burned she could not tell if it was a man or woman, or even if the person still had legs. Syslo held her hand the whole way; his face was so swollen that he could hardly breathe.

The hospital report written by the doctor at Singapore General documents Sureau's injuries in exacting detail. "Deep dermal" burns on her left arm and forearm, left hand, right arm and right foot. "Mid dermal" burns on her back, face and thighs. "Total burn surface area 23%." The hospital report goes on to describe her "bilateral central eardrum perforation with an inflamed left external auditory canal." The explosion had left her with mild hearing loss. And then there was the "post traumatic stress reaction and depression." A psychiatrist put her on Prosac (30 mg), Prothiaden (75 mg), Epilim Chrono (500 mg) and Atarax (10 mg, 10 mg and 50 mg daily). To top it off, she had chipped several teeth—her incisors and right molars.

Sureau's parents decided that one of them should go to Singapore. Real thought his wife should be the one, but she was "too emotional" and said she would rather he went. Berthelot met him at the airport and took him straight to the hospital. "It was quite a shock at first." He wanted to kiss his daughter but she was almost entirely wrapped in bandages. The only exposed flesh was on her left toe. He kissed it. "She was alive and still smiling as usual, and confident." He came back to the hospital the next day and Sophie was upset. She wanted to get out of there and go back to work. The news got worse. Sophie's health insurance company would not pay her bills, and the Canadian government was refusing to accept responsibility because she had been working in Brazil for three years.

Sophie Sureau stayed at Singapore General for thirty-five days while surgeons peeled skin from her thigh and grafted it onto her burns. Meanwhile, her father returned to Montreal and held a joint news conference with the Canadian Red Cross, appealing for donations to bring Sophie home. Canada gives welfare to terrorists and funds their front organizations, but until Sophie's father's appeal, had not been willing to pay to help this stranded Canadian victim of terror get home. The federal government, shamed by the publicity, relented and agreed to cover her costs. Dr. Lennard Chan of Singapore General Hospital's department of burns and plastic surgery pronounced her fit to travel. She flew to Toronto and then to Montreal, where she was admitted at Hôtel Dieu, the burn hospital. When I met Sureau nine months later, she was still going to physiotherapy five days a week for three to four hours.

"I don't understand why people would do such a thing," she told me. "I can understand you want to kill someone because that person killed your whole family or something ..." The fact that she had never done anything like that didn't matter. The bombers said nightclubs were targeted because they were places of sin. The terrorists did not care who was inside; all that mattered was that they were infidels. "Australians, Americans, whatever—they are all white people," one of the bomb makers, an Indonesian named Ali Imron, remarked.

"It goes beyond our understanding of humans that we would willfully want to go out and exterminate people for no other reason than they're different," Syslo says. "It's like Hitler going out to kill the Jews. It's crazy. It's beyond understanding."

Sureau does not know what she would say if she ever met the men behind the plot, some of whom have since been arrested. "I don't think it's worth saying anything. They're so brainwashed. Do you have a heart inside of you? There are so many better ways to spend your days than getting ready to kill people."

As it turns out, if Sureau wanted to deliver her message to a member of the terrorist organization responsible for the bombing plot, she would not have to go far from home.

A Canadian flag hangs limply from the steel pole at Holy Cross Secondary School, "Home of the Raiders." The students sitting on the curb outside wear gray slacks and white shirts. The sign above the door reads Spes Unica. I ask a girl with a long chestnut ponytail what it means. She turns to her friends. "What does that mean?" she yells. She turns back and says, "No idea." What it means is "Only Hope," as in God is humanity's sole hope for salvation.

A few blocks away, Abdullah Jabarah sits in the garage of his parents' suburban house with two friends, who are slouched on an old couch eating their lunch from McDonald's bags. Abdullah is clearly not interested in talking. I show him a copy of an FBI report that says his little brother, Mohammed Jabarah, is an Al Qaeda terrorist.

"I don't have time to read it," he says. "Just tell me what it says."

"It says your brother has admitted to everything," I tell him.

"Burn it," one of the kids on the couch says.

Abdullah is unfazed.

"They give him drugs and he'll admit to anything. You saw what they did in Iraq, in Afghanistan."

He tells me to leave. As I'm walking back down the driveway, one of the kids on the couch says, "You got off easy."

The Jabarahs moved to Canada from Kuwait in 1994, three years after Allied troops liberated the country from Saddam Hussein, who had invaded and plundered his oil-rich neighbor. "After the Gulf War, it was really scary in the Gulf area and I wanted to have a good life and a good education for my sons and a new home," Mansour Jabarah told me. He brought his wife and four sons to a two-storey home with a porch on a quiet street in St. Catharines, Ontario. The father served as vice-president of the Islamic Society of St. Catharines; the boys helped out at the mosque, a sandstone building with twin minarets next to a Sunoco gas station. "None to be Worshipped but God" reads the inscription on the mosque wall.

The Jabarah boys did not stand out at Holy Cross high school, although Mohammed was serious about his Islamic faith. "He was a religious boy. He didn't drink, he didn't have girlfriends," his father said. In his high school yearbook photo, the young Jabarah sports a thin mustache and does not smile. "The boy was a gentleman," recalled Hussein Hamdani, a family friend and an official at the Islamic Society of St. Catharines. "He was working here in the mosque, nice polite boy ... I'm damned sure they got the wrong man."

Although Mansour Jabarah wanted his children to become Canadians, he also wanted them to maintain their Arab and Islamic roots, so in 1996 he began sending the boys back to Kuwait during the summer school break. During Mohammed's first trip home, he met up with a childhood friend named Anas Al Kandari, who had grown up in the same neighborhood of Kuwait City. Al Kandari introduced him to Sulaiman Abu Gaith, a high school religion teacher and hard-core Islamist. Abu Gaith showed Jabarah and Al Kandari Al Qaeda propaganda videos about the war in Chechnya and told them about Abdullah Azzam, one of the founders of Al Qaeda.

Jabarah returned to Canada for school that fall, but he nurtured his interest in jihad from his home in Ontario. He spent a lot of time on the Internet, visiting websites that glorified the mujahedin holy warriors in Chechnya and the Palestinian territories. He also began hanging out with a few jihadi veterans, who had participated in training and combat in places like Bosnia. And he began raising money for the jihad in Chechnya, which he sent to Abu Gaith. Shortly after his high school graduation in June 2000, Jabarah flew back to Kuwait City; this time, he did not come home to Canada at the end of the summer. Instead he went to Karachi, where he met up with Al Qaeda operatives who arranged his passage to Afghanistan.

In Jalalabad, he was reunited with his older brother, Abdul Rahman, and Al Kandari, who had also traveled to Afghanistan for jihad training. From there, they entered bin Laden's boot camp system. Al Qaeda quickly saw Jabarah's potential. His fluent English and Canadian passport made him a valued addition to the terror network. He could travel freely without raising suspicion. He was also young and unworldly. "He grew up in Canada, he never went to any Asian countries before," his father said.

The Jabarah brothers trained together at Camp Sheik Shaheed Abu Yahya, north of Kabul, then Mohammed went on to take addition training. In the winter of 2000, he fell ill with Hepatitis and was treated by none other than Ayman Al Zawahiri, the doctor who was Al Qaeda's second-in-command.

At the Al Farooq training camp near Kandahar in 2001, Jabarah continued his training. He then took a sniper training course. It concluded with a shooting competition. The winners got to have dinner with bin Laden. Jabarah fired off his AK-47, and when the dust had settled, he had won. Later he sat in bin Laden's home in Kandahar, listening. It was only then that he began to think about formally joining Al Qaeda. He talked it over with Abu Gaith and then went to bin Laden. The two of them sat together, and Jabarah made bayat, or the martyr's oath. He pledged his allegiance to bin Laden's jihad.

Bin Laden initially sent Jabarah to Karachi to meet Khalid Sheikh Mohammed, who was then in the final stages of planning the 9/11 attacks. Khalid was a plump engineer with a bushy black beard and over-sized eyeglasses. A Kuwaiti educated in North Carolina, he was a womanizer who hung out at bars and beaches. *Time* magazine dubbed him "Al Qaeda's agent 007." Mohammed's face has long been on the FBI's most wanted list, with a US$25-million reward that testified to his importance in the ranks of global terrorism. Name any major Al Qaeda plot, and Khalid was probably involved. He first came to the attention of intelligence agencies after the February 1993 attempt to bring down the World Trade Center with a truck bomb. Investigators traced the plot to Ramzi Youssef, his nephew. By the time they found Khalid's trail, however, he and Youssef had fled to the Philippines. From Manila, Khalid and his nephew plotted the assassination of the Pope, but his main preoccupation was Project Bojinka (Croatian for "Bang"), which involved planting bombs on a dozen American airliners and timing them to detonate over the Pacific. He also wanted to crash a plane into CIA headquarters. But a fire in the apartment where the bombs were being manufactured betrayed the plot. Khalid escaped to Afghanistan.

From his new base in Kandahar, Khalid used his international web of terrorists to help plan the 1998 bombings of the U.S. embassies in Kenya and Tanzania, and the bombing in 2000 of USS *Cole* in Yemen's port city of Aden. Eventually he returned to one of the scenarios that had been discussed during Bojinka: hijacking a plane and ramming it into a building. He assembled the hijacking team and planned the attacks in great detail. He wired tens of thousands of dollars to the hijackers and met at least once with Mohammed Atta, the ringleader.

Later, he would boast about the attacks in a videotaped interview. "We had a large surplus of brothers willing to die as martyrs," he told Al Jazeera. During an interview with the Arab-language network, he was told that he was considered a terrorist by many people. His reply: "They are right. That is what we do for a living." His colleague, Ramzi bin al-Shibh, added: "If terrorism is to throw terror into the heart of your enemy and the enemy of Allah then we thank Him, the Most Merciful, the Most Compassionate, for enabling us to be terrorists."

Even before 9/11, Khalid Sheikh Mohammed was planning follow-up attacks. In August 2001 he met Mohammed Jabarah, who was then just nineteen years old. The meeting took place in Karachi. Khalid gave Jabarah US$10,000 and told him to organize attacks on Western embassies in Southeast Asia. The plan was to ram truck bombs into the U.S. and Israeli embassies in Manila. It was to be a joint operation, with Al Qaeda supplying the suicide bombers and the money. Jemaah Islamiyah was to procure the explosives and take care of the details. "Jabarah advised that he was in charge of the financing for the operation," according to a classified FBI report.

For two weeks, Jabarah underwent intensive training at a house in Karachi, learning techniques for operating in urban environments. Operational security was central to the training—how to live, travel and plot without arousing suspicion. Eventually Jabarah was introduced to Hambali (an alias for Riduan Isamuddin), an Al Qaeda member who served as operations chief of Jemaah Islamiyah. The meeting took place at the Karachi apartment of one of Hambali's four wives. Hambali instructed Jabarah to contact his two point men in Malaysia—Mahmoud (an alias for Faiz Bafana) and Saad (an alias for Fathur Rahman Al Ghozi).

"Make sure you leave before Tuesday," Khalid cautioned Jabarah.

The Tuesday he was referring to was September 11.

Jabarah left Pakistan for Hong Kong on September 10. He was staying at a Hong Kong hotel when nineteen Al Qaeda operatives hijacked four planes and brought down the World Trade Center. As he watched on television, he began to doubt he could carry off the assignment he had been handed. But he remembered bin Laden's words. And in a testament to his conviction, even after the atrocities of 9/11, he vowed to carry on with his mission to cause even more human carnage. After three days in Hong Kong he flew to Kuala Lumpur, Malaysia, and met an agent code-named Azzam, as well as Mahmoud, a bomb-making expert who had learned his tradecraft at an Al Qaeda camp in Afghanistan. Mahmoud told Jabarah to speak to Saad, who was then training with Moro Islamic Liberation Front rebels in the Philippine mountains. "Jabarah told Mahmoud that he needed to go to the

Philippines and Mahmoud said he would get in touch with Saad, as he is the person who could obtain any of the needed explosives," says the FBI report.

Jabarah, the planner, and his associate, Ahmed Sahagi, who was to be the suicide bomber, flew to the Philippine city of Makati on September 22 and checked in at the Horizon Hotel. A few days later, Saad e-mailed his Manila phone number to Jabarah and they made plans to meet. "When Saad arrived at the hotel, Saad informed Jabarah he only had 300 kilograms of TNT and he needed additional time and money. Saad informed Jabarah he wanted four tons of explosives," the FBI report said.

There was another complication. Saad thought the U.S. embassy in Manila was not a good target because it was set back too far from the road. They scouted the U.S. and Israeli embassies together and Saad decided to return to Malaysia to discuss the plot with Mahmoud. They met again in Kuala Lumpur to talk about targets, and decided the embassies in the Philippines were no good. They wanted to try somewhere else. Mahmoud advised Jabarah to go to Singapore to record videotapes of potential targets there with his Canadian passport, he could travel freely around Asia.

In a parking lot at Singapore's Marina South, Jabarah held a meeting with local terrorist operatives and asked for their suggestions about targets. In addition to the U.S. and Israeli embassies, they identified the Australian and British High Commissions, as well as several commercial buildings that housed American companies. Using a Sony video camera, Jabarah posed as a tourist to film sites such as the American Club and American International Assurance. The videos were labeled "Visiting Sightseeing Singapore." They were then transferred to CD-ROMs for distribution up the chain of command. Jabarah rented an apartment in Kuala Lumpur in November 2001, but he was already running short of money and asked Khalid for more. A few days later, at a mall, an Al Qaeda agent named Youssef handed him a number of envelopes. Inside were wads of US$100 bills, tied with elastic bands—US$10,000 in total. Two more bags of cash were delivered over the next few days, each containing $10,000.

Because TNT was difficult to obtain in the region, the cell decided to use ammonium nitrate to amplify the blast. Six trucks were to be used in the operation. Each would carry three tonnes of ammonium nitrate (by comparison, the truck bomb used in Oklahoma City in 1995 contained two to three tonnes of the explosive). "Sammy would bring his people down to Singapore to rig the bombs at the secured warehouse," said a report on the plot by the government of Singapore. "The trucks would then be driven and parked at designated points near the targets. The local cell members would then leave the country as unknown suicide bombers arrived. These suicide bombers (believed to be Arabs) would be brought down to Singapore just a day before the planned attack."

Early in December, Jabarah met Hambali and Azzam at an apartment in Malaysia. Jabarah asked about his brother in Afghanistan, and about Mohammed Atef, the Al Qaeda military chief who had recently been killed by a U.S. air strike. Hambali told Jabarah that Atef had wanted an attack to be carried out right away. They could not wait for the Singapore plot to come together. Hambali wanted to move the target back to Manila. The advantage of attacking in Manila, Hambali said, was that the explosives were already in the Philippines and would not have to be shipped to Singapore. The attack could therefore be done sooner—as Al Qaeda wanted. If the embassies proved too difficult, they would find other targets in the Philippines, Hambali said. By then, however, videos and notes about the Singapore plot had been found in the ruins of an Al Qaeda safe house in Afghanistan that had been bombed by U.S. warplanes. Police moved in to break up the cell. On December 9, 2001, Singapore's Internal Security Department made the first in a series of arrests. Within a week they had arrested thirteen Jemaah Islamiyah members.

Jabarah was in Malaysia when a message landed in his Yahoo account. It was from Azzam. The subject was "Problem." Mahmoud, Jabarah's point man, who knew everything about the plot, had been arrested in Singapore, it said. Jabarah left immediately for southern Thailand. At a hotel in Bangkok, he met with Hambali, who advised him to get out of the region before he was caught. He was too valuable to Al Qaeda to end up behind bars. "It will be a very big hit for us if you're arrested," Hambali said.

Hambali was furious that the Singapore plot had failed, and he began discussing attacks elsewhere. "The last contact Jabarah had with Hambali was in mid-January 2002, in Thailand," the FBI report said. "During this time Hambali discussed carrying out attacks with his group. His plan was to conduct small bombings in bars, cafés or nightclubs frequented by Westerners in Thailand, Malaysia, Singapore, Philippines and *Indonesia* [italics mine]."

Jabarah tried to take a bus to Myanmar, but could not get a visa. He went to Chiang Mai, Thailand, and flew to Bangkok and then Dubai. Using his e-mail address, honda_civic12@yahoo.com, Jabarah contacted Hambali and Khalid. Jabarah sent them a copy of an article from a Canadian newspaper that linked him to the bombing plot in Singapore. He said he had to run and needed money. He met his brother Abdulrahman and they stayed together in Dubai. Jabarah wanted to go to Saudi Arabia but could not get a visa, so he went to Oman, where, according to the FBI, he was helping "Al Qaeda operatives traveling through Oman to Yemen" when he was arrested in March 2002.

A few weeks later, CSIS got a call from the Omanis. They said they had arrested a young Canadian, and he wanted to talk to the Canadian authorities. Once the devoted jihadi, Jabarah had all of a sudden become remarkably cooperative. The jihad had seemed like an adventure at first, it was fun. He could run around playing the game of secret terrorist. But this was no game anymore. Sitting in an Omani jail was no fun at all.

Two CSIS officers brought Jabarah back to Toronto and then a veteran intelligence officer named Mike Pavlovic took him to a hotel in Niagara Falls. Jabarah was a big catch. Pavlovic wined and dined him, and coaxed him into telling what he knew. The interviews continued at a condo in downtown Toronto. CSIS passed their intelligence to the Americans and other allied intelligence agencies. Jabarah had remarkable inside knowledge about Al Qaeda and its key players in Southeast Asia. CSIS contacted the RCMP to see if criminal charges could be brought against Jabarah, but the Mounties said they could not make a case. Not so for the

Americans. Jabarah knew the FBI was after him for trying to bomb their embassies. He decided to make a deal with them. At his request, U.S. officials drafted a surrender agreement. Jabarah signed it and went into U.S. custody.

After news of the case was publicized in Canada in July 2002, a Toronto newspaper claimed there was no evidence against him and that the only reason Canadians were not outraged by his treatment was that he was Muslim, "not a Jones or a Bouchard." The Canadian Arab Federation (CAF) and Canadian Civil Liberties Association held a news conference to demand a government probe. Instead of facilitating his transfer to the United States, Canada should have "been advising him not to go to the United States where he will get lost in the hellhole of secret detentions, secret evidence and secret hearings," said Raja Khouri, the CAF president.

The Security Intelligence Review Committee, the watchdog agency that oversees CSIS, launched an investigation. But the truth was, Jabarah wanted to go to the U.S. He thought he could barter his knowledge for leniency. He chose to talk, and one of the most dangerous terrorists to emerge from Canada became one of its most valuable contributions to the war on terrorism.

In New York, the FBI Joint Terrorism Task Force established a rapport with Jabarah and began to extract intelligence from their young Canadian prisoner, including the code words used by Al Qaeda cells in Southeast Asia. "Market" was code for Malaysia, "Soup" meant Singapore, and "Hotel" meant Philippines, he told the agents. A "Book" was a passport, and Indonesia was referred to as "Terminal." And then there was the code word for Americans: "White Meat."

Jabarah also told them about Khalid Sheik Mohammed and the bomb plots in Singapore and Manila, and about Hambali's plan to attack Westerners in Southeast Asia. In the FBI's account of its interrogations, Jabarah spoke about the bombing plots with cold detachment, sounding like a university student tackling an exam question. When he was asked about the bombing plot in Singapore, he said it "would not have been difficult. This embassy is very close to the street and did not have many barriers to prevent the attack," he told the agents. When asked about the plot to bomb the U.S.

embassy in Manila, he added that "a plane would be needed to attack this building because the security was very tough." No mention was made of the lives that would have been lost.

The inside account was distributed to police and intelligence services on August 22, 2002, and some responded by heightening security at their embassies. It was not enough, though, to prevent the worst act of terrorism since September 11. In Thailand, Hambali had ordered his deputy, Mukhlas, to plan attacks at places where Western tourists were known to hang out. Mukhlas recruited his younger brothers Ali Imron and Amrozi for the task. All three were former students of an Islamic boarding school in southern Malaysia run by Abu Bakar Bashir, the spiritual leader of Jemaah Islamiyah, who had fled Indonesia during the reign of Suharto. Hambali also frequented the school, and now he was calling on his alumni to complete the task that Jabarah had helped set in motion. "Ironically, before the Bali tragedy, the U.S. intelligence community communicated this specific threat to Southeast Asian security and intelligence services," said Rohan Gunaratna, a terrorism scholar and author of *Inside Al Qaeda.* "However, the Southeast Asian services failed to develop the contact or ground intelligence essential to detect and disrupt a terrorist attack."

The bombers blew up Paddy's Irish Bar and then parked a minivan packed with explosives on the narrow street outside the Sari Club. More than two hundred were killed, among them Mervin Popadynec, an oil industry engineer from Wynyard, Saskatchewan, and Rick Gleason, an adventurous traveler and outdoorsman who worked as a financial adviser in Vancouver. Hambali was captured in August 2003. Amrozi was also caught and put on trial. His lawyers said he was remorseful, but Amrozi never showed any signs of being sorry. He earned the nickname the "Smiling Bomber" by grinning throughout his court proceedings. Reporters could hear him in his prison compound singing "continue the holy struggle, get rid of Zionists, get rid of Christian filth. God is great, this is my song." He was convicted and sentenced to death.

The U.S. drafted a plea agreement with Jabarah, charging him with multiple counts of terrorism, but it was torn up after he lunged at his prison guard and stabbed him in the eye. The incident took place after Jabarah learned about the deaths of Al Kandari, who was killed in Kuwait by U.S. Marines after he opened fire on them while they were training, and then his brother. Abdul Rahman had gone to Saudi Arabia, where he joined an Al Qaeda cell. Saudi authorities, anxious to show they could fight terror, got wind of a plot and on May 6, 2003, raided what they called a "terrorists' lair" in Riyadh. They found a huge cache of explosives-almost four hundred kilograms in total-as well as AK-47s, four dozen hand grenades and 2,500 rounds of ammunition. The occupants escaped during a shootout, but the Saudis identified the nineteen wanted men and released a wanted poster. Number 18 on the list was Abdulrahman Mansour Jabarah, citizen of Canada.

A week later, gunmen shot their way into Western housing complexes in Riyadh and set off a series of car bombs. Twenty-nine were killed. Crown Prince Abdullah bin Abdulaziz called the attackers "vicious animals" and said: "The entire Saudi nation, and not just its valiant security forces, will not hesitate to confront the murderous criminals." Saudi security authorities began hunting down the men behind the attack. At 5:00 a.m. on July 3, in the northern province of Al Jouf, security forces cornered Turki Nasser Mishaal Aldandany, a top Al Qaeda operative and mastermind of the bombings. The security forces surrounded the house in which Aldandany was hiding with four other fugitives; the neighbors were ordered to leave their homes. Using a loudspeaker, police urged the men to surrender. One did but the others opened fire with machine guns and grenades. The police fought back and killed all four men. One of the dead was Abdul Rahman Jabarah.

Mansour Jabarah insists his son had no advance knowledge of any terrorist plots and called the claims lies. "No, this is false information, 100 percent, because Mohammed's situation, he doesn't know this kind of information," he said. "And in the meantime his wish is now to go back home to Canada to continue his education as a doctor.

"He's an excellent boy."

What may be most frightening about Jabarah is that he was raised in Canada and yet was still somehow indoctrinated into radical Islam. He was, it turns out, Canada's first example of what would later become known as a homegrown terrorist.

In March 2003, Sophie Sureau was watching television in the apartment in Montreal where she was recovering, when all of a sudden every channel was broadcasting live reports of the invasion of Iraq. The war images thrust her back to Bali and she started having a panic attack. "She was crying and shaking," Syslo said. Her heart was racing. She said there were men in the hall pointing guns at her, trying to kill her. Through the window she thought she saw gunmen in the neighboring condo.

Syslo has had similar moments. He was riding a bus from downtown Montreal to Nun's Island when he saw a passenger clutching a backpack against his chest. It was odd, and it gave him an uneasy feeling. Was there a bomb in the backpack? "This is really strange," he thought. He had to get off the bus before his stop and walk the rest of the way home. These were just irrational moments, to be expected from anybody who has survived such trauma. Then again, maybe they weren't so irrational at all. "The enemy is not only at our door, but inside our house, in practically every room," the Second World War spymaster Sir William Stephenson once said. He was talking about the Cold War Soviet threat, but two decades later his words apply equally well to the new preeminent threat to global security. The terrorists who want to kill people like Sophie Sureau live among us, even as they plot to kill us with their cold terror.

CONCLUSION

FROM HOMELAND TO HOMEGROWN

THE DURHAM REGIONAL POLICE Service building in Pickering, Ontario, has probably never been so secure. Behind streamers of yellow plastic police tape, tactical team members decked out in full battle gear pace the parking lot in the dark. The guns they carry were built not for policing, but for war. White squad cars block the entrance roads and a brown, short-haired dog sniffs for explosives. The security precautions seem like overkill to passers-by, until they find out that inside the police station, suspected terrorists accused of planning to ignite a small war in Canada are being booked and fingerprinted.

The young Muslim extremists had, only a few hours earlier, waited at a warehouse north of Toronto for a potentially deadly delivery: three tonnes of ammonium nitrate. They did not know that RCMP national security investigators had intercepted the shipment and substituted the fertilizer for a harmless look-alike substance. When the delivery was completed, police donned their equipment behind a mall. A couple of shoppers who stumbled across the heavily armed officers were told, "It's all right. We're just making a movie." Ten adults were arrested. By morning, five juveniles under the age of eighteen had been picked up as well. Together with two men already behind bars for gun smuggling, a total of seventeen were charged under the Anti-terrorism Act.

The biggest terrorism bust in North America since 9/11 had gone off without a hitch.

At 10:00 a.m. the next morning, the RCMP summoned the press to a news conference to announce the arrests. To underscore the gravity of the case, a sample of evidence seized in the raids was laid out on a folding table: a bag of the (fake) ammonium nitrate, a handgun, a computer hard drive and a remote detonator fitted inside small tool box. Plastic evidence bags filled with boots and camouflage combat gear allegedly used for terrorist training, as well as a door with bullet holes that had been used for target practice, were displayed in a corner. "After a lengthy investigation, the RCMP in cooperation with our partners, through our Integrated National Security Enforcement Team or INSET in Toronto, have arrested individuals who were planning to commit a series of terrorist attacks against solely Canadian targets in southern Ontario," RCMP Assistant Commissioner Mike McDonell said. "This group took steps to acquire components necessary to create explosive devices using ammonium nitrate which is a commonly used fertilizer. Three tonnes of ammonium nitrate was ordered by these individuals and delivered to them. It was their intent to use it for a terrorist attack."

A news release identified the men facing charges: Fahim Ahmad, 21; Zakaria Amara, 20; Asad Ansari, 21; Shaareef Abdelhaleen, 30; Qayyum Abdul Jamal, 43; Mohammed Dirie, 22; Yasin Mohamed, 24; Jahmaal James, 23; Amin Durani, 19; Steven Chand, 25; Ahmad Ghany, 21; and Saad Khalid, 19. The juveniles were not named. "The men arrested are Canadian residents from a variety of backgrounds," said Luc Portelance, the CSIS Assistant Director, Operations. "For various reasons, they appear to have become adherents of a violent ideology inspired by Al Qaeda." They were, in other words, homegrown Canadian terrorists waging a jihad against Canada.

That afternoon, as police snipers kept a watch from the rooftops, the suspects were taken to the courthouse in Brampton, Ontario, to be formally charged. The sight of the young men in handcuffs and leg irons, some of them so youthful they were struggling to sprout beards, made the allegations that much more startling: a terrorist training camp in the woods of Canada's cottage country; plots to blow up the Toronto Stock Exchange and the CSIS regional headquarters in Toronto; a plan to storm the Parliament buildings, take hostages such as the prime minister and behead them unless Canada withdrew its troops from Afghanistan and released Muslim prisoners. All of a sudden, Canadians were asking themselves the same question that Europeans had posed after Madrid, the Hague and London: What on earth could drive young Canadians to embrace the martyrdom death culture of Osama bin Laden, Ayman Al-Zawahiri and Abu Musab al Zarqawi? How do young men described by their families and neighbors as nice, polite and well-adjusted become little terrorists, training in the snowy forests in combat camo gear, preparing for the murder of their countrymen?

The arrests were a turning point for terrorism in Canada. The country's top national security problem used to be the homeland terrorism that occurs when foreigners bring to Canada the violent causes of their countries of origin. Other people's wars had been seeping into Canada for decades as a result of the "spillover effect," which is what happened when Sikh militants in B.C. bombed the Air India planes in 1985 in support of a far-away cause. This kind of terrorism will probably always be a feature in Canada. As long as immigrants continue to find Canada a receptive place to call home, homeland sympathies will continue to exist and terrorist groups will attempt to exploit them to advance their violent causes.

But the Toronto arrests were a sign that since 9/11, the threat to Canada had evolved. It had shifted from *homeland* terrorism to *homegrown* terrorism. The new generation of terrorists is not fighting the wars of the motherland. These are, for the most part, youths who were either born in Canada, or immigrated at a young age. Their motherland is Canada. They are homegrown in the sense that they are emerging from within Canada, rather than infiltrating it from abroad. They have not only been raised in Canada but radicalized here as well. They are "insiders," as opposed to "outsiders" like Ahmed Ressam. "Increasingly, we are learning of more and more extremists that are homegrown," says a de-classified Canadian intelligence report. A "high percentage" of the Islamic extremists in Canada are now Canadian-born, CSIS says. "These individuals are part of Western society, and their 'Canadianness' makes detection more difficult."

The members of Generation Jihad come from a variety of ethnic backgrounds. They include South Asians, Africans, Caribbeans and Canadians who have converted to Islam. Some are educated and computer-literate, while others have criminal records and more closely fit the profile of gang culture. They share only one thing: a zealous devotion to extreme Islam. That extremism causes them to look at the world and see only the worldwide oppression of Muslims. By selectively citing scripture, they come to justify terrorism as a legitimate response to the "war on Islam" that they believe the West is waging in places like Afghanistan and Iraq, as well as within Western countries that have arrested Muslim terrorists. While they look to Osama bin Laden for inspiration, they are not formal members of al-Qaeda. They often have no apparent connection to any terrorist groups. Most have never been to a terror training camp, (although some have taken weapons training in Canada and abroad in places like Pakistan). Rather than taking orders from overseas terror leaders, they plan and execute their activities locally, "without input from masterminds abroad," says one CSIS report. The Internet provides all the indoctrination and instruction they could possibly need.

What truly distinguishes the new generation from the old guard is that whereas homeland terrorists usually went overseas to fulfill their violent fantasies, homegrown terrorists want to fight their jihads right here in Canada. They see Canada as just another battlefield in the global Muslim conquest. They want to kill Canadians, not just exploit Canada as a base for waging terror elsewhere. These deluded young radicals are "a significant threat to national security" and "a clear and present danger to Canada and its allies," according to de-classified CSIS reports. "A small number of Islamic extremists in Canada advocate violent jihad in pursuit of their political or religious aims," says a "Secret" Canadian intelligence report written in the days after the London bombings. "The reasons for this radicalization are varied and include a general sense of anger at what is seen as oppression of Muslims throughout the world [and] parental influence."

The Toronto operation was the first major operation under the Anti-terrorism Act passed by Parliament in the aftermath of 9/11. After September 11, the Canadian government defined terrorism made it illegal, outlawed terror fundraising and created a list of designated terrorist organizations. The government dedicated $8-billion to national security, created Integrated National Security Enforcement Teams, the Integrated Threat Assessment Centre and FINTRAC, to monitor financial transactions, as well as the Smart Border Action plan. The Communications Security Establishment, the signals intelligence service, got new powers to intercept over-seas terrorist communications with one leg in Canada and to set up an anti-terrorism unit. The Canadian military also played a major role, sending troops to Afghanistan and dispatching the navy to hotspots.

Despite the measures introduced immediately after 9/11, Canadian security and intelligence was still disorganized and decentralized. When Paul Martin came to power in December 2003, he began to create a more centralized homeland security system. He created the Department of Public Safety and Emergency Preparedness, which oversees CSIS, the RCMP and the Canada Border Services Agency. A Cabinet committee on security, public health and emergencies was set up, and a national security advisor was appointed. In the wake of the Madrid bombings and public outrage over the return to Canada of the "Al Qaeda" Khadr family, the government also began to publicly admit that Canada was "a named target" for terror. Anne McLellan, the Minister of Public Safety, told the Canadian Club of Ottawa in a March 25, 2004, address that "we need to continue to ensure Canada is not a base for threats to others ... We have a choice in Canada—to be in denial or to be prepared." Two days later, the government tabled its National Security Strategy, which asserted that the government's primary responsibility was to protect its citizens and ensure that Canada would not be a safe haven for the world's terrorists.

Yet on March 30, the Auditor General of Canada, who had studied the post-9/11 anti-terrorism initiative, found that gaping holes remained, particularly at borders and airports—the two major places of concern to Canada's allies. The audit found that the government lacked a framework for directing its anti-terror spending to respond to major threats, that departments were still unable to share certain types of security information, that watch lists were not accurate or even up to date and that information about the 25,000 Canadian passports lost or stolen every year was not shared with frontline officers. In addition, the audit examined a sample of airport employees who worked in sensitive areas where freight was handled or aircraft were serviced and found that 5.5 percent—or 4,500—"had possible criminal associations" and needed further investigation. "These matters are serious and need to be addressed," Auditor General Sheila Fraser said.

The flaws in Canada's security policy left Ottawa "open to criticisms that the document is nothing more than a 'short-term fix' to win points in Washington that will not lead to any profound changes in the near future," the Center for Strategic and International Studies wrote. The Bush administration reacted cautiously to the changes, it said. "This reaction reflects the fact that while what has happened in Canadian security circles in the past year is significant, it only represents a blueprint that will mean little if current commitments do not translate into future action, and if other issues [refugee policies, for example] remain outside the current debate on future security policies in Canada."

Another paper, this one published in Canadian Foreign Policy, argued that while Canada had made progress, "potentially dangerous chinks remain in the Canadian armour." One weakness is the shortage of analysts to take raw information and turn it into useful intelligence in a timely fashion, wrote Professor Martin Rudner. "Although there has been a steady building up of Canada's intelligence analytical capacity in PCO [the Privy Council Office] and also in individual agencies, this still remains modest by comparison to other G-7 countries." Another problem is that Canada does not have an adequate capacity to train Canadians for jobs in intelligence. "There is a generally recognized and urgent need to acquire analytical and linguistic skill, and international area and cultural proficiencies relating to unfamiliar societies that figure prominently in contemporary security concerns: the Arab world, the Muslim umma, and Southern and Central Asia."

In the aftermath of 9/11, CSIS and the RCMP mounted several operations. Project O-Canada was one such effort, aimed at a group of Toronto extremists who according to CSIS Deputy Director of Operations Jack Hooper "had designs to execute an act of serious violence in the Toronto area." Prosecutors were not satisfied with the evidence gathered by police, however, and would not approve criminal charges, so Canadian agencies switched to "diffuse and disrupt mode." CSIS and the RCMP made sure the targets knew they were being watched. Some of them got spooked and left the country voluntarily, and the plot was broken.

The first arrest under the Anti-terrorism Act occurred on March 29, 2004. Mohammad Momin Khawaja was born in Canada to Pakistani parents. He went to Sir Wilfrid Laurier Secondary School in Ottawa, and studied computer programming at Algonquin College before starting work in 2000 with the Canadian government. In 2002, he took a trip to Pakistan. "When the Kuffur Americans invaded Afghanistan that was the most painful time in my whole life 'cause I loved the Mujahedin and our brothers in Afghanistan so much that I couldn't stand it," he wrote in one e-mail found on a computer seized from his company in Ottawa. "It would tear my heart out knowing these filthy kaafir dog Americans were bombing our Muslim brother and sisters. Beside that, Osama bin Laden is like the most beloved person to me in the whole world. I wish I could even kiss his blessed hand. So I hooked up with some bro's from the UK and else and we all went over to Pakistan to support jihad in Afghanistan in 2002. We got there and stayed about three months. It was amazing. Best experience in my whole life. I made my intention in Ramadan that I wanna go and help out with the Jihad in Iraq. Just making plans for that. Many of my mates from the UK also might wanna come there."

They never made it. After training in Pakistan, Khawaja returned to Ottawa, where he worked as a contract computer expert at the Department of Foreign Affairs, but he kept in contact with his British friends by e-mail. According to the British and Canadian authorities, under the direction of a ringleader named

Omar Khyam, the group began developing a plot to carry out terrorist attacks in the U.K. that would target nightclubs, pubs, trains and a shopping mall. Khawaja played "a vital role in this plot," British prosecutor David Waters said. "A great deal of preparation was undertaken in Pakistan, and also in Canada through the work of Momin Khawaja."

The group amassed 600 kilograms of ammonium nitrate fertilizer, as well as a quantity of aluminum powder and detonation devices. As part of an investigation codenamed Operation Crevice, Britain's MI-5 conducted surveillance of Khyam and his associates. In February 2004, as MI-5 watched, Khawaja visited London and took some of his alleged co-conspirators to an Internet café to show them an image of a remote detonation device he was working on, the prosecutor alleged. Britain notified Canadian authorities and the RCMP began watching Khawaja when he returned to Ottawa later that month. "I am putting together up to 30 devices for you," Khawaja wrote in an e-mail to Khyam on March 26, 2004. "We will test out stuff too." When the RCMP raided Khawaja's house three days later later, they found documents about jihad, hundreds of electronic components and three rifles. Within hours of Khawaja's arrest, British police rounded up his alleged co-conspirators. Khawaja's trial is scheduled to begin in Ottawa in January 2007. His father says his son is innocent and it is all a misunderstanding.

Around the time the Khawaja investigation was wrapping up in Ottawa, CSIS was paying increasing attention to a small group of Muslim youths in Toronto. The probe revolved around young men described as "The Sons of the Father." All were radicalized, Canadian extremists who had grown up in extremist households. They included a Canadian of Egyptian origin who had travelled to Afghanistan, where he is believed to have participated in terrorist training, and two others, who would gather in household basements for prayer meetings and post their views on several pro-jihadist Internet forums. Others then joined in. As the group began to swell, investigators got a break when they succeeded in recruiting an agent to penetrate it. His name was Mubin Shaikh.

A Canadian-born Muslim of Indian origin, Shaikh had served in the Royal Canadian Army Cadets since age thirteen, and reached the rank of staff instructor. He worshipped at a small mosque in Toronto's York neighborhood, and by his own admission had become radicalized to the point that he was ready to go off to Chechnya or Afghanistan to "do some jihad-oriented thing," but he was able to "correct" his understanding of Islam before doing any harm. He then devoted himself to interfaith harmony and served as multiculturalism coordinator for his local Member of Parliament, Liberal Alan Tonks.

Upon returning to Canada from a trip to Syria in 2004, Shaikh discovered that his friend Momin Khawaja had been arrested for terrorism. He contacted CSIS and offered to help. CSIS asked if he would be willing to work for them, to get close to the Toronto youths they were watching and to report back what he heard and saw. He agreed. His motive, he said later, was to protect Canada and particularly the Muslim community, which he felt would suffer terribly should a terrorist attack occur. CSIS gave him his lines and sent him out to penetrate the emerging network that was forming around a young man named Fahim Ahmad.

CSIS was dealing with a variety of threats at the time. There were mounting reports of target-scouting in Canada. Intelligence officers disrupted a Toronto cell of the Salafist Group for Call and Combat, an Algerian terrorist faction loyal to bin Laden. The cell was allegedly led by a one-legged Afghan war veteran name Nourddine "Haji" Zendaoui, who worked as a school bus driver in Toronto. On weekends, he was the goaltender for an Algerian soccer team whose players included jihadi veterans suspected of involvement in terrorist activities in Chechnya.

Before coming to Canada in 1998, investigators claim, Zendaoui had been an instructor at the Khaldun terrorist camp in eastern Afghanistan and had been involved in the conflict in Chechnya. CSIS confronted Zendaoui, and he left Canada in 2004. The remaining members of the group were arrested and eventually deported, with the exception of Zendaoui's lieutenant, a landed immigrant, who remains. "We may never know if these guys would have taken things to the next level and carried out an attack in Canada or the United States," Larry Brooks, the CSIS chief of counterterrorism for the Toronto region, told delegates at a national security workshop in the fall of 2005. "But one thing I can say with certainty is they are not here any more and that's because you, the people who were involved, made the system work."

The threats in 2005, however, were at a manageable level, which allowed CSIS to pay more attention to Operation Claymore, the homegrown terror investigation. Fahim Ahmad and Zakaria Amara were identified as the ringleaders of the amorphous group. CSIS initially tried to break the group with a disruption campaign. Intelligence officers approached some of the members and, since they were so young (some were still in high school), even their parents. The tactic had worked before, but this time it didn't seem to have any effect. The youths continued to meet and feed their anger by swapping propaganda videos, such as *The Martyrs of the Encounters*, a thirty-eight-minute production that calls the 9/11 hijackers heroes. "Those who believe do battle for the cause of Allah," says the video. "Come forth to kill the Jews and Americans, for killing them is foremost of obligations and the greatest form of worship."

There were several international connections to the Toronto group. On March 6, 2005, two Georgia men, Ehsanul Islam Sadequee and Syed Haris Ahmed took a Greyhound bus to Toronto, according to the FBI, and spent a week in Ontario with two of the Operation Claymore targets, Fahim Ahmad and Jahmaal James, discussing "strategic locations in the United States suitable for a terrorist strike" including oil refineries and military bases. They also talked about traveling to Pakistan for military training at "terrorist-sponsored camps," the FBI says. The son of Bangladeshi immigrants, Sadequee was born in Fairfax, Virginia in 1986 and studied at an Islamic boarding school in Ontario, before moving to Roswell, Georgia, on the outskirts of Atlanta, with his mother, brother and sister. At Atlanta's Al-Farooq mosque, he met Ahmed, a twenty-one-year-old Georgia Institute of Technology student who had come to the U.S. from Pakistan in 1997 after his family won a green card lottery.

A month after their visit to Toronto, Ahmed and Sadequee traveled to Washington and filmed what a U.S. prosecutor has described as a "casing video" of the U.S. Capitol building, World Bank, a Masonic temple and a fuel storage depot. The first arrests related to the broad CSIS case came on August 13, 2005. At 5:30 a.m., a Buick with Ontario licence plates veered into one of the fourteen primary inspection lanes at the Peace Bridge border crossing near Niagara Falls. Canadian Customs officers checked the plates and ordered the men in the rented car to pull over for an inspection. The border agents soon found a loaded Hi-Point CF380 semi-automatic taped to the groin of Yasin Mohamed. He was also carrying sixty .380 caliber bullets and twenty-five rounds of .357 Magnum ammunition. Ali Dirie had two guns in his pants.

The Canada Border Services Agency called the Niagara Regional Police Service at 5:40 a.m. Police officers took the two men to 22 Division in Niagara Falls, where the two Somali–Canadians were charged. Canadian authorities now allege they were smuggling guns for terrorist purposes.

Investigators soon discovered that the car had been rented using the credit card of Fahim Ahmad.

The next round of arrests began two months later, when Bosnian authorities moved against a man they believe to be a terrorist codenamed Maximus, who had allegedly recruited Europeans to fight in Iraq and plotted a bombing attack. At 3:55 p.m. on October 19, Bosnian counterterrorism officers armed with a search warrant rang the doorbell outside a ground-floor apartment in Sarajevo, according to the indictment. Mirsad Bektasevic, aka Maximus, answered. The eighteen-year-old Swede had arrived in Bosnia on September 27. "Who are you to search my house, you trash," he raged at the investigators.

The officers overpowered Bektasevic and entered the apartment. Their search turned up twenty kilograms of explosives, a suicide belt and a Sony 60 Hi 8 VHS tape that contained instructions on how to make a bomb and warned of a pending attack against an unnamed country. "God is great," said the voice on the videotape (a British forensic expert determined the voice was "more than rather likely" that of Bektasevic). "These brothers are ready to attack and, God willing, they will attack the non-Muslims who are killing our brothers and Muslims in Iraq, Afghanistan, Chechnya and in many other countries."

Just forty-eight hours after the arrests in Sarajevo, the Metropolitan Police Anti-Terrorist Branch in London took three men into custody who had been in contact with Maximus: Waseem Mughal, 23; Younis Tsouli, 22; and Tariq Al-Daour, 19. Police searches turned up a number of items of interest including, according to the Bosnian indictment, Swedish and Bosnian telephone numbers used by Maximus. Under Mughal's bed, police found a DVD containing instructions on how to make suicide bomb vests, a piece of paper with "Welcome to Jihad" written in Arabic and a recipe for rocket propellant. Tsouli is believed to be a young Internet hacker who used the on-line handle Irhabi 007, and who was a member of al-Tibyyan, a password-protected Web forum that was also used by terror suspects in Australia, Sweden, the U.S. and Canada. During the police search of his bedroom, police found a computer hard drive containing instructions on how to make a car bomb as well as video slides showing "a number of places in Washington, D.C.," according to the British charges. Authorities claimed the images were from the video filmed that spring by Sadequee and Ahmed. Arrests followed in Sweden and Denmark. Ahmed was arrested after returning to Atlanta from Pakistan. Sadequee was detained in Bangladesh and sent back to the U.S. to face charges.

The RCMP launched its own investigation in November, 2005. As the Toronto cell had started to go beyond talk, CSIS officially notified the RCMP and "O" INSET, the Integrated National Security Enforcement Team in Toronto, began a criminal investigation under the Anti-terrorism Act. It was called Project OSAGE. There is no shortage of trash-talk on the Web about jihad and killing infidels, but when the RCMP began looking into the Toronto group, they felt there was reason for concern. To begin with, the subjects of the investigation, whose fresh faces were plotted on an elaborate organizational chart, were using jargon that suggested they were not just wannabes, a source familiar with the case told me. They were clearly familiar with Al Qaeda ideologues like Abdullah Azzam ("jihad and the rifle alone") and Ayman Al-Zawahiri (sidekick to bin Laden). "The terminology and use of words stood out," the source said. A month into the investigation, members of the group traveled to a remote property near Orillia, Ontario and underwent several days of weapons training. Mubin Shaikh, who by now was working for the RCMP, was there. There were growing indications the group was trying to purchase equipment, and that they were collecting intelligence about possible targets.

In the eyes of police, this was more than just a bunch of angry youths. They were beginning to talk about what they were going to do and how they were going to do it. Analysts responsible for figuring out which threats to take seriously and which to ignore know that terrorists become a concern when they possess both intent and capability. This group had made no secret of its desires, and seemed to be becoming rapidly capable. "These guys were expressing intent, they were trash-talking away, they'd obviously been reading some ideological tracts and they'd also got off their butts to do training, they'd actualized their intent," my source said. The group allegedly manufactured an electronic detonation device with a cell phone rigged to a light-sensitive switch. It was simple, but fully functional. Although the suspects knew they were being watched, they allegedly carried on, even as some of their associates began to get picked up by police abroad. They knew they were being watched. They even discovered some listening devices that had been sloppily installed. They didn't care.

In the winter of 2006, Fahim and Amara split, and Amara allegedly began developing the truck bomb plot. Once the plot reached the point where public safety was deemed seriously at risk, police moved in. An eighteenth suspect, Ibrahim Alkhalel Mohammed Aboud, 19, was arrested on August 3. Family and friends of the accused have voiced doubts about the strength of the case, calling the charges "baloney" and suggesting the suspects were targeted because they are Muslims. Aly Hindy, imam of the Salaheddin mosque, where the Khadrs and the like worship, claimed the case had been manufactured to appease George W. Bush. "He's a great kid. Never in a chance in hell could this ever occur," said Gary, who played soccer with Saad Khalid, nineteen, who is charged with terrorist training and intent to cause an explosion. But police believe they have a solid case, backed up by electronic intercepts, physical surveillance and other evidence. What is apparent, however, is that some members of the group appear to have been more intensely involved than others.

The case described by the prosecution has all the hallmarks of a homegrown terror plot, albeit with some outside instigation and assistance. The key Toronto suspects had not only communicated with like-minded extremists on Internet forums, but also met with foreign co-conspirators both in Canada and abroad. There were international links to Pakistan, in particular to Lashkar-e-Tayyiba, the armed Islamic group fighting in Kashmir that has opened its training camps to foreign Muslims. A key Lashkar operative named Abu Umar traveled to Canada in 2005 and a few suspects associated with the Toronto cell trained at Lashkar camps. "The threat of this type of terrorism is global, complex and sophisticated," Jack Hooper, the CSIS Deputy Director of Operations, testified to the Senate national security committee. "The individuals and groups involved are often internationally inter-connected and highly mobile in their travel patterns."

Since the July 7, 2005 bombings in Britain, intelligence services have struggling to explain the rise of homegrown terror. Why are Western Muslims becoming radicalized to the point that they are willing to commit acts of terror at home? A particularly articulate explanation comes from a 2006 report by the Dutch General Intelligence and Security Service, which described radicalization as the result of the struggle among young Muslims to reconcile Islam with an increasingly modern, global and secular world. "Although Muslims worldwide are faced with globalization and modernization, young Muslims growing up in secular Western societies, in which Islam is just one more religious and cultural movement, are much more acutely confronted with problems of existential and religious orientation." These youths may turn to the Koran for guidance, but lacking Muslim cultural roots and ignorant of true Islamic teachings, they can fall into the trap of believing that to be a "good Muslim" they must adhere to intolerant, extremist interpretations of the faith. "With the help of radical websites and chat sessions they compile a radical 'cut-and-paste' version of Islam from Koran quotations which they reshape into a revolutionary pamphlet of global violent jihad."

FBI Director Robert Mueller offered his own theory in a speech that followed the arrest in Miami of seven alleged homegrown terrorists whom police said had pledged loyalty to bin Laden in the company of an undercover agent. "Radicalization often starts with individuals who are frustrated with their lives or with the politics of their home governments ... Some may be lonely or dissatisfied with their role in society. Others may have friends or mentors who encourage membership for social reasons. Once a person has joined an extremist group, he or she may start to identify with an ideology—one that encourages violence against a government and its citizens."

The conclusion of CSIS is that "there does not appear to be a single process that leads to extremism: the transformation is highly individual." But the service has identified a number of factors it says can lead youths down the path of extremism. One is family ties. CSIS has been reporting a trend in which fathers with extreme beliefs are raising their children to be extreme believers. The Khadr family of Toronto is a tragic example.

Radicalization is also occurring as a result of the influence of self-proclaimed spiritual leaders who guide youths into extremism. The two young men described as the key figures in the Toronto plot were, according to those who knew them, followers of a forty-three-year-old director of the Al-Rahman Islamic Centre, who once welcomed a Canadian Member of Parliament to his mosque by railing against Canada's military presence in Afghanistan, saying the troops had been sent to Kandahar to rape Muslim women.

A third factor is religious conversion. CSIS reports that terrorists are actively seeking Western converts, who are "highly prized by terrorist groups" for their familiarity with the West and the relative ease with which they are able to move through Western society. "The issue of radicalized converts will grow over the next few decades," the intelligence report predicts. Adds another study, "Much like the attraction of extreme ideologies of past decades, radical Islam will continue to appeal to the disenfranchised and those struggling with a personal or spiritual crisis." Finally, there is the Internet, which has made it possible for Western Muslims to network with like-minded believers and completely immerse themselves in the global jihadi subculture from the comfort of their bedrooms.

Once Canadians get over the jolt of the Toronto arrests, they will have to begin confronting the extremism that many thought they would only ever see on television. This will mean targeting incitement and recruitment, as Britain has started to do. Canada has a law that makes it a crime to incite hatred against identifiable groups. It has never been used against firebrand jihadist lecturers or writers. It should be. Canada will also have to do something about the veterans of terror training camps and jihadi volunteer brigades who have seen combat in Afghanistan, Bosnia and Chechnya. Several cases, including that of Jabarah, have highlighted the critical role played by these veterans in the indoctrination and recruitment of youth, but efforts to deport them have proven mostly unsuccessful and politically problematic due to concerns they might be tortured in their homelands. Equally important is the need to find novel ways of fighting the jihadist propaganda that is now so pervasive. Extremists have been very effective at spreading their "war on Islam" victimhood message. Until Canada does a better job at countering this, youths will continue to be drawn into extremism and terrorism with deadly consequences.

Whether the measures introduced by the government since 9/11 will be enough to change Canada from a source country of terrorism to a responsible ally in the war on terrorism remains to be seen. The world's terrorist networks are, in some cases, so deeply entrenched in Canada that it will not be an easy task. What can be said with certainty is that the threat is not going away. The world has seen its share of terrorists over the past half-century, but radical Islamic extremists are by far the most dangerous. Anyone who has peered down into the crater and up into empty sky where the Twin Towers used to stand understands that implicitly. Islamic extremists are not only arrogant and violent, but patient. Their hatred arises from centuries-old grievances and their aim is long-term: a world under the rule of Islam, the one true faith. "The real battle has not started yet," Ayman Al Zawahiri, bin Laden's right-hand man, said in a message broadcast on Al Jazeera on the second anniversary of the 2001 World Trade Center attacks. Radical Islamists are willing to wait it out until things die down, until the inconveniences imposed since 9/11 in the name of national security no longer seem necessary and public pressure builds to rescind anti-terror laws. Then the extremists will be able to start plotting freely again. They know it will happen, and they are probably right.

Despite 9/11, Madrid, London, Toronto and direct Al Qaeda threats against Canada and its allies, not to mention a growing number of incidents of target scouting in Canada, counterterrorism still faces significant political opposition from uninformed lobby groups that are narrowly concerned about protecting their rights from the state, while ignoring the ways in which terrorists threaten and undermine those rights. These lobbyists have found a voice through the Maher Arar affair and protests against the deportation of terror suspects under the security certificate process. They are pushing the notion that the government has gone too far in fighting terrorism, a conclusion hardly supported by close study. "Never has a combined physical and economic threat to the Canadian homeland been more palpable," the Standing Senate Committee on National Security and Defence wrote, "but rarely have Canadians been more sanguine about their well-being."

The war on terrorism has rightly put those who kill for their causes under unprecedented pressure, but the fight is far from over. Technological advances and globalization have all but removed the need for a base such as Afghanistan. Terrorists can now recruit, train and conspire within the comfort of the West simply by exploiting the liberal democracies of the world and their technological advances. Those nations that are most open and advanced, and least attuned to the terrorist threat will become the most likely havens of tomorrow. At the same time, the global dominance of the United States will continue into the foreseeable future, and with it will come a backlash from terrorists who resent America and its world vision. The fanatical causes that drive terrorism have hardly been exhausted. Indeed, they are growing. "Canada's increased participation in Afghanistan, its close political relationship with the U.S. and the increasing media profile of Canada's law enforcement and intelligence actions continue to give Canada a significant profile in the ongoing global war on terrorism," the Integrated Threat Assessment Centre wrote in an

April 2006 report. "Consequently Canada, like other Western nations, must maintain its vigilance for the foreseeable future."

Perhaps it is only natural that there should be so many Canadian terrorists. Canada, after all, takes in immigrants and refugees from all over the world, many of them from zones of conflict. But what makes Canada a refuge for some makes it a haven for others. An RCMP intelligence report that deals partly with the recruitment of terrorists from within Canadian ethnic communities notes that 17 percent of Canada's population is foreign born, as opposed to 9 percent in the United States, "making Canada more vulnerable to these tendencies than are other developed nations." Given the opportunistic nature of terror, it is hardly surprising that agents of violence cynically seek to exploit the vulnerabilities of Western society—but that only makes Canada's political weakness in the field of counterterrorism all the more difficult to comprehend. A country such as Canada, a top destination for global migration, should logically have the toughest antiterrorism policies and the lowest tolerance for terrorists, because in such a society the potential for exploitation by terrorists is so great. Instead, Ottawa has traditionally found such measures tedious and politically inopportune, and has tried to pretend there was nothing to worry about.

Counterterrorism may be distasteful to some, and it will rightly set off debate about the balance between civil liberties and state security, but so be it. If that debate is fairly argued, the lies, exaggerations and naiveté of interest groups opposed to counterterror measures will lose out. The state's primary function is the security of the nation and its citizens, not the rights of terrorists. There is no rational defense for the kind of random violence directed at noncombatants that is the essence of terror. Political and public complacency about terrorism was perhaps understandable in the years before the Air India bombing, when the Cold War was still the preoccupation of Western security agencies, but not anymore. Ignoring the threat today would be inexcusable. For over two decades, Canada tried to smother terrorism with kindness. That has been the Canadian approach since the first major attacks in Canada, and to an extent it continues today. It is perhaps a typically Canadian approach. But it is wrong, dead wrong.

NOTES

INTRODUCTION

The immigration study referred to is:
Glyn Custred, *North American Borders, Why They Matter*
(Washington, DC: Center for Immigration Studies, May 2003).

The official Canadian documents cited are:
Special Senate Committee on Security and Intelligence,
"The Report of the Special Senate Committee on Security and Intelligence"
(chair William M. Kelly), January 1999.

Canadian Security Intelligence Service (CSIS),
"Submission to the Special Committee of the Senate on Security and Intelligence,"
delivered by CSIS director Ward Elcock, June 24, 1998.

CSIS, "Counter Terrorism Presentation to Solicitor General Wayne Easter,"
November 22, 2002 ("Top Secret").

CSIS, "Bin Laden's November 2002 Statement: What Does It Mean?"
intelligence brief, IB 2002-3/15, November 14, 2002 ("Secret").

Integrated Threat Assessment Centre, "Is Canada Next?" Intelligence Assessment
06/23, April 13, 2006, (Unclassified—For Official Use Only).

CSIS, "Sunni Islamic Extremism and the Threat to Canadian Maritime Security,"
March 4, 2004, ("Secret—Canadian Eyes Only").

CSIS, "Threats to Canada's National Security," October 10, 2003, ("Secret—
Canadian Eyes Only").

Privy Council Office, "Memorandum for the Prime Minister: Contacts of Ministers
with Groups or Individuals Who May Have Undesirable Connections,"
May 23, 2000 ("Secret—Canadian Eyes Only").

RCMP (criminal extremism analysis section), "Chronology of Criminal Extremist Incidents from 1989," Annex 3, Project [name censored] 1998, File 92-CI-874, February 5, 1999 ("Secret—RCMP Eyes Only").

Canada v. Mohamed Harkat, "Statement Summarizing" pursuant to section 78 (h) of the Immigration Act and Refugee Protection Act, FCC, file DES-4-02, December 2002 ("Unclassified").

Canada v. Adil Charkaoui, "Statement Summarizing" pursuant to section 78 (h) of the Immigration Act and Refugee Protection Act, FCC, file DES-3-03, May 2003 ("Unclassified"). Supplementary evidence, July 17 and August 14, 2003.

"Al Qaida: Terrorist Group Profiler," CSIS, September 2001 ("Unclassified: For Official Use Only"). The report contains the following disclaimer: "Terrorist Group Profiler is compiled from a variety of open sources and does not imply CSIS authentication or endorsement. The following information is intended for official use only." But CSIS would not circulate a report that contained information it did not endorse.

RCMP (Criminal Intelligence Directorate), "Strategic Assessment of the Nature and Extent of Organized Crime in Canada," April 30, 2003 ("Protected 'B').

I also relied on:
Colin Kenny, "So many threats. So few officers," *National Post*, June 15, 2006.
John Mintz, "Detainees at Base in Cuba Yield Little Valuable Information," *The Washington Post*, Oct. 29, 2002.

For a tongue-in-cheek take on Canada's terror problem, see: Mike Pearson, *Waging War from Canada: Why Canada Is the Perfect Base for Organizing, Supporting, and Conducting International Insurgency* (Port Townsend, WA: Loompanics Unlimited, 2001).

Jack Granatstein and David Statford, "The Terrorist Threat," in *Spy Wars: Espionage and Canada from Gouzenko to Glasnost* (Toronto: Key Porter Books, 1990), outlines some of the early terror-related issues faced by Canada up to the late 1980s.

CHAPTER ONE

The Bagri speech was translated by the RCMP and released by the B.C. Supreme Court as part of the Air India trial proceedings. Bagri's lawyers dispute parts of the translation and downplay the significance of the speech.

Bagri described his affiliation with the Babbar Khalsa in "Affidavit of Ajaib Singh Bagri," SC, file CC010287, B.C. Supreme Court, Vancouver registry.

The CSIS analysis of Babbar Khalsa activities in Canada is from: *Canada v. Iqbal Singh*, "Statement Summarizing the Information Pursuant to Paragraph 40.1 of the Immigration Act," FCC.

James Littleton, "The Reform of Security Service," in *Target Nation: Canada and the Western Intelligence Network* (Toronto: Lester & Orpen/CBC, 1986) describes the creation of CSIS.

Anthony Kellet, a Department of National Defence analyst, described the "waves" of Canadian terror in "Terrorism in Canada 1960–1992," in Jeffrey Ian Ross (ed.), *Violence in Canada: Sociopolitical Perspectives* (Oxford University Press, 1995).

The Mackenzie Institute traced the development of Canadian terror in the report *Other People's Wars: A Review of Overseas Terrorism in Canada,* prepared by John C. Thompson and Joe Turlej (Toronto: Mackenzie Institute, June 2003).

Larry Hannant, Camosun College and University of Victoria, "RCMP Innovations in Response to Sons of Freedom Doukobor Terrorism in the late 1950s and 1960s" (paper, Canadian Association of Security and Intelligence Studies conference, Vancouver, October 16–18, 2003).

Haig Gharakhanian described the Canadian operations of ASALA in an interview with the author on September 14, 2003.

The judge's comments about Gharakhanian are cited in a ruling by the Immigration and Refugee Board, *Haig Gharakhanian v. The Minister of Citizenship and Immigration,* IRB, file T91-02163, January 22, 1996.

Nicoghas Moumdjian's case is described in: *Nicoghas Moumdjian v. Security Intelligence Review Committee, the Attorney General of Canada, the Minister of Employment and Immigration and the Solicitor General,* FCC, file A-1065-88.

The RCMP's Air India investigation is partly documented in *B.C. v. Bagri and Malik,* "Air India," vol. 1, *Unopposed Exhibits & File Material, Release to Media,* B.C. Supreme Court, April 25, 2003.

The CSIS investigation is detailed in Security Intelligence Review Committee, "CSIS Activities in Regard to the Destruction of Air India Flight 182 on June 23, 1985: A SIRC Review," File 2800-5, November 1992 ("Top Secret").

Other documents:
Integrated Threat Assessment Centre, "Jama'at ul Fuqra: A Threat to Canada?" Intelligence Assessment 05/33, May 16, 2006, (Unclassified—For Official Use Only).

Government of India, "Important Sikh Extremists Operation from UK, Canada," Jain Commission Report, sect. 5.18 to 5.20.

CSIS, *A Historical Perspective on CSIS,* updated September 1, 2001.

CSIS, *The CSIS Mandate*, amended August 2001.

SIRC, "Air India," in *SIRC Annual Report*, 1991–92.

Canadian Aviation Bureau Safety Board, "Aviation Occurrence Air India Boeing 747-237B VT-EFO Cork, Ireland 110 Miles West," June 23, 1985.

CSIS, "Recent Media Coverage on the Canadian Security Intelligence Service's Activities Prior to the Air India Bombing of 1985," news release/communiqué, June 2, 2003.

For a thorough account of the Air India case see: Kim Bolan, *Loss of Faith: How the Air India Bombers Got Away With Murder*, McClelland & Stewart, 2005.

Press reports I relied on:
John Kessel, "Chronology of Terror: The Plot To Kill a Turkish Diplomat," *Ottawa Citizen,* June 14, 1986.

Iain Hunter, "Armenian Terrorist Applies To Stay," *Ottawa Citizen*, March 10, 1988.

Kim Bolan, "Charges at Last, Air India," *The Vancouver Sun*, October 28, 2000.

Camille Bains, "Man Argued About Getting Suitcase onto Air India Flights," Canadian Press, May 5, 2003.

Kim Bolan, "Parmar's Village Remembers," *The Vancouver Sun*, April 1, 2003.

CHAPTER TWO

A large volume of intelligence documentation exists concerning the LTTE's activities in Canada. The most useful documents I have obtained, through leaks, court disclosures and Access to Information requests, are:

CSIS (research, analysis and production branch), "LTTE Front Organizations in Canada," 1999 ("Secret").

RCMP (criminal intelligence branch), "Middle Eastern and Tamil Criminal Extremism," RCMP, file # 98-CID-1342, January 20, 2000 ("Secret").

Metropolitan Toronto Police Tamil Task Force, "Pilot Project, Tamil Organized Crime," February 1998.

Canada v. Muralitharan Nadarajah, RCMP Sgt. Fred Bowen, "Information to Obtain a Search Warrant," September 15, 1998.

Manickavasagam Suresh v. the Minister of Citizenship and Immigration Canada and the Attorney General of Canada, respondents factum, SCC, file 27790, February 2001.

CSIS, "Liberation Tigers of Tamil Eelam," open sources brief, information dated May 1999 ("Unclassified").

RCMP (Criminal Intelligence Directorate), "The Liberation Tigers of Tamil Eelam and Its Front Organizations in Canada," criminal intelligence brief, vol. 9, no. 5, October 2, 2002 ("Secret").

RCMP (Criminal Intelligence Directorate), "Immigration and Passport Branch Targets and Their Connections to Criminal Activity in Canada and to the LTTE," criminal intelligence brief, vol. 9, no. 9, November 27, 2002 ("Secret").

RCMP (Criminal Intelligence Directorate), "The Sri Lankan Peace Process," criminal intelligence brief, vol. 9, no. 6, October 10, 2002 ("Confidential").

RCMP (Criminal Intelligence Directorate), "Suicide Bombings—Canadian Perspective," criminal intelligence brief, vol. 10, no. 3, March 18, 2003 ("Protected 'A'").

RCMP (Criminal Intelligence Directorate), "Connections between Tamil Criminal Activity in Canada and the LTTE," vol. 10. no. 9, April 25, 2003 ("Secret").

The role of LTTE front organizations is analyzed in the November 19, 2001, decision of the Immigration and Refugee Board in the case of Muralitharan Nadarajah, the former leader of the Swiss LTTE, who was captured living in Canada in 1998 under a false name.

Sivakumar Thalayasingam described his relationship with CSIS in an affidavit filed in federal court as part of his attempt to avoid deportation. He argued that he would be harmed if he was sent back to Sri Lanka because he had cooperated with CSIS. The government denied he had been offered refugee status in return for his cooperation.

Two other informative background articles:
Rohan Gunaratna, "LTTE Fundraisers Still on the Offensive,"
Jane's Intelligence Review, December 1997.

Anthony Davis, "Tamil Tiger International," *Jane's Intelligence Review,* October 1996.

CHAPTER THREE

Most of the material concerning Fauzi Ayub comes from censored transcripts of his in-camera testimony at the Tel Aviv–Yaffo District Court on February 18, February 25 and March 19, 2003.

I also interviewed senior Canadian and Israeli officials and referred to the following documents:
Israeli Prime Minister's Office, *ISA Arrests Senior Hezbollah Terrorist,* media advisory, Jerusalem, October 29, 2002.

Solicitor General Canada, "Update on Canadian Citizen Detained in Israel," briefing note, November 2, 2002 ("Secret").

CSIS, "Hezbollah and Its Activities in Canada," Report #2002-3/17 ("Secret—Canadian Eyes Only").

Solicitor General Canada, "North Carolina," briefing note, October 28, 2002 ("Secret").

CSIS (counter-proliferation branch), "Shiite Terrorism," November 14, 2002.

RCMP (criminal intelligence branch), "Middle Eastern and Tamil Criminal Extremism," file 98-CID-1342, January 20, 2000 ("Secret").

RCMP, "Project Sparkplug," prepared for director, criminal intelligence, file 97-CA-93 ("Protected 'A'").

U.S. Department of Treasury, "Holy Land Foundation for Relief and Development, International Emergency Economic Powers Act," action memorandum, November 5, 2001.

Immigration and Refugee Board, "Summary of a Detention Review Hearing," Omar El Sayed adjudication file 0002-99-00124, Foss ID 3721-5230, 28 May 1999.

USA v. Hani Al-Sayegh et al, U.S. District Court, Eastern District of Virginia, Alexandria Division.

B'nai Brith Canada v. Attorney General of Canada, Minister of Foreign Affairs, Her Majesty the Queen, notice of application, FCC Trial Division, November 26, 2002.

The case of Mohamed Hussein Al Husseini is documented in FCC file DES-8-93. The results of the CSIS investigation are in "Statement Summarizing the Information Pursuant to Paragraph 40.1 (4) (b) of the Immigration Act, 1993."

The U.S. Department of Justice detailed its investigation into the Charlotte Hezbollah cell in:
"Panel One of a Hearing of the Senate Judiciary Committee, Terrorism Financing," Washington, DC, chaired by Senator Arlen Specter, November 20, 2002.

I obtained copies of the surveillance photos, shot by CSIS during Harb's visit to Vancouver, from the U.S. Department of Justice.

USA v. Mohammad Youssef Hammoud, CSIS summaries, redacted copy, trial testimony, and *USA v. Mohammad Youssef Hammoud,* CSIS summaries, redacted copy, deposition testimony, April 29, 2002, Ottawa.

The prime minister's encounter with the leader of Hezbollah is mentioned in Department of Foreign Affairs, "Copies of All Documents Concerning the Presence of Sheik Hassan Nasrallah, the Leader of Hezbollah, at the October 2002 Francophone Summit in Beirut," no. A-2002-00310/jal, January 28, 2003.

For an authoritative report on Hezbollah and Imad Mugniyah, see Jeffrey Goldberg, "In the Party of God," *The New Yorker,* October 28, 2002.

For a look at the development of Shia Islam, see Bernard Lewis, *The Middle East: A Brief History of the Last 2,000 Years* (New York: Touchstone, 1995).

CHAPTER FOUR
This chapter is adapted from Stewart Bell's "The Terrorist Next Door," *Saturday Night,* April 28, 2001.

The case against Fateh Kamel is detailed in a lengthy document written by French investigators, who were headed by antiterrorism investigating judge Jean-Louis Bruguiere.

Sheik Omar Abdel Rahman's visit to Canada is discussed in SIRC, "Counter-Terrorism Study 93-06," file 2800-43, May 31, 1993 ("Secret").

I obtained a transcript of Abul-Dahab's interview with Egyptian police from the SITE Institute in Washington, DC. The interview took place November 1–3, 1998. His lawyer was present.

Ahmed Ressam did not testify at his own trial, but he told his story later when he appeared as a witness in the trial of his colleague Mokhtar Haouari in U.S. District Court, Southern District of New York, before Judge John F. Keenan. The transcripts of his testimony on July 3 and 5, 2001, are the basis of this part of the story.

The connections between Ahmed Ressam and Samir Ait Mohamed are detailed in the affidavit of FBI Special Agent Frederick W. Humphries, Seattle, August 8, 2001.

Other documents that I relied on for this chapter include:
CSIS, "Terrorist Group Profiler, Armed Islamic Group (GIA)," May 2003 ("Unclassified for Police and Security Officials' Use Only").

Department of National Defence, "Where Did Bin Laden Come From?", Ottawa, September 2001 ("Confidential—Canadian Eyes Only").

Ministry of Interior, France (Unité Coordination de la Lutte Anti-Terroriste), "Training Volunteers for Jihad at Training Camps" (translated from French), December 27, 1996 ("Confidential").

Canada v. Mourad Ikhlef, "Fatah Kamel, Alias Mustapha," Annex G, CSIS, FCC, file DES-8-01, 2001 ("Unclassified").

Canada v. Mourad Ikhlef, "Said Atmani (Karim)," Annex F, CSIS, FCC, file DES-8-01, 2001 ("Unclassified").

Canada v. Mourad Ikhlef, "Ahmed Ressam," Annex H, CSIS, FCC, file DES-8-01, 2001 ("Unclassified").

Canada v. Mohamed Harkat, "The Armed Islamic Group (GIA)," Annex IV, CSIS, , FCC, file DES-4-02, December 2002 ("Unclassified").

Abdel Ghani, aka Eduardo Rocha, Southern District of New York. Sealed complaint, FBI, Dec. 30, 1999; *USA v. Mokhtar Haouari and Abdel Ghani Meskini,* indictment, S1-00-Cr. 15, U.S. District Court, Southern District of New York, January 19, 2000.

US Attorney, Southern District of New York, "Press Release," January 19, 2000.

USA v. Ahmed Ressam, "Nature of the Case and Short Procedural History," U.S. District Court, Western District of Washington at Seattle, CR99-666C, March 7, 2001.

USA v. Ahmed Ressam, "Statement of Facts," U.S. District Court, Western District of Washington at Seattle, CR99-666C, March 7, 2001.

Mourad Ikhlef's ties to the Ressam group are outlined in FCC file DES-8-01.

The Ressam conspiracy is described in detail in Hal Bernton, Mike Carter, David Heath and James Neff, "The Terrorist Within," special report, *Seattle Times,* June 23–July 7, 2002.

Other press articles I relied on:
Salim Jiwa, "Bin Laden Trainer Was Here," *The Province* (Vancouver), December 21, 2001.

Susan Sachs, "Merger Spreads Al-Qaeda Tentacles," *National Post*, November 21, 2001.

CHAPTER FIVE

Kassem Daher is described as an Islamic extremist in *Minister of Citizenship and Immigration and Solicitor General Canada v. Mahmoud Jaballah*, transcript of proceedings vol. 3 and 4, FCC Trial Division, DES-4-01, December 17 and 18, 2001.

Details about Daher's business activities in Canada come from a report I commissioned: The Search Company, "Confidential Investigation Intelligence Report on: Daher, Kassem, Capitol Theatre, Ponoka, Leduc Twin Cinemas, Leduc," Toronto, January 15, 2002.

Daher's arrest is described in: *L'Orient du Jour* (Beirut), "Neuf islamistes du maquis de Denniyé capturés dans la Békaa," February 3, 2000.

Sharq al Awsat (Beirut), "Telegrams from Interpol Washington, Canada, Switzerland, Moscow: Canada Acquiring Information about Individuals Tied to Terrorism in N. Lebanon," October 9, 2001.

I first reported the case of Kassem Daher in my article "Lebanon Holds Alberta Men as Terrorists: Allege Links to Bin Laden" and "Canadian and Muslim, but Are They Terrorists?" *National Post*, February 9, 2002.

CHAPTER SIX

Official documents used in this chapter:
Canada v. Mohamed Harkat, "Ahmed Said Khadr," Annex V, CSIS, FCC, DES-4-02, December 2002 ("Unclassified").

CSIS, "Ahmed Khadr," July 31, 1996 ("Secret—Canadian Eyes Only").

Privy Council Office, "Information on Khadr Family" (R.S. Heatherington was director, PCO Foreign Intelligence Division), September 2, 2002 ("Secret—Canadian Eyes Only").

Privy Council Office, "Canadians Detained in Afghanistan," memorandum for Alex Himelfarb, August 23, 2002 ("Top Secret").

Privy Council Office, "Canadians Detained in Afghanistan," memorandum for the prime minister ("Secret").

Department of National Defence, "Briefing Note—Detention in Afghanistan of an Individual Claiming To Be Canadian," August 23, 2002 ("Secret").

Privy Council Office, "Canadians with Al Qaida Links in Detention Abroad," (R.S. Heatherington was director, PCO Foreign Intelligence Division), August 20, 2002 ("Secret—Canadian Eyes Only").

Department of Foreign Affairs, "Canadian Held in Afghanistan," press release, September 5, 2002.

Privy Council Office, "Factual Information Gathering, Ahmed Khadr Family," no date ("Secret").

Department of Foreign Affairs, "Afghanistan, Khadr," case note, July 30, 2002.

Privy Council Office, "Omar Khadr," press lines, September 4, 2002.

Canada v. Mohamed Harkat, "Background Brief: The Bin Laden Network," Annex I, CSIS, FCC, DES-4-02, December 2002 ("Unclassified").

Mohamed Zeki Mahjoub, FCC, file DES-1-00.

Mahmoud Jaballah, FCC, file DES-4-01.

Minister of Citizenship and Immigration and Solicitor General Canada v. Mahmoud Jaballah, transcript of proceedings vol. 3 and 4, FCC Trial Division, DES-4-01, December 17 and 18, 2001.

Canada v. Hassan Almrei, "Background Brief: The Bin Laden Network," Annex A, CSIS evidence, FCC Trial Division, 2001.

CIDA, "Human Concern International," memorandum for the minister ("Secret").

HCI v. Minister for International Cooperation and Minister of Foreign Affairs, FCC Trial Division, file T-435-99, March 9, 1999.

Department of Foreign Affairs, "Case Note 95-ISBAD-11199, Pakistan Khadr," December 12, 2000.

Testimony of Abdurahman Khadr, *Canada v. Adil Charkaoui,* Federal Court of Canada, July 13, 2004.

U.S. Military, Combatant Status Review Board, "Summary of Evidence for Combatant Status Review Tribunal," August 31, 2004.

I also relied on the following press articles:
Isabel Vincent, "The Good Son: Omar Khadr: From Toronto's Suburbs to Bin Laden's Army," *National Post,* December 28, 2002.

Tim McGirk, Hannah Bloch and Massimo Calabresi, "Has Pakistan Tamed Its Spies?" *Time*, May 6, 2002.

CBC-TV, "U.S. Most Wanted Man," March 4, 2003.

Ottawa Citizen, "Readers Express Views on Afghanistan, Soviet Soldiers," December 15, 1986.

Ottawa Citizen, "Canadian Aid Worker Seriously Wounded," May 2, 1992.

Dave Rogers, "Ahmed Saeed Khadr: Muslim Groups Hope Chrétien Will Intercede," *Ottawa Citizen*, January 3, 1996.

Jacquie Miller, "PM to Raise Issue of Canadian Held in Pakistan," *Ottawa Citizen*, January 10, 1996.

Muhammad al-Shafi'I, "Daughter of Al-Qaida's Reported Financier Speaks about Bin Laden," Al-Sharq Al-Awsat, March 18, 2004.

Kevin Bissett, "Mulroney criticizes Liberals' handling of Khadrs at Conservative dinner," *Canadian Press*, April 24, 2004.

Other sources:
The dispute involving Ahmed Khadr surfaced in a document discovered during the FBI investigation into Benevolence International Fund, whose leader was convicted of terror financing.

Jean-Charles Brisard, JCB Consulting, "Terrorism Financing: Roots and Trends of Saudi Terrorism Financing," report prepared for the president of the Security Council, United Nations, December 19, 2002, New York.

Steven Emerson, "Inside the Osama Bin Laden Investigation," *Journal of Counterterrorism & Security International*, Fall 1998.

Rohan Gunaratna, "Blowback," *Jane's Intelligence Journal*, August 2001.

Sgt. Morris gave his account of the firefight involving Omar Khadr to *National Post* reporter Michael Friscolanti at his home in Utah. We wrote about the incident in Stewart Bell and Michael Friscolanti, with files from Sarah Schmidt and Isabel Vincent, "Americans Are Coming. Get Ready to Kill Them," *National Post*, September 21, 2002.

The official U.S. military description of the battle was found in U.S. Department of Defense, "Afghanistan Firefight," prepared by Major Gary Tallman, Centcom, Public Affairs, September 11, 2002.

Reporter Sarah Schmidt interviewed Ms. Speer by e-mail for the *National Post* on September 19, 2002.

Paul McGeough of the *Sydney Morning Herald*, whom I met in Afghanistan, also wrote about the Northern Alliance offensive against the Taliban in *Manhattan to Baghdad: Dispatches from the War on Terror* (Crows Nest, NSW, Australia: Allen and Unwin, 2003).

CHAPTER SEVEN

Sophie Sureau provided a copy of her hospital report from Singapore. I am grateful to her and the Sureau family for patiently answering my many questions.

Jabarah's confession is detailed in U.S. Department of Justice, FBI, "Information Derived from Mohammed Mansour Jabarah," August 21, 2002. I obtained a copy from a confidential source. Thanks also to Jay Solomon of the *Wall Street Journal* for sending me a copy. I first wrote about this document in my article "Canadian Admits to Role in Hunt for 'White Meat'," *National Post*, January 18, 2003.

I also referred to the following official documents:
Department of Foreign Affairs, "Canadian Linked to Singapore Bomb Plot," July 19, 2002 ("Protected 'A'").

Solicitor General Canada, "Canadian Citizen Held in U.S. Custody in Relation to an Alleged Singapore Bomb Plot," House of Commons Book, July 29, 2002 ("Unclassified").

Solicitor General Canada, "Jabarah Case: UPDATE," House of Commons Book, August 1, 2002 ("Unclassified").

Republic of Singapore Ministry of Home Affairs, "White Paper: The Jemaah Islamiyah Arrests and the Threat of Terrorism," January 7, 2003.

Royal Embassy of Saudi Arabia (Information Office), "Death of Top Al Qaeda Fugitive," Washington, DC, July 3, 2003.

Royal Embassy of Saudi Arabia (Information Office), "Saudi Arabia Foils Terrorist Plot," Washington, DC, May 7, 2003.

Canadian Civil Liberties Association to Lawrence MacAulay, Solicitor General, letter, August 2, 2002.

The following press articles and books were also useful:
Alex Spillius, "Terrorism: A Family Affair for Laughing Bali Bomber," *The Daily Telegraph*, August 8, 2003.

David Case, "Terror in Paradise," *Men's Journal*, January 2003.

James Hookway and Jay Solomon, "Sent to the Front: How Al Qaeda Groomed a Youth From Canada To Be a Terrorist," *The Wall Street Journal*, January 21, 2003.

Eric Hoffer, *The True Believer: Thoughts on the Nature of Mass Movements* (New York: Harper and Row, 1951).

Robert D. Kaplan, *Soldiers of God: With Islamic Holy Warriors in Afghanistan and Pakistan* (New York: Vintage Departures, 2001).

CONCLUSION

RCMP, "Twelve Arrested on Anti-Terrorism Charges," News Release, June 3, 2006.

RCMP, "Assistant Commissioner Mike McDonell, News Conference, June 3, 2006."

CSIS, "Statement by Assistant Director, Operations at Press Conference, Saturday June 3, 2006."

Integrated Threat Assessment Centre, "Illegal Immigration and Terrorism," Intelligence Assessment N05/01, April 29, 2005, ("Secret").

Integrated National Security Assessment Centre, "Al Qaeda Attack Planning Against North American Targets," SABRE 04/24, May 21, 2005, ("Secret—Canadian Eyes Only").

CSIS, "Canadian Converts to Radical Islam," Intelligence Brief, IB 2004-5/29, Canadian Security Intelligence Service, Oct. 13, 2004, ("Secret").

CSIS, "Is Radical Islam A Problem in Canadian Prisons?" Intelligence Brief, IB 2004-5/39, Dec. 10, 2004, ("Secret").

Integrated National Security Assessment Centre, "Sunni Islamic Extremism: Use of Converts," SABRE, 04/19, April 27, 2004, ("Unclassified/For Official Purposes Only").

CSIS, "Paths to Radicalization of Home-Grown Islamic Extremists in Canada," July 29, 2005, ("Secret").

CSIS, "Sons of the Father: The Next Generation of Islamic Extremists in Canada," IB 2004-5/07, April 16, 2004, ("Secret—Canadian Eyes Only").

Martin Collacott, "Canada's Inadequate Response to Terrorism: The Need for Policy Reform," The Fraser Institute, 2006.

The text of the Anti-Terrorism Act is available at
http://canada.justice.gc.ca/en/anti_terr/act.html

Standing Senate Committee on National Security and Defence, "Canada's
Coastlines: The Longest Under-Defended Borders in the World" (chair Senator
Colin Kenny), October 2003.

RCMP (Criminal Intelligence Directorate), "Strategic Assessment of the Nature and
Extent of Organized Crime in Canada," April 30, 2003 (Protected 'B'").

Andre Belelieu, "Canada Alert: The Recent Evolution of Canadian Security Policy,"
Hemisphere Focus, Volume XII, Issue 10, Center for Strategic and International
Studies, Washington, September 2, 2004.

Martin Rudner, "Challenge and Response: Canada's Intelligence Community and
the War on Terrorism," Canadian Foreign Policy, Ottawa, Winter 2004.

Report of the Auditor General of Canada to the House of Commons, Chapter 3,
"National Security in Canada—The 2001 Anti-Terrorism Initiative," Ottawa,
March 29, 2004.

Ian Macleod, "Ottawa man made bomb triggers," *Ottawa Citizen*, March 23, 2006.

Ian MacLeod, "Khawaja lauded 'beloved' bin Laden," *Ottawa Citizen*, July 20, 2006.

Ian MacLeod, "Khawaja said his device could trigger bomb, court told," *Ottawa
Citizen*, July 22, 2006.

Ian MacLeod, "Crown says Ottawa man spent months on detonators for London
bomb plot," *Ottawa Citizen*, July 21, 2006.

CBC.ca, "Interview with Mubin Shaikh," July 15, 2006.

AUTHOR'S NOTE AND ACKNOWLEDGEMENTS

THIS IS THE STORY of the terrorists who have used Canada as a base; the carnage they caused around the world; and the political leaders in Ottawa who let it all happen. The accounts come from my investigative work as a newspaper and magazine journalist, my travels to countries wrenched by war and terror and my own archive of intelligence files on Canadian terrorists, which fills many boxes and may well be the largest collection outside of government.

When I started writing this book, most people had never heard of Osama bin Laden, and 9/11 was just a number you dialed on the telephone in an emergency. But even before the 2001 attack on the United States, it was clear that Canada had a serious problem. I first started writing about the infiltration of terrorist groups into Canada in 1988, when I published articles on Sikh and Armenian extremism. Later, I investigated the Canadian operations of the Tamil Tigers, Hezbollah and Al Qaeda. After September 11, 2001, I dug deeper into the workings of Islamic terrorist networks and ventured off to Afghanistan and Pakistan to witness the war on terror from the front lines.

The first two chapters of this book deal with the homeland wars that characterized the early days of Canadian terrorism. Chapter 3 examines the Canadian activities of Middle East terrorist groups, focusing on Hezbollah. And the final four chapters chronicle the rise of the Canadian Al Qaeda network. Many of the names and terms throughout, as well as some of the documents and statements, are translated from other languages, notably Arabic. Dollar figures are in Canadian currency, unless otherwise noted.

A great deal has happened since *Cold Terror* was published in hardcover in March 2004. Canada was directly threatened by Al Qaeda for a second time, and the bombings in Madrid showed that bin Laden's network was not only an anti-American terrorist group; it would not hesitate to massacre Western civilians anywhere given the opportunity. Canadian authorities laid their first charges under the Anti-Terrorism Act. The Khadr family, whose remarkable story is told in Chapter 6, became known across Canada. A Jewish school in Montreal was firebombed by a Hamas sympathizer. The Auditor General of Canada released a devastating assessment of Canadian security post–9/11 and sketchy stories of yet more Canadian terrorists began to emerge, and the RCMP arrested eighteen alleged "homegrown terrorists" in Toronto in the summer of 2006. I have incorporated these important developments into this new edition.

Talk of terrorism inevitably gets misconstrued as an attack on ethnicity, race or religion. And so it must be said that this book does not take a position against any segment of society, aside from that which supports the use of terrorist violence to further its agenda. The organizations examined here are those that have created the most serious security threats for Canada because of the way they have tried to use the country as a base for terror.

But for those who require such reassurance, I quote from the preface of the U.S. State Department's *Patterns of Global Terrorism* report, which worded the issue particularly well: "Adverse mention in this report of individual members of any political, social, ethnic, religious, or national group is not meant to imply that all members of that group are terrorists. Indeed, terrorists represent a small minority of dedicated, often fanatical, individuals in most such groups. It is those small groups—and their actions—that are the subject of this report."

I'm grateful to many people. Regrettably, most of them cannot be named. To do so would put their jobs and perhaps even their lives at risk. But suffice it to say that they include police, intelligence, immigration and foreign affairs officials, from the most senior levels to the rank and file. They also include members of the public who have been my eyes and ears inside closed ethnic communities, and the fixers, translators, diplomats, soldiers and rebels who guided me, often at great peril, when I traveled abroad. As for those who can be named, I am grateful to Don Loney for his enthusiasm, encouragement and suggestions, and to the team at Wiley Canada. I would also like to thank Jeff Stephen and Kevin Newman of Global TV, and Jane Kokan. Thanks also to Mark Stevenson, Dianna Symonds, Ken Whyte, Martin Newland, Sarmishta Subramanian, Adrian Humphreys, Mike Friscolanti, Steve Meurice and Doug Kelly. Professor Martin Rudner of the Norman Paterson School of International Affairs at Carleton University has been very kind to me, and so has Professor Wesley Wark of the University of Toronto. Both read early drafts of my manuscript and made helpful suggestions. Thanks also to George Jonas, Martin Collacott, David Harris, Lee Lamothe and David Frum, all of whom read my manuscript as well. I am indebted to Rohan Gunaratna, author of Inside Al Qaeda; Rita Katz and Josh Devon of the Search for International Terrorist Entities (SITE) Institute in Washington, DC; and Steven Emerson, who heads The Investigative Project (also in Washington, DC) and wrote American Jihad. Thanks to Peggy Lumpkin at the United States Department of Justice. Many thanks to the Sureau family for their kindness and cooperation during a difficult time. Most of all, thanks to Laura, and M., K., and J.

Stewart Bell
Toronto

July 2006

INDEX

A

Abdelhaleen, Shaareef, 246
Aboud, Ibrahim Alhalel Mohammed, 257
Aboughousch, Ahmed, 177, 180, 181–182, 184
Aboughousch, Fatima, 178
Aboughousch, Sarab, 180, 183–184
Abu Gaith, Sulaiman, 234, 235
Abu Mezer, Gazi Ibrahim, 4
Abu Osama, 127
Abu Sahil, 126–127
Abu Shanab, 134–135
Abul-Dahab, Khaled al-Sayed Ali Mohamed, 192, 194, 196
Access to Information Act, 2
Adora (Israeli village), 133
Adoum, Adnan, 176–178
Afghanistan
  refugee camps, 188–190, 197
  Soviet war, 149, 151, 187–188, 190–191, 192
  training camps, 4, 5, 22, 164–165, 235
  U.S.-led war, 208–216
Agel, Iyad, 126, 129, 130
Ahmad, Fahim, 246, 253, 254, 255, 257
Ahmed Khadr group, 6
Ahmed, Syed Haris, 254–255, 256
Air India bombing (1985), 2, 4, 9, 34, 35–40, 247, 262
  lessons learned, 42–43, 44–45
  problems with case, 38–40, 41–42

Airport security, 19, 250
AK Kannan (Tamil gang), 74, 75, 76
Akkal, Jamal, 126–130
Aklil, Pierre, 154–155
Al Aqsa Martyrs Brigade, 132
Al-Daour, Tariq, 256
Al Husseini, Mohamed Hussein, 111–116, 138
Al Jihad, 193–194, 197, 199, 224
Al Kanadi, Abu Abdurahman
  see Khadr, Ahmed Said
Al Kandari, Anas, 234, 235
Al Qaeda, 15, 138, 149–151, 157, 170, 174, 192, 217
  presence in Canada, 6, 10, 11
  Toronto arrests (2006), 245–247
  U.S. embassy bombings (1998), 202
  see also bin Laden, Osama; Khadr, Ahmed Said
Al Rahman Islamic Centre, 259
Al-Sayegh, Hani Abd Rahim, 117
Al-Tibyyan, 256
Al Yamani, Issam, 131
Al Zawahiri, Ayman, 157, 192, 198–199, 235, 256, 260
Aldandany, Turki Nasser Mishaal, 243
Algerian extremists see Kamel, Fateh
Almrei, Hassan, 15
Altikat, Atilla, 29
Amal, 110
Amara, Zakaria, 246, 254, 257
Amhaz, Ali, 119, 121, 122, 123–124, 125

281

Y

Z